GW00728982

# GETTING FREE

BY THE SAME AUTHOR

*The Ins and Outs of Moving*

*Frauds, Swindles and Rackets*

*The Money Book:*
*Financial Planning for the Young Family*

*Rosefsky's Guide to Financial Security*
*for the Mature Family*

# GETTING FREE

## How to Profit Most Out of Working for Yourself

Robert S. Rosefsky

Quadrangle/The New York Times Book Co.

*A Speaking Dollar-Wise Book*

 For information, address: Quadrangle/The New York Times Book Co., Inc., Three Park Avenue, New York, New York 10016. Manufactured in the United States of America. Published simultaneously in Canada by Fitzhenry & Whiteside, Ltd., Toronto.

**Library of Congress Cataloging in Publication Data**

Rosefsky, Robert S
Getting free.

1. New business enterprises—Management.
2. Self-employed. I. Title.
HD69.N3R67 1977 658'.04'1 76-9728
ISBN 0-8129-0663-2

# Contents

# GETTING FREE

# Why Not . . . ?

*People are always blaming their circumstances for what they are. I don't believe in circumstances. The people who get on in this world are the people who get up and look for the circumstances they want, and, if they can't find them, make them.*

GEORGE BERNARD SHAW

Time flies too swiftly.

On a bleak night late in November of 1963, an elderly woman sat in her modest apartment, weeping to herself. Her once sturdy frame was now gnarled by arthritis, and was beginning to show the ravages of a disease that would claim her two years later. The room was lit only by the glow from the television set. The sound had been turned down; yet sound wasn't needed, for the sad, muted face of the commentator was repeating for the hundredth time the shocking details of a nation's tragedy.

As a visitor entered the room, the old woman didn't wait to be asked why she was weeping.

"My God, my God," she managed between sobs. "First McKinley. Now Kennedy."

Sixty-two years. How swiftly. Yet how full.

The old woman, and tens of millions like her, had had the courage to escape her homeland around the turn of the century and seek freedom in the United States. The immigrants came from the world over—from Eastern and Central Europe, from Ireland, Italy, China, Japan, Mexico. They were smuggled across borders in the bottoms of hay wagons, and they crossed oceans, packed like sardines into the rotting holds of whatever ship they could afford. They came to escape a life—had they been permitted to live—of persecution, of unrelenting poverty, of serfdom.

To them, getting free meant surviving.

Like her countless peers, this old woman had come over as an illiterate peasant lass to marry the lad from her native village who had sent for her.

He was a peddler, and he criss-crossed the towns and villages of New York State and New England to provide a modest living for his family, which in short order had been expanded by five children. Then, when his oldest child was only 8, and his youngest was still in diapers, he went off on a winter trip and returned with a fatal pneumonia.

In 1904, there was no welfare, no life insurance, no Social Security, no aid to families with dependent children. But there was work.

Somehow, perhaps intuitively, the young widow knew that mere survival was not enough. Her children had the freedom to achieve, and they would do so.

The small backyard of their home became a miniature farm, and the front parlor became a tiny grocery store. By the age of 10, each child was well accustomed to fifty-hour work weeks.

All minority groups had to cope with quotas and degrees of social ostracism. But opportunity with a quota is better than no opportunity at all. In the decades that followed, the woman's three sons worked their way through high school, through college, and through graduate school to emerge as a doctor, a lawyer, and an accountant. The two daughters married independent businessmen, who themselves had struggled along the same path.

They had struggled. They had achieved. And the next priority for these and millions of other similar families was to create a harbor of security for their own children. Children who should not have to worry about quotas, about social ostracism, about making a living.

To the second generation, getting free meant security.

Then came the grandchildren. The first entered Harvard at age 16, en route to medical school. In short order, the grandchildren matriculated through Cornell, Yale, Syracuse, Vassar, and the University of Pennsylvania. Their personalities and their aspirations differed widely. Midnight escapes in hay wagons and ocean voyages in steerage were like fairy tale legends to them, yet they all passed through the powerful force field that drew them back home to the family bosom, to the harbor, to the security that their parents and grandparents had struggled so to achieve for them.

Yet, now in the last quarter of the twentieth century, getting free no longer meant mere survival, nor mere achievement, nor mere security—it meant, as the saying goes, "Doing your own thing."

## Freedom to Choose

*What is freedom? Freedom is the right to choose: the right to create for oneself the alternatives of choice. Without the possibility of choice and the exercise of choice, a man is not a man, but a member, an instrument, a thing.*

ARCHIBALD MACLEISH

The old woman, my grandmother, died in 1965. I think that we, the generation of her grandchildren, probably took her struggle for freedom too much for granted. She had chosen, at the risk of her life, to escape from a world in which freedom did not exist. Her choice, very simply, was to risk her life in leaving rather than risk her life in staying. Because of such people, I, and my cousins, and tens of millions of others like us, live in a world where the freedom of choice is probably greater than for any other people at any time in the history of the earth.

Yet even today we take our freedom of choice so much for granted that we fail to see it as it really is. We neglect to see clearly the alternatives that we have at our disposal. We fail to appreciate the choices we can make.

Some of the most elementary freedoms of choice were largely denied our parents and grandparents, and indeed have come upon us rather swiftly, due to rapid changes in social mores and technology. With the demise of marriage by parental contract and consent, we're free to wed anyone of our choice, regardless of race, creed, place of national origin, and, in some cases, even sex. And not only does society no longer frown when we choose to avoid the marital bonds altogether by living, unmarried, with a chosen partner, but we're free to change our minds about our marital status. The rate of this change of mind is alarming; the ratio of marriages to divorces is currently only about 2 to 1, as compared with roughly 10 to 1 earlier in this century.

We're free to live where we choose—parental bonds being easily replaced by long-distance telephone calls and ever-swifter jets. And we're free to change our minds about where we originally chose to live, as evidenced by the 15 million American families who change residence each year.

But there's one area of our freedom of choice that is all too often ignored, or at best just daydreamed about. That area is the choice of our work.

Accurate statistics are not maintained on job satisfaction or career changes, but it has been estimated that roughly 40 percent of the American work force has given serious thought to changing their jobs; yet only a very small percentage ever really do.

Someone you know, probably yourself, has pondered, perhaps with dismay, "How can I get out of this rut I'm in and be what I really want to be?"

The aim of this book is to help you answer that question.

## Getting Free—What Does It Mean?

*Four things come not back—the spoken word, the sped arrow, the past life, and the neglected opportunity.*

ARABIAN PROVERB

*Without work all life goes rotten. But when work is soulless, life stifles and dies.*

ALBERT CAMUS

If you are thoroughly convinced that you're as happy at your work as you're capable of being, and are likely to remain so for the duration, then there's nothing that this book can do for you. If you are content that you are now, and will continue to be, at the maximum level of income, responsibility, status, security, and recognition from your work, this book is not for you.

But if you have that elusive itch that you can't scratch, that sense of something missing, that concern that something is holding you back or tying you down, then you're a candidate for getting free.

It would have been tempting, though misleading, to title this book, *How to Quit Your Job, Go Into Business for Yourself, and Earn More Money Than You've Ever Dreamed of Earning!* The first two elements aren't necessarily a solution, and the third is a pipe dream. Perhaps the end result of your having read this book will be that you quit your job and go into business for yourself. If this works for you, fine. Or perhaps you will merely examine your situation from a vantage point that you never used before. Perhaps you will find the cause of that nagging itch, and a simple shifting of gears or a changing of directions will allow you to break free of its grasp. Perhaps you will realize that your innate skills needed some polishing, some updating, some new challenges—and you will get free of the rut you had dug for yourself.

Perhaps you will find that you were working not to please yourself, but to please others—spouse, parents, social peers. "Okay, Mom, are you happy now? I'm a goddamned doctor making $120,000 a year!" You can scratch someone else's itch all you like, but it's never going to do much good for your fingers. It's time to get free and work for your own satisfaction, not for the satisfaction of others.

> *Money may be the husk of many things, but not the kernel. It brings you food, but not appetite; medicine, but not health; acquaintances, but not friends; servants, but not faithfulness; days of joy, but not peace or happiness.*
>
> HENRIK IBSEN

Just as "getting free" does not necessarily mean walking out on your job and going out onto the streets, "profiting most" does not necessarily mean making vastly greater sums of money than you had been making before. There is more to life than the acquisition of things, yet so many of us dedicate our working hours to nothing more than the acquisition of things. How to profit most implies embarking upon career activities that will bring you the most fulfillment, not just in terms of money, but in terms of personal joy, personal growth and development, and a true sense of achievement.

This book is divided into three parts. The first part is "Thinking About It," in which you are asked to take a deep and serious look at your own career to date. What brought you here, and where will you be going from here?

The second part is "Reading About It." I've compiled a few dozen case histories of individuals like yourself who have made substantial changes, mostly work-oriented, in their personal circumstances. Each of these individuals willingly spent hours with me, allowing me to delve into their innermost thoughts and motivations. They did so with the hope that their experience might be helpful to others. I herewith express my deepest gratitude to them, individually and as a group, and hope that you'll have occasion to do the same.

The third part is "Doing It," in which we explore some of the specific steps that can be taken, and some that should be avoided, by those interested in establishing their own new career identities. This part includes discussions on financing, professional assistance, taxes, and much more.

Interspersed throughout these pages, you'll also find a choice selection of the words of others—poets, philosophers, dreamers, and doers. Since my primary aim is not to motivate you to act, but rather to motivate you to think, to reflect, to examine, to explore, I'm hopeful that these other bits of thought will serve as provocative stimuli to help you create your own positive course of action—for example:

> *Hell begins on the day when God grants us a clear vision of all that we might have achieved, of all the gifts that we have wasted, of all that we might have done that we did not do.*
>
> GIAN-CARLO MENOTTI

Part One

# Thinking About It

*This is a world of action, and not for moping and groaning in.*
CHARLES DICKENS

In a rut?

Is there some seething, perhaps inexplicable, discontent bubbling below the surface? And does it erupt now and then in some form of antisocial behavior? How does it manifest itself—fits of anger, depression, insomnia? Are there bouts of overindulgence, either with food or with drink? Or does some marvelous skill of self-control keep it bottled up inside to gnaw away at the tender lining of your stomach?

You can't run away from home again—you're too old, and there are mouths to feed and an image to maintain.

What are you going to do about it? Are you going to suffer? or get free?

Let's examine the problem coolly, rationally, dispassionately. Let's see if we can get to the root of the troubles. If we can define them clearly, we can arrive at a viable solution. You already know that the head-in-the-sand approach doesn't work. The troubles don't go away. More likely, they get worse. And if you don't already know it, I can assure you that the flying-off-the-handle approach won't work either. Like an unrequited lover on the rebound, your unsatisfied passions can too easily lead you even further astray.

Let's think, analyze, explore together. Let's talk about how we got this way in the first place. Let's see if we can zero in on specific elements of satisfaction or dissatisfaction with your work or other daily routine. Let's make a careful appraisal of where we would really like to be. And let's see if we can knock down some of the common obstacles that may be preventing us from achieving what we feel we truly can achieve.

Before we examine the first of these situations, how we got this way, I want to relate two incidents that occurred within the short span of twenty-four hours, some years ago. They jolted me into a new awareness about work—what it's all about, and what it means to us.

It was summer 1969, and to celebrate our tenth wedding anniversary, my wife and I had treated ourselves to a two-week vacation at the Club Méditerranée on the South Pacific island of Moorea, just fifteen miles from the romantic Tahiti. As commonly happens before any vacation, the weeks just before our departure were hectic, taxing, overloaded. Among the eighty or so people awaiting the midnight flight out of Los Angeles International Airport, there was no doubt more pent-up energy than there was in the fuel tanks of the DC-8 that would, some seven and a half hours later, deliver us to the airport in Papeete. It was just your typical vacationing entourage, overwrought, overwhelmed, anxiously awaiting a vacation that would, on average, take the first five days to wind down, the next five days to relax, and the last four days to start getting wound up again for reentry into the real world.

We arrived in Papeete as dawn was breaking—a sight to relieve many tensions right off the bat—and had a two-hour wait until the boat took us across to Moorea. We shared a cab to the boat dock with a couple from San Francisco, and spent our early-morning hours touring the fascinating Tahitian farmers' market. Our conversation with the other couple, John and Gunilla, was pretty much limited to mutual oohing and ahing over the exotic sights, sounds, and smells of the market. Our small talk continued during the boat ride to Moorea, the bus ride to the club, and the buffet lunch that greeted us on our arrival.

After a few hours' nap to recuperate from the relatively sleepless night spent on the airplane, John and I donned our snorkling gear to explore the wonders of the coral reef lagoon that lay at the doorstep of our native Tahitian bungalows. More small talk ensued as we examined the fluorescent fish, the moray eels, the coral formations, and the occasional octopus that came within our view.

Enough of this idle banter, I thought to myself. It seemed as though John and I and our wives had hit it off nicely, and that we'd be good friends at least during our stay at the Club. It was high time, I thought, for us to identify ourselves properly so that we could communicate properly in the normal channels expected of fine upstanding American citizens.

Thus, as we bubbled up to the surface and took off our snorkling masks, I turned to John and asked, "By the way, what do you do?"

He looked at me with a wry yet kind smile, and answered in a way not to offend, but to suggest a bit of a lesson: "What difference does it make?"

And then, he compounded the matter by not asking me what I did!

For a moment, I was stunned. What does he mean, "What difference does it make?" I thought to myself. How can we communicate if we haven't put the proper labels on our foreheads? How can we talk about that which is of most interest to each of us if we don't know what the other does? Is he ashamed of what he does? Is he so callous as to not care what I do? How can we be friends if we don't know what the other does?

I glanced back at John, and his smile was now accompanied by a twinkling in his eyes, a realization that he had succeeded in opening a little window in my mind. I looked around at my surroundings—the stunning emerald green mountain jutting up out of the sea, the powder white sand beach rimmed with majestic coconut palms and not a trace of telephone wires, television antennae, beer cans, or any other semblances of civilization as we know it.

The place, the surroundings, the circumstances all caused the realization to dawn on me: "You're right," I replied to John, "What difference does it make?"

John apparently came by it naturally; I had to learn it. For so many of us, the work that we do is a medallion, a label, a list of ingredients that we hang upon ourselves. Some of us may do it compulsively; others defensively; others unconsciously. Whatever our reason, we're telling those around us, "It's what I do, not who I am, that I want you to recognize and communicate with." It can become, in effect, a mask. As such, it can shape your own way of thinking, or nonthinking. It can affect your relationships with other people. And it can limit your ability to learn from others or impart yourself to others. A vital dimension of life can be lost to one who too frequently tries to function behind the mask.

To my pleasant surprise, the total atmosphere at the Moorea Club Méditerranée underscored John's reply. Not only were vocations left unmentioned, but even last names—another indicator of certain aspects of a person—were left unstated. It was strictly a people-to-people environment, with no pretenses, no masks.

Getting to know people in this kind of environment was a rather astounding experience. I suspect it would be virtually impossible to duplicate back home, where the trappings and symbols of our identity are compounded even more by our clothing, our offices, our automobiles, and our homes. I had thought that the initial experience might have been a fluke, but I was fortunate enough to return to Moorea three years later, and found the same attitude prevailing. Ever since those trips, I've tried to meet people as people, without the mask of "What do you do?" I'm often looked at as though I'm a bit foolish, but the experience enables me to see people as they really are, and they're more worth knowing without the masks.

Certainly, anyone should be proud of his work and related achievements. I don't mean to be demeaning of anyone's career. But one can demean himself when he takes refuge behind the mask. The loss of identity of your inner self is difficult indeed to replace.

The second experience happened just a day after the initial confrontation with John. Eight of us rented small motor bikes to take a tour around the island. Moorea is a heart-shaped volcanic island encircled by a coral reef. Virtually all of its 4,000 population lives along the forty-mile perimeter of the island, with the *fare* (fa-ray), or thatched-roof bungalow, being the common form of dwelling. Nature has amply blessed Moorea: the low-lying lands around the perimeter of the island abound with papaya, coconut, mango, and breadfruit trees. The lagoon, which extends for about 2,000 yards from the shoreline, is crystal clear and as smooth as glass. It abounds with more kinds of fish than I could ever count. With few exceptions, the fruit of the trees and the fish in the lagoon appear to be owned commonly by the people of Moorea.

We set off on our excursion over the semipaved and badly rutted one-lane road that circles the island. We had about completed our course when my luck with renting things held true to form: both my bike and my wife's bike broke down within fifty yards of each other, leaving us some four or five miles from the Club, just as the sun was beginning to near the horizon. The others in our group went on ahead, saying they would have a truck sent back to pick us up, and we were to wait patiently at the side of the road for our rescue.

It would be unnatural for strangers in a strange land not to feel some apprehension in such a predicament, particularly with no grasp of the Tahitian language, or its commonly spoken alternative, French. Along the stretch of the road where we stood there were perhaps a half-dozen bungalows stretched out, nestled in the mango and papaya groves. We saw small children playing, and occasionally the parents would emerge from their bungalows to observe the crazy Americans with their broken bikes.

Then my eye was attracted to the opening of a door of one of the bungalows about fifty feet away from us on the inland side of the road. Through it emerged a native Tahitian, who at first glance resembled a trimmed-down sumo wrestler. He was about five feet six inches tall, perhaps equally wide, and he carried a long, thin spear in one hand. He was heading toward us, and I listened anxiously for the sound of our rescue truck.

The whole incident took at most three minutes. The Tahitian strolled toward us. Along the way, he picked up a bucket with his other hand. He approached us directly, his face expressionless. As he neared us, a slight smile wrinkled his full face, and he walked on by us and down a mild slope toward a tree at water's edge. We had not noticed before that there were two piglets tied to the tree. Apparently, they were the family's livestock, and the bucket held slops for the animals who would later become the main ingredients in a native feast. After pouring the slops, the Tahitian wandered out waist deep into the lagoon, and with his spear artfully impaled three or four fish in the course of a few seconds. He strung the fish onto a line, tossed it over his shoulder, and headed back out of the water toward his bungalow.

He stopped at a breadfruit tree a few paces from his front door and shook it until some of the ripe fruit fell to the ground. He repeated this process with other trees and then gathered up an armload of breadfruits, papaya, mangoes, and coconuts. Now, laden with fruit and fish, he proceeded back into the bungalow. Moments later, a few of the handsome little children who had been observing us, scampered into the bungalow behind their father.

As during the electric pause that follows a nearby bolt of lightning, I suddenly realized that this peaceable and well-fed individual had performed all of the necessary day's work in the few minutes that we were observing him. He had fed his livestock and gathered up the needed ration of food for his family, the remnants of which would feed his livestock the following day, as the cycle repeated itself. I was compelled to ponder my typical day's work, the typical day's work of any of our companions at the Club. I'm not sure that I, or any of us, would be willing to change places with the Tahitian for more than a short time (though I'd be willing to give it a try), but the concept of the meaning of work to different peoples took on a whole new perspective for me.

Tahitians, or more particularly Mooreans, are not noted for their industriousness. Fortunately for them, nature has seen to it that they don't have to be industrious. The saying goes on the island that if you offer a native a choice of a broom and some money if he'll use the broom, or a guitar and no money if he'll play the guitar, he'll take the guitar every time.

There are no banks on Moorea, but there are no psychiatrists either.

Now, let's get back to the reality of the workers that we know, and the ruts that many of them find themselves in. First, a word of caution to those who may feel totally content with their current work situation: proceed at your own risk. While I'm not in any way advocating that anyone abandon a good thing, the discussions that follow are liable to spark in you some thinking as to whether or not you are fulfilling your potential.

If you're set in your ways and have no thought whatsoever of changing them, beware: we're going to plumb deep, and we may touch a raw nerve that you had thought was safely covered up and out of reach.

> *What I am interested in doing is finding and expressing a new form of life. People do not live nowadays—they get about 10% out of life.*
>
> ISADORA DUNCAN

# How Did We Get This Way?— The Rut Syndromes

## 1. The Cookie-Mold Syndrome

It happened, and probably still does happen, in thousands of schoolrooms around the nation every week of every year. I remember it from my seventh- or eighth-grade classrooms in Binghamton, New York, in the late 1940s.

Binghamton, like countless other cities around the country, was a factory town that grew relatively prosperous as a result of attracting cheap immigrant labor early in the century. Binghamton, with its neighboring communities of Endicott and Johnson City, was the home of Endicott Johnson Shoe Company, or EJ, at the time the largest shoe manufacturing firm in the world. It was said that immigrants from Poland, Czechoslovakia, Yugoslavia, and other Eastern European nations would disembark at Ellis Island with their only words of English being, "Which way EJ?"

These fine people streamed into Binghamton, and other cities like it, where work was available and a family could live freely.

My recollections of Endicott-Johnson are of an extraordinarily paternalistic company, who paid the minimum wages that their consciences and existing laws would allow, but lavished other benefits upon their workers: medical care, legal services, parks, playgrounds, low-rate mortgages on company-sponsored housing, and so on. It was difficult for one member of the family to bring home a living wage, so it was quite common that the mother and father both worked, plus any aunts, uncles, and grandparents on hand. As soon as they reached the proper age, the children would also punch the EJ clock. Thus, a family could make itself a substantial income, at least compared to what it was capable of earning in the motherland.

That it was a zealously guarded, captive labor force was made clear in the late 1930s, when the Ford Motor Company proposed establishing an assembly plant outside of Binghamton. The plant, as hindsight now indicates, would have enhanced the economic fortunes of the community considerably. But the powers that were, fearful of losing their captive labor force to the automotive people, successfully exerted every possible pressure to prevent the Ford people from settling in.

The specific incident that comes filtering back through the memories of those musty brown classrooms is that of a teacher, or teachers, telling the students to study hard so that they would get through high school, and if they did so with good grades and a clean behavior record, they'd be fortunate enough to get a job in the shoe factory just like their moms and dads had.

Thus, a level of aspiration was imposed upon the minds of these impressionable children. In retrospect, I have to surmise that the clout of the company was so strong that they could have influenced the local board of education, at least subliminally, not to put any notions in the heads of the children that might cause them to leave the community. They were the fodder for the mill. They were needed. The schools had no business teaching the town's future laborers that there were better opportunities elsewhere.

We'll never know how many fertile young minds were unwittingly shaped, as by a cookie mold, into a situation of minimal aspiration. For all the Binghamtons, and for all the Endicott-Johnsons, there could be millions of workers today who would have to go through depth analysis in order to determine why they never aspired to anything higher than the situation that was created for them by economic circumstances during their youth.

A curious thing, though, did happen to Endicott-Johnson on its way to oblivion. As the first wave of immigrants reached middle age in the 1930s and 1940s, many of them started to buy a relatively strange new product: life insurance. By the 1950s, when the end came for the original pioneers, their children suddenly found themselves with $10,000, $15,000, $20,000 cash in hand. And for many, the migration out of Binghamton was swift in coming. This newly affluent breed realized that they didn't have to struggle through life in the dingy factories that had captured their parents—they could depart and strike out on their own. The company-town paternalism of the twenties and thirties didn't sit well with the postwar, GI Bill–endowed, insurance-rich children. Endicott-Johnson had lost touch with the times, and its fortunes dwindled rapidly.

In the meantime, the cookie-mold syndrome had taken—and takes still—its toll.

## 2. The 20/40 Syndrome

Today's world is full of 40-year-old men (or 35, or 45, or whatever age) whose careers were chosen for them by an impetuous, impulsive, and perhaps irrational 20-year-old. Now who could that be? Indeed, it's himself, twenty years earlier. How common it is for the 20-year-old, perhaps under pressure from parents or peers to choose a career, to embark on a life's adventure without ever consulting with his alter ego twenty years hence.

In our precious world of instant gratification, we can so eagerly reach out for the brass ring on the first spin around the carousel. Then, perhaps having grabbed it, pride enters the scene and forbids letting go. If the 20-year-old had chosen a career that, in fact, time proved him to be unsuited for, it's the 40-year-old who suffers for it. When the early gratifications have subsided, the dregs at the bottom of the cup may prove bitter and of little sustenance at all.

"Who was that smart aleck kid who got me into this rut?" the victim of the 20/40 syndrome might ask. He'd like to kick the responsible party square in the butt, but nature has constructed us so as to render that feat impossible. Thus, we have to deal with him rationally.

## 3. The I-Don't-Know-What-I-Want-to-Be-When-I-Grow-Up Syndrome

Some people will just never settle down. They may be called drifters, job hoppers, opportunists. But that doesn't make them bad people.

Their situations may be caused by a number of factors: a short span of attention or concentration; a lack of challenge or an inability to rise to a challenge; the failure to have ever set specific career goals; or, simply, a restless, maverick-type spirit, which afflicts many of us.

Many of these victims may never find anything of lasting meaning to them, and they may only be content in their restive search for the ultimate happiness. Still others, however, will, because of societal and financial pressures, hang on to a situation far beyond their ability to tolerate it in order to bring home the bread and maintain the image. This victim suffers more, for he isn't letting his own natural instincts and/or abilities carry him wherever he should be going.

## 4. The Rosebud Syndrome

Orson Welles' classic film *Citizen Kane* is a fictionalized version of the life of newspaper magnate William Randolph Hearst. The opening scene of the film shows the once immensely wealthy and powerful Kane on his deathbed, being tended to by a nurse. His last living word is "Rosebud."

Why, wonders a newsreel producer, would one of the most dynamic men of the age die with the word "rosebud" on his lips. He sends forth a reporter to investigate this phenomenon, and in the course of the reporter's interviews with all of Kane's former friends and associates, the man's life is spun out before us.

But nobody knows anything about "rosebud." Not until the final scene does the audience learn what "rosebud" meant: a thing so innocent, so unexpected, so trivial, and yet so deeply important to the child Kane that it carried through his entire life, and was all that he could think of as his long and hectic life expired. (An unwritten bond among all viewers of *Citizen Kane* prohibits us from identifying "rosebud" to the multitudes who have yet to see the film. Sorry about that.)

As some of the case histories in the section that follows will reveal, rosebud seekers are more numerous than we may suspect. From my observations, this is particularly true among those who during their youth enjoyed an artistic or creative bent that was later sidetracked because of other considerations.

There's no assurance that finding one's rosebud will assure happiness, but, more important, the failure to go out and actively seek rosebud can cause a person even greater frustration than he is already experiencing. As Charles Foster Kane's life so amply illustrated, even with all the power and affluence, if you don't find your rosebud, there's a big aching void, and all the deathbed utterances can't fill it.

## 5. The Please-the-Parents Syndrome

"Okay, Mom and Pop, now I'm a goddamned doctor/lawyer/merchant/manufacturer/whatever you wanted me to be. I know it cost you plenty to set me up, and I know that you did it for my own good—for my security, so I'd never have to work like Papa had to work. Sure, I'm making all the money you said I'd make, maybe even a little more. But I've got to tell you this, Mom and Dad—I'm not very happy with it all."

## 6. The Displease-the-Parents Syndrome

"Okay, Mom and Dad, you were always telling me to do as you told me, to think as you told me, to eat what you told me, to date whom you told me, to study what you told me, to have the friends that you told me, to be what you told me to be. Well it shouldn't come as any surprise to you that I'd had it up to my ears by the time I was old enough to do what I damned well felt like doing on my own. So whatever it was you told me to be when I grew up, there was no way in the world I would be that. I just wouldn't give you the satisfaction any longer. And all these years you've still been telling me that's what I should have been. You'll just never reconcile yourselves to the fact that I am what I am because *I* chose to be that, not *you*. Yet, you still keep needling me. And you know, damn it, after all these years, it still gets to me. Why don't you just leave me alone?"

These two parent-related syndromes, and their myriad variations, are common to us all to one degree or another. The extreme examples illustrated here are probably the least common but certainly the most painful types. All of us, at one time or another, have felt some form of parental influence on our ultimate careers. It may have been gentle and proper guidance, it may have been a shove, it may have been total apathy. Very few of us are immune to the fact that our parents did raise us and did have goals for us. If we've pleased them at the expense of our own satisfaction, or if we've spited them for our own satisfaction, the scars left by such acts can be deep and slow to heal. The longer we continue to throw salt in the wound, the longer the pain will persist.

## 7. The Professional Menopause Syndrome

Everything was chosen with precision and due concern for all possible contingencies. The career was well suited to your natural abilities and fulfilled your own sense of personal aspiration. There was ample progress in both job status and income. Everything moved along nicely, smoothly, progressively, inevitably toward that brick wall that is now standing firmly in front of you. The challenges have been surmounted, the goals have been reached, and here you are with decades of productive working years left, and the thrill is gone. Now it's drudgery, boredom, apathy. Every new task is just a dull variation on one that you completed long ago. You've gone about as far as you can go within your company, within your community, within your career.

What are you going to do for an encore?

Professional menopause is perhaps the most insidious of the rut syndromes, for it's the least expected. It may build quietly and secretly over the years, or it may come crashing down around us without any warning. It can happen to anyone. The money and the status may still be great enough, but the sense of personal achievement has eroded completely, or soon will.

A particularly aggravating aspect of the professional menopause syndrome is that it seems to arrive at a time of life when you think yourself unsuited for any other endeavor. Thus, you feel locked in with it. No escape. No way to get free.

You may not recognize soon enough, or fully enough, that the skills you've developed over the years can be shifted into another mode, and can be used productively in another environment.

Professional menopause is very likely an adjunct to the formerly mythical male menopause—the change-of-life phenomenon that is signaled by the apparent passage of youth and the necessary settlement into the less exhilarating days and years of maturity.

In the career appraisal suggestions that follow, you may spot an incipient case of professional menopause lurking in your future. If that's the case, you can prepare for it, and contend with it successfully. If it has already attacked, you can get free—but only if you really want to.

## 8. The Housewife Blues Syndrome

"The kids can take care of themselves now, and I can't stand another game of bridge, mah-jongg, tennis/watch another soap opera/clean another closet/polish another spoon. My role as housewife/mother is nearing its end, and what do I have to show for my life? I've done only what I've been obligated to do, and though I've done the best I could, I still feel an aching void. My husband tells me it would be awkward within his business community if it were known that his wife was working. It could be detrimental to his career. I've never been trained for anything. I have no skills that I can use beyond those of the housewife/mother. The years are speeding by. It scares the hell out of me. What am I supposed to do?"

This syndrome has been spreading like wildfire, no doubt brought on in part by the heightened consciousness that the Women's Liberation Movement has caused. It's an ever-increasing cause of marital discontent and alcoholism (for both spouses). The sad truth is that many women currently lack the training to handle much more than menial jobs, which very likely would provide as little satisfaction as would continuing with their housewife role.

But there are ample opportunities for education, vocational training, and on-the-job training that can provide a sturdy set of bootstraps for the multitudes of women, otherwise lacking skills, who wish to lift themselves up. Many career opportunities for women have opened in recent years, particularly in such areas as real-estate sales, life insurance, and even stock brokerage. Some of the case histories in the next section will reveal success stories along these lines.

You can get free, if you recognize the problem and are willing to take the steps to cope with it.

*Restlessness and discontent are the first necessities of progress.*
THOMAS ALVA EDISON

*Truly there is a tide in the affairs of men; but there is no Gulf Stream setting it forever in one direction.*
JAMES RUSSELL LOWELL

Mull over the potpourri of "rut syndromes." You may find yourself picking and choosing a little here, a little there, to account for that seething discontent inside of you. Ask yourself questions, and don't be afraid to speak the answers honestly. Before you can get free, you have to know precisely the kind of locks and chains that are holding you down.

Let's turn now to some of the specific elements that can cause satisfaction or dissatisfaction in your working routine. In effect, let's take a closer look at the chains that bind.

# Elements of Satisfaction and Dissatisfaction at Work

## 1. Personal Factors

When you get right down to it, it may turn out that you're perfectly happy in your work situation, but that something else outside of your working environment is bothering you and causing all the grief. Problems get to vexing us so that we often can't pinpoint their origin. Our anxieties cloud our common sense, and we fail to recognize the true nature of many problems. We may think a problem is work-related, when, in fact, it may be marital, medical, financial.

I'm still bemused by a letter that I received some years ago. It was from a woman in her mid-thirties, living in a major midwestern city, who was apparently seeking some budgeting advice for her family. They just couldn't seem to make ends meet, she claimed, as do so many such letters. Normally, readers seeking my advice on budgetary matters will proceed to outline their income fairly accurately. Then comes the outgo; after listing the basic monthly expenses of rent, or mortgage, utilities, food, insurance, etc., they come to what is generally the biggest category of all—miscellaneous. And there, normally, is the root of the problem. I ask them to send me a breakdown of the miscellaneous if they really want my help, and usually that's the last I hear from them.

But this particular case was more interesting, for the husband was a doctor and the wife was a lawyer, and they were earning close to $70,000 a year! They lived in a rather modest home, and the expenses outlined by the wife were, if true, quite reasonable under the circumstances. She didn't have a "miscellaneous" entry in her outgo column, but she had something far more perplexing.

Her husband, it seemed, was fond of taking trips to Las Vegas and engaging in some gaming wagers. To the best of her knowledge, he went two or three times a year, and she was certain that he would never lose more than $500 to $1,000 on each trip. There were a few "fishing trips" at other times of the year, that her husband took with his "boyfriends," but she was sure that those were relatively inexpensive. One last item that she included was the purchase of a townhouse in Lake Tahoe, for which the husband was making payments on a $25,000 debt.

The woman's letter went on in some detail, explaining her relationship with her husband, their attempts at frugality, their desire to spend their money prudently. But it became quite obvious to me that we had here not a budgetary problem, but a psychological problem. Her husband apparently was a compulsive gambler, and my guess was that the fishing trips were also gambling trips, that the payments on the supposed Lake Tahoe townhouse were really payments to bookies or casinos for back debts, and that the maximum $1,000 losses on each trip may have been many times that.

Why couldn't the wife have seen this? Why should she write to a financial counselor for what turned out to be a psychological problem? I never asked her, but I'm sure it's a common problem, neatly summed up in the cliché about seeing the forest for the trees.

Just as distressing personal factors can cause dissatisfaction in the working environment, so can pleasant personal factors make an unpleasant work routine more tolerable. The amount of tedium one is able to endure can be vastly increased by the promise of various joys or pleasures once the hours of tedium have ended. A happy home and sex life, intriguing hobbies, an active social routine, invigorating community involvement, even extramarital affairs can help cast a glittering rainbow over the dull mud puddle of work. The danger is that if the outside pleasant personal factor is removed or terminated, the drudgery of work can suddenly come rushing to the surface.

Evaluate carefully all of the personal factors that can have an effect on your work routine. And all of the work factors that can have an effect on your personal life. Something of a minimally unsettling nature in your work routine could be creating friction outside of work, which can compound itself back into a heightened dissatisfaction with work—which in turn reflects back on your personal life. And round and round it goes.

Only in very rare cases can we totally separate our working life from our personal life. There are bound to be elements on one side affecting elements on the other side. It's necessary to analyze all of these factors carefully if you're going to be able to remove the causes of the problems, to scratch the itch, to get free.

## 2. Status

Has your work gained you the recognition you think you deserve, both with your co-workers and within your community? Status can be an easy, but dangerously misleading, indicator of the amount of satisfaction you're deriving from work. At best, it's an imperfect measuring device, since it necessarily has to weigh what you think of yourself against what *you* think *others* think of you. Lack of status, whether real or imagined, would probably be one of the more flimsy reasons for seeking a change in career direction. It's not that it isn't meaningful; just be careful not to make it more meaningful than it really deserves to be.

## 3. Working Conditions

Working conditions can include many factors: the personal comforts and conveniences available to you at work, your attitude and the attitude of your co-workers, your relationship with your co-workers; the ease with which undesirable conditions can be altered.

Among the comforts and conveniences might be the availability and quality of employee parking, public transportation, the cafeteria, rest rooms, the infirmary, employees' lounges, recreational facilities, library and other learning facilities, temperature controls. I don't know that anyone ever left a job because the tapioca pudding in the cafeteria was too loose, but an accumulation of negatives within the category of working conditions will certainly get you thinking. The importance you give these items is strictly individual. There may be those who prefer to work for less money and less chance of advancement, but in a country club surrounding, and others who would choose an opposite situation. If the working conditions do measure out on the negative side, is it really negative enough to warrant contemplating a career change? Or might you be putting too much emphasis on small points? Analyze. Evaluate. You have to be the judge. But judge on the basis of facts, not whimsy.

## 4. Company Policy

Company policy is one of the more basic elements of job satisfaction or dissatisfaction. Do you, in fact, understand your company's underlying policy with respect to many important functions, such as unions, promoting from within, stockholder relations, employee relations, community relations, risk taking, lack of risk taking, incentives for both management and employees, profitability targets, fringe benefits, nepotism, and autonomy (who has what right to make what decisions at what level, with or without checking with whom)?

Even when all other factors are favorable, negative feelings about basic company policy, even though it may not affect you directly, can cause a level of dissatisfaction that can turn into bitterness. You may, for example, feel offended that your company did not contribute adequately to a particular charity, one for which you were involved in making the pitch. Or you may feel irked that an outsider was brought in to assume a managerial position that you felt someone on the inside deserved. Or you may be provoked when the president's son is made executive vice-president when you feel he's an incompetent, even though it has absolutely no bearing on your own personal situation within the company.

As with the other elements of work satisfaction, an accumulation of negatives in this category is going to start gnawing at you. Attach proper, but not undue, significance to each of these elements, and evaluate the potential for changes in company policy that may make it more to your liking. If you're uncomfortable with company policy now, and you can rationally envision that it's probably going to get worse, you're starting to build yourself an ulcer by trying to battle the foe that's bigger than you are. It's time to start thinking about getting free.

## 5. Income and Security

Nothing can be more vexing than not to be receiving what you think you're worth for the work you're doing. But before you use this as a 'umping-off point for a career change, it's essential that you determine what you might be worth to someone else for the same or similar work. Any kind of career change is going to involve many trade-offs—more money, but a longer commute; better chance for advancement, but less attractive working conditions; a more progressive company, but a lower wage scale; and so on.

Income and security tend to be the most visible elements of work satisfaction. Indeed, when the kids ask what you're having for dinner that night, you can't very well tell them pride or contentment. The paycheck, and its promise of continuing in the foreseeable future, is the tangible evidence of the reward you're receiving for your energies and abilities. It can't be measured solely by itself. It has to be evaluated along with the other factors included in this section.

As with the section on syndromes, take your pencil and do some inventorying of these various elements of job satisfaction. It's likely to be a little here, a little there, that will add up to something you can put your finger on and say, "That's what's bugging me." I hope that we're now starting to close in on what may have been an elusive bogyman, taunting you from dark corners, without ever showing its face. When you come face to face with your tormentor, it's much easier to handle him. As long as he remains elusive, you'll never know what steps to take to bring him under control or get rid of him.

> *The prudent, penniless beginner in the world labors for wages for a while, saves a surplus with which to buy tools or land for himself another while, and at length hires another new beginner to help him. This is the just, and generous and prosperous system which opens the way to all, gives hope to all, and consequently energy and progress, and improvement of conditions to all.*
>
> ABRAHAM LINCOLN

# A Self-Appraisal of Your Career Future—Where Do You Go from Here?

Even assuming general satisfaction with your work, a periodic appraisal of your career potential is in order, if for no other reason than to anticipate and/or avoid the woes of professional menopause. As later chapters will illustrate, a successful career redirection will usually require some advance preparation, either a new learning experience, the raising of capital, the development of markets for a new product, the acquisition of competent partners and helpers, or simply the time to prepare yourself psychologically for the change. Your periodic appraisal should provide you with advance signals as to the feasibility of preparing for a change and then actually making the change. Without this kind of up-front planning, you could stumble dangerously into a wrong career change, and never be able to recover. The need for self-appraisal is particularly important for military personnel anticipating a career change. The shift from the military routine to the less rigidly structured civilian career can pose unique problems which must be anticipated in advance of any change.

## 1. Getting a Clear Focus on Your Personal Goals and Desires

This element is of the highest priority, if not the total priority for many people. Your goals and aspirations will definitely shift over the years, very likely in pace with the growth and development of your family, and with your own personal energies. The lack of focus on our own goals often takes us off in the wrong direction. We may be lured by a money-making opportunity, when at that moment greater emphasis should be placed on improving professional skills. We may be lured by an opportunity to broaden outside contacts, when greater emphasis should be placed on broadening inside contacts. We may be misled into thinking that office politics, rather than productivity, is the path to ultimate success, or vice versa. In any of these cases, or dozens of others like them, we simply have failed to focus on our ultimate short-term and long-term goals, and we find ourselves taking detours, which may end up only leading us back to the starting place.

This goal focusing may involve a technique as simple as charting out on a piece of paper just where you want to be one year, three years, five years, and ten years from now, in terms of income and the corporate hierarchy. Naturally, the farther out you project, the fuzzier the projections have to be. But with the short-term projections, you should be able to come up with realistic appraisals of what you're seeking, and of the chances for achieving those goals.

You may realistically conclude that the company, as it is now structured, won't be capable of allowing you to achieve your goals. That's an early warning signal that should be heeded. But make sure the signal is a valid one. Beware of false signals that can detour you—such as rumors, suppositions founded on rumors, and wishful thinking.

In addition to the strictly financial goals (and these include fringe benefits), what about your professional goals? What additional skills and capabilities do you hope to acquire, and will your present position allow you to acquire them? What new avenues for your particular skills are being opened up by advancing technology within your field, and is your present company capable of giving you access to these new developments?

## 2. The Future of the Company

Will the company's growth pattern be able to accommodate your own desired growth pattern? This refers to income, skills, personal achievement, responsibility levels, and whatever symbols of recognition you're seeking for yourself.

This is not a time for pie-in-the-sky guesswork. It is a time to study carefully the company's recent years' operating history and development, and its stated projections for the future. Develop whatever opportunity you can to learn about future plans from the highest possible sources within the company.

What plans for management succession does the company itself have? In small, closely held and/or family-owned companies, there's always a likelihood that the company will be sold or merged when the owner decides to retire. This can have a drastic effect on your future. It could enhance it, or it could spell danger. If the company doesn't have a well-plotted management-succession program, you have to be on guard for some kind of disruption should top management, be it an individual or a group, depart.

If the company does have a well-ordered plan for management succession, how far down does the plan reach? Does it encompass your own activities? And if so, how? These factors can have a very important effect on your career, and if you don't already know the answers, you must seek them out.

How is your company doing with respect to the competition in your community, or with companies across the country? Is it keeping pace, falling behind, getting ahead? Are you riding a winning horse or a loser? Is there a sense of dynamism and growth about the company? Or are there signs that it is beginning to wither on the vine? Any tip-off you can get as to when it would be timely to make a change will work in your favor.

## 3. Personal Opportunity

Considering your own newly defined goals and your newly gained knowledge of your company's potential, how do you view your own personal opportunity within that framework? What income, benefits, and security do you foresee for yourself? Will there be ample opportunity for you to make the most use of your existing skills, to enhance your skills, and to put those enhanced skills to the best possible use? Is your own need for productivity fulfilled in the overall work environment now? Will it be fulfilled in the future?

What opportunities are there for personal diversification for you within the company, as it now exists and as you foresee it growing? This element of career direction is too often overlooked. Can the skills you've acquired up to now in your career be put to use in another area of the company, thus affording you a greater chance for advancement or job satisfaction? Or are the skills that you've acquired to date capable of serving you better if you move into another form of work?

For example, the advertising copywriter has a facility with words. They are his stock-in-trade. He can turn out jingles and rhymes and slogans by the carload. He is, in short, a wordsmith. He is able to discern that his future with the company, as the company's future is projected, will be that of a copywriter until the last slogan is wrung out of him. Perhaps that will satisfy him. But on the other hand, a simple redirection of his skills might enhance his overall career. Perhaps instead of writing slogans for the Fizzy Whizzy Soda Pop Company in their ad agency, he can improve himself by moving to the Fizzy Whizzy Soda Pop Company as in-house public relations coordinator, writing press releases and speeches for management. Here he has transferred himself from a horizontal career future to a vertical one—there's a chance for upward movement within the new company, opportunity for greater responsibility, and greater rewards. "But," you might protest, "he's a copywriter, not a public relations writer." The fact is that he's a writer and he's using the same tools, just applying them differently. The case histories in the following section will illuminate this concept much more clearly.

# 4. Sacrifices

As was said earlier, most career changes will involve a trade-off—security for freedom, income for ego satisfaction, hypertension for ulcers. To each his own, the list is endless.

*A man's reach should exceed his grasp, or what's a Heaven for?*

ROBERT BROWNING

Naturally, you want to strive for all of the possible satisfactions you can achieve: maximum income, maximum security, maximum pleasure, optimum working conditions, and so on. But early on, you'll have to start figuring out the trade-offs, the balances, the sacrifices of some things that you'll have to make in order to achieve others. And that, quite frankly, is a very good thing. It can be like a purge, an exorcism of some of the musty spirits that inhabit us. At first, it may seem like a sacrifice. Maybe, in fact, it will be. But, in many cases, it may be like removing a millstone from your back.

For example, it may be that in order to accomplish a career change, it will be necessary to sell your house and use the equity for capital investment, or simply to lower your living costs. A sacrifice? It certainly appears to be. But why did you buy this house in the first place? Could it be, as is the case with many, that you bought it not for your own satisfaction, but to satisfy what others wished for you, such as your parents and social peers?

I recall a case of a young couple from Cleveland, who sought my advice regarding whether or not they should sell their existing home and buy a new one. Both husband and wife were working and making a very good living in broadcasting. Some years earlier, they had purchased a ramshackle old house a few miles out of the city at the edge of Lake Erie. It was, as they described it, rather dingy and unappealing, but they liked it. They had enjoyed fixing it up, they enjoyed living away from the bustle of the city, they enjoyed the lakeside environment. But eventually parental and peer-group pressure began to make itself felt. They were asked, "Why are you living way out of town in that clunker? Why don't you move into the city, into such and such a swanky neighborhood, into such and such a swanky type of house?" They could certainly afford it. Money wasn't the problem. They were succumbing to the pressure, and feeling that they'd be doing the wrong thing if they didn't move up into the fancier quarters.

I asked them, "Who is it, after all, that you're trying to satisfy? The other people or yourselves?"

Had they succumbed to the pressure and bought the new house, they would have tied up $20,000 in non-income-producing brick and mortar. That's a rather expensive mask to dwell behind. But they didn't. They shunned the so-called advice of their status-conscious parents and peers, and remained in their ramshackle home by the lake, their $20,000 well invested, and their peace of mind well assured.

As you appraise the sacrifices and trade-offs that you may have to make in getting free, consider carefully this fact: change and sacrifice are not synonymous. Change represents a break from the status quo, an opportunity to expand, to enlarge, to improve. You may lose some status points in the process, but when you get right down to it, what are those points really worth in terms of your overall personal make-up?

Many career changes do, in fact, involve a loss in income, sometimes temporary, sometimes long-term. This obviously necessitates a trimming of one's life style. But what good is a life style that is hindered and hobbled by dissatisfaction with one's career?

*There is more to life than increasing its speed.*

MOHANDAS K. GANDHI

# Obstacles to Getting Free

Let's examine briefly some of the most common obstacles to getting free, to making a career change. If we can look these fears and doubts straight in the eye, evaluate them, analyze them, and weigh them, we can begin to formulate ways to overcome them. Frequently, these fears and doubts are vague and unspoken thoughts that drift around in the back of our minds. We may suppress them because we're reluctant to meet them face to face. That's compounding the felony. Let's get them out on the table and have a clear and honest look at them.

## 1. Relearning

*If a man empties his purse into his head, no one can take it away from him. An investment in knowledge always pays the best interest.*

BENJAMIN FRANKLIN

*The expectations of life depend on diligence; the mechanic that would perfect his work must first sharpen his tools.*

CONFUCIUS

Yes, old dogs can learn new tricks, if we are motivated and if we try hard enough. Many of us may have unpleasant recollections of our early career learning experiences. We were in our late teens and early twenties, anxious to conquer the world and the opposite sex, and to experience our new independence. Formal education and/or on-the-job training may have seemed like reins holding us back from our natural instincts. We had to study when we wanted to be out playing. We had to perform menial tasks when our energies told us that we were capable of much more important things. We were tested, quizzed, pressured, and disciplined.

It's no surprise that when we look back on such experiences, we feel that we do not wish to go through all that again.

Well, we don't have to. The information explosion of the last decade has reached such proportions that abundant training materials and courses are available for virtually every kind of vocation, in a form that you can follow yourself, at your own pace, to suit your own needs. The wildfire growth of the community college systems throughout the nation, and of their adult-education adjuncts, has provided literally hundreds of basic career-opportunity courses in their curricula. Whether you're starting from scratch, or just need some updating of your existing skills, the materials are out there.

Visit your local library, bookstores, community college, and high school adult-extension programs. Talk to people who are already involved in the field you wish to enter, and ask them to direct you to additional learning sources, either in the form of an on-the-job apprenticeship or in a formal training situation. The learning sources are out there. You just have to look for them.

What about going back to school in the formal sense? Spending four to six hours each day taking courses, subjecting yourself to exams and the like? If it's financially feasible to do so, you're probably going to find it far more palatable than you may have when you did it for the first time, as a youth. You won't be bothered by many of the typical pressures of the college environment that you suffered the first time around. There were pressures to date, to be socially acceptable, to join the right organization, to please your parents, to get the grades you were seeking. Those pressures can be quite distracting to the typical 18- or 19-year-old. But they're gone now.

You're there for the sole purpose of learning skills that you can put to use in a new career. Your powers of concentration will be far more focused than they were then. Your ability to absorb will be at a much higher level because you are motivated toward a more definite goal. And without the normal diversions and distractions that tempt the typical college youth, you very likely can accomplish your goals in a much shorter time than the normal college curriculum dictates.

One source of relearning requires a word of caution. The mass media abound with advertisements for "learn-at-home" programs. The pitches can be quite appealing. And misleading. And costly. And unproductive.

Some learn-at-home programs may be excellent. But in every industry there are a few bad apples. Perhaps the learn-at-home industry has more than its share. It requires diligence on your part to determine if the course you're signing up for can deliver what you're hoping to get out of it. Are you getting what you bargained for? It's always wise to determine if the same course of instruction is available through a local community college or high school extension program before you spend the not inconsiderable dollars on the learn-at-home program.

One common type of learn-at-home education, which has faded from the scene but is likely to return again, is the school, purportedly conducted by famous writers, artists, photographers, that allegedly will teach you the particular art in the comfort of your own living room. The lure and the glamour were readily apparent. And with teachers like that, how far wrong could you go?

All the way wrong was the most common answer. These particular arts involve a certain innate talent that, if you don't have it in you, can't really be taught adequately via the U.S. Postal Service. But the promoters preyed on the vanity of the victims, convincing them that they had all the talent required, and just needed this $750 course to bring it out. That was the approximate price of a one-way ticket for an ego trip with these programs.

Applicants would be asked to take a test that would, theoretically, determine their aptitude for art, writing, photography, etc. The result of the test was that you did have the talent, however deeply hidden it might be. All it would take to bring it to the surface was the money. Thus were many misled down the primrose path, and the disappointment that followed was enough to completely discourage them from making any attempt to get free for the rest of their lives.

Other learn-at-home programs were aimed at the trade and vocational skills—driving a truck, jockeying a disc, drafting a blueprint, surveying a subdivision, managing a motel, and on and on.

With dependable regularity, I receive information from the Federal Trade Commission and from various state attorney generals' offices alleging complaints against operators of these schools. Legal procedures are frequently instituted to bring a halt to these deceptive practices, but equally frequently they spring up again a few months later under a different guise. (I repeat—there are legitimate home-study programs, but you must beware of the few that besmirch the name of the good ones, and that can be hazardous to your bank account.)

Among the typical complaints in these proceedings are the following:

—Despite what the advertisements allege, there is not, in fact, an urgent need or demand for graduates of these schools.

—Testimonials used in the advertising don't truly reflect the typical job opportunities that are available to graduates.
—Some of the testimonials in the advertisements by purported graduates of the school are untrue or fictitious.
—Contrary to what the advertisements say, the course of training will not completely equip graduates for the job they're seeking. Further on-the-job training may be necessary to reach the salary levels that the ads indicate are available to students upon graduation.
—Contrary to the advertisements, enrollment in the school is not selective. Anybody who pays the money can get in.
—Contrary to the advertisements, the school may not be an accredited institution, and credit is not transferable to accredited institutions.
—Often, it's very difficult to get a fair refund on tuition paid if you do decide to drop out of the course. (Naturally, a portion of the tuition for any learn-at-home course may be kept by the school to offset the initial costs of setting up the program for you. But a fair refund should be available and should be stipulated in the agreement that you sign.)

Don't let these cautions discourage you from seeking the training that you'll need to further yourself. Just look upon them as situations to avoid or carefully scrutinize on your route to getting free.

## 2. Financial Security

*Security is mostly a superstition. It does not exist in nature, nor do the children of man as a whole experience it. Avoiding danger is no safer in the long run than outright exposure. Life is either a daring adventure, or nothing.*

HELEN KELLER

What, after all, is job security? The president of the United States only gets a four-year contract, and he has to spend the last of those four years jockeying for position to get a renewal. U.S. senators get six years, but there are only 100 of them; and the chairman of the Federal Reserve Board gets fourteen years, but there's only one of him.

Heads can roll in seconds in the executive offices of major corporations, due to one or many slight improprieties, bad earnings reports, or a frontal assault from the next lower rung on the ladder. A slight shift in the monthly Nielsen ratings (wherein some 1,200 people presumably reflect the television viewing habits of the entire nation) can at least temporarily doom the careers of hundreds in the television industry. If a lawyer loses an important case, if a doctor is successfully sued for malpractice, if an accountant lets his client get into income-tax troubles, the question of security in a profession becomes instantly shaky.

The boss's wife doesn't like your spouse. The boss's nephew covets your job. The boss covets you.

The critics don't like your book/movie/play/painting/sculpture/restaurant/song/dance/music/juggling routine and the public stays away in droves. Or the critics like any or all of the above, but the public doesn't.

Your company bids on a major contract, and success will mean five years, or ten years, or a lifetime in the planning, development, and manufacture of the product. But the company loses the bid, and months and years of research go down the drain.

A competitor introduces a better product than the one you are involved in, and your own sales dwindle away.

The nation's economy, or a state's economy, or a city's economy goes into a slump, and whatever product/service you are designing/assembling/selling/advertising/delivering is no longer in demand.

Your company is a major supplier of another larger company, and the big one goes bust. The domino effect is soon felt.

The ladder you've been slowly and steadily climbing is swiftly kicked out from under you when your company is absorbed by a larger company, which has ample personnel, thank you very much, to take over your duties.

Even civil servants—government employees—are finding their historic job security in jeopardy, as cities, counties, states, and even the federal government curtail programs, run into financial difficulty, cease the expansion of programs in certain areas.

What is job security? The lifer in prison has the ultimate. At least he knows where his three meals a day will be coming from for the duration. Short of that, do you really have the security that you've led yourself to believe you have?

I don't mean to alarm you. I just want you to be aware of the tenuous nature of job security, particularly in view of the economic upheavals the nation has gone through in recent years. If you do your work well, if you're loyal and productive, if you follow the "book," you probably have a measure of security that shouldn't be interrupted short of a drastic change within your company or the industry in which you're working. But those changes can occur.

Is security the comfort of knowing that you get a regular paycheck each week? Granted, not knowing whether or not a check will be forthcoming each week can be very traumatic, particularly if you have a family and no other means of support for them. Fear of loss of financial security is a very natural and formidable obstacle to making a career change.

But if you do make a change, is your ship really going to sink? If you make an impulsive and poorly reasoned change, taking great financial risk in the process, you're putting yourself into danger—if not for the present, then possibly for the future if you blow your nest egg in the process.

But if your change is planned carefully, capitalized adequately, and approached rationally, your chances of success are greatly enhanced. Naturally, there's no assurance that any particular new venture will succeed, just as there is no automatic certainty that it will fail. If worse comes to worst, if you've done the proper planning, can't you always go back to the job or the type of work that you're now contemplating leaving? At the worst, you might find yourself saying, "I wasn't happy, I tried something new, but I failed, so now I'm going back to what can at least provide for my family." This is an outcome that you may have to confront, but at least you will have tried.

You can assure your own security with the proper planning, with the proper professional advice, and with a proper frame of mind. You put your security at risk if you act impetuously, if you listen to the wrong advice, if you have faulty timing.

Enhancing your security, then, is really up to you. You can do it and leave yourself in a situation with little to lose, and something to fall back upon. The case histories that follow will further illustrate this point, and the final part of the book on "doing it" will give you some of the specific guidelines you'll need to overcome this really not so formidable obstacle.

## 3. The Family Is Too Settled

*The mass of men lead lives of quiet desperation.*

HENRY DAVID THOREAU

"Everything is nice and smooth and comfortable and under control. My spouse and I and the kids have each got our own little niche, worn and secure, and we move along one step at a time, one day at a time. We're settled, we have roots, we know where we are and where we're going. Then why do I wake up in the middle of the night and feel like screaming so often? I'd really like to, but I know it would ripple the waters."

Certainly, family contentedness is not to be sloughed off. But the possibility does exist that an apparently well settled and content family is suffering from the same enslavement, once removed, as the breadwinner. They're grinning and bearing their situation just as their breadwinner does. If that seething discontent that we discussed earlier is bubbling within you, you may be kidding yourself in thinking that you're hiding it from those around you. They can sense it, and they can react instinctively, withdrawing into a protective little niche that can, in its own turn, send them off into their adulthood or future years with an exceptionally high vulnerability to distress.

Family stability and contentedness are among the highest goals of any person. But if these are built upon a weak foundation, they can do as much harm as good. Yet, even with a flaw in the foundation, this might be the last area that you'd want to tamper with in trading off goods and bads for a new career for yourself. You're tinkering with the lives of others, and you don't know what the outcome will be—if you stay put or make a change.

The situation definitely calls for maximum communication among the members of the family, including the children who are old enough to comprehend what is going on. Some families, or individual members of some families, may be very flexible, easily capable of riding out even turbulent changes without their own psyches being affected. Some family members might indeed welcome a change—much to your surprise, for you had thought all these years that they were so content in their little niche. Other families or individual members will indeed have a natural resistance to change.

Perhaps a decision in this area will require some professional guidance. Acting on your own, even with ample communication among the family members, you might not be able to determine if your actions will be harmful (either staying put or getting free) until after the damage has been done. Consider discussing your plans with a family counselor, a clergyman, or another trusted advisor—someone who can see the situation from a different perspective, objectively and honestly.

"But what will my friends think if they hear we're talking over our problems with a family counselor?" I can hear some of you asking yourselves.

Nonsense. What will your friends think when they hear you've been waking up in the middle of the night screaming? All of which brings us to the next obstacle.

## 4. Social Effects

*The eyes of other people are the eyes that ruin us. If all but myself were blind, I should want neither fine clothes, fine houses, nor fine furniture.*

BENJAMIN FRANKLIN

"Roger, you must be crazy thinking of leaving a good secure job. You've got a wife and kids to feed. A mortgage to pay off. You've got position in the community. Are you going to give all that up?"

"Tell me, what is it with Roger, keeping his wife and kids in those shabby clothes? Is it true what I hear about his saving up all his money so that he can open up an antique book shop? I pity poor Zelda. Is there anything we can do?"

"Hey, Rog! We've been missing you lately at happy hour. Get with it, kid. Hoist a few. Christ, Rog, you're getting to be a real drudge."

"Daddy, the Braunschweigers just got a new car. When are we going to get rid of our old rattletrap?"

"Roger, you may not give a damn, but your boss's daughter didn't invite our Emily to her birthday party, and Emily's been in her room crying all afternoon."

The social effects and reverberations of making a career change may not affect you in the slightest. But this will not be the case for everyone. People being what they are, the little digs and jibes and nasties can take their toll, if not on ourselves, then on the members of our families.

But the main obstacle is not in the actual occurrence of such unpleasantness, it's in the worrying that such unpleasantness will occur. In short, "What *will* the neighbors say?" The family that communicates well should be able to gird itself for any such petty problems, which probably won't occur anyway. What the neighbors say aloud may sting and then fade. But what they're likely to be saying to themselves, in the quiet confessions of their own minds, is, "I envy him/her."

This issue, if it is one at all, should be the slightest obstacle in your path. But you can let it get out of hand by treating it disproportionately in the first place. People will dig deep to find petty reasons to criticize and make jibes at others. It's a form of cheap therapy to cover up their own anxieties. If you let it get you down, perhaps you deserve it. This is an obstacle you should overcome without any strain.

# 5. Fear of Lack of Capital

*A man is rich in proportion to the number of things he can afford to let alone.*

HENRY DAVID THOREAU

Ascetic hippy or clever economist? Thoreau suggests that doing without can be translated into wealth, in a sense. Indeed, the feeling that you don't have enough capital to embark on your desired adventure can easily be manifested in your unwillingness to forego some of the pleasures you're now enjoying. Again, we come to a question of a trade-off. Later, in this book, we'll discuss various ways of raising capital, or cutting down the need for capital, in various business endeavors. But in this section, where we're still thinking about getting free, I want you to simply consider what trade-offs you can make in your current life style that will generate the extra dollars you may need in order to get free. If you're not willing to forego certain things, perhaps you really don't want to get free that badlv. Only you can answer this question.

It boils down to this: if you can't raise the capital that you need (once you've given the matter careful study with the proper professional help, as discussed later), or you can't trim down your capital needs to suit the capital that you can raise, what, if anything, are you willing to give up of your present life style in order to achieve your goals? The answer to this question may tell you a lot about how much those goals really mean to you. It's a question that may be hard to answer, but it must be asked.

Fear of lack of capital is an easy disguise for a lack of commitment on your part to get free. But it's a weak excuse. Don't let yourself succumb to it. Plans can be modified, delayed, trimmed back to bring them in line with capital availability.

In fact, one of the most frequent causes of new-business failure is under-capitalization. But that's a matter of poor planning, which can be avoided. But reluctance to embark on a new venture because of the initial *fear* of lack of capital is simply a premature admission of defeat.

"I can never raise the capital that I'm really going to need, so I'll just forget the whole thing." That's foolishness. Plot out your program. Determine how much you'll need. Be ready to move. Then, if you can't get the capital you need, you can start making adjustments. If, ultimately, you do strike out, that's the time to decide to abandon the project. At least, give it a chance to live. Don't let fear of lack of capital be an obstacle.

## 6. Fear of the Unknown/Lack of Confidence

*Freedom lies in being bold.*

ROBERT FROST

*There is one thing stronger than all the armies in the world: and that is an idea whose time has come.*

VICTOR HUGO

*I think I can, I think I can . . . I know I can, I know I can . . . I knew I could, I knew I could . . .*

THE LITTLE ENGINE WHO COULD

Of course you can! Who do you think is out there right now making the world go round? It's the doers, the entrepreneurs, the individualists, big and small, who one day said to themselves, "There is something that I must do, and I will do it." They didn't ask, "Can I do it?" They said "I *will* do it." Sure, many failed, and then again many of them bounced right back to succeed. Many failed and never recovered. They may have had bad breaks, bad timing, bad advice, or the wrong idea to begin with.

It's not going to be a garden of roses. Anything as tasty and juicy and desirable as the freedom you're seeking is going to take some hard work, some luck, some guts, a whole lot of patience, and an abundance of determination. It's not certain whether you'll succeed beyond your wildest dreams, or whether you'll have to settle for half a dream. But one thing is certain: you have to open that door and you have to walk through it. Otherwise, you'll never know.

As you'll see in the case histories that follow, confidence was never really in question in most of them. You'll see a glint of what I felt when I made my major career change in my early thirties. I was enjoying the epitome of financial security and stability. It was the *known* that I feared. I could clearly see the income that I'd be making, the committees that I'd be serving on, my role in the community, my activity at work at age 35, 40, 45, 50, and onward. And that scared me. I sensed that I would thrive more on a diet of adventure, unknown, come-what-may. Fortunately, the predictability of my life succumbed to the maverick spirit within me. You have that same maverick spirit within you. Otherwise, you wouldn't have read this far.

Now, onward to some intimate glimpses of people like yourself who have gotten free.

Part Two

# Reading About It: How Others Got Free

# How Do Other People Do It?

You are about to read twenty-two actual case histories of people who have gotten free. How and why did they do what they did? What motivated them? What risks did they face?

I had to delve into the childhoods of some of these people to determine some hidden factor that later surfaced and moved them along a chosen path. Others shifted direction due to some factor in their later life—a divorce, a firing, an "awakening."

You may find that one or more of these cases mirror your own personal situation. Or you may find factors from the whole group that combine to resemble your own situation. Even though specific careers among these case histories may differ from your own, you may find a common ground in the underlying causes and motivations.

Some of these cases represent a complete turnabout in career, such as those of Larry, who gave up his law practice to become a clothing designer and haberdasher; Mike, who left a career in engineering to open his own auto-repair shop; and Hal, who worked in personnel for a large industry until he got free and started his own franchised printing shop. Others have grown within an existing vocation, working for a company until they had enough skills to embark on their own enterprise, such as Fred, first the advertising manager for a large financial institution and later the owner of his own ad agency; Liz, who worked in public relations until she felt ready to open her own firm; and Ken, a real-estate entrepreneur who cut his teeth with a major firm for many years before getting free.

I've not attempted to measure or compare the so-called success of each of these ventures, for indeed success is a personal and relative thing. All of these people are happy that they have done what they have done, though some aren't sure that yet another change might not be in store for them. Some have exceeded their previous earnings, others have not. But, generally, earnings didn't seem to matter to them. While all were motivated to some extent to earn an acceptable living from their venture, none of them were compelled only by the desire for money. Thus, money, which is the most commonly accepted measurement of success in our system, is not a valid criterion for measuring success in these case histories. Nor should it necessarily be a valid criterion for you.

All of the people involved in these case histories voluntarily allowed me to probe deep into their personal lives and thoughts. To protect their anonymity, I have changed their names and locations. Each of them, in one way or another, expressed a thought to me that I now pass along to you, "I hope that my story will help others see the light and do what's best for them. If I can do it, so can anyone else."

# How Do You Get to Be a Bank President at 34, and What Do You Do for an Encore?

*There's a man in the world who is never turned down,*
*Wherever he chances to stray;*
*He gets the glad hand in the populous town,*
*Or out where the farmers make hay;*
*He's greeted with pleasure on deserts of sand,*
*and deep in the aisles of the woods;*
*Wherever he goes there's a welcoming hand—*
*He's the man who delivers the goods.*

WALT WHITMAN

WAYNE'S STORY: Wayne was ambitious and industrious even during his high school days in St. Louis during the late 1940s. During the summer vacations, he worked in factories and on construction projects, but he had no particular career goals in mind. A good student, and curious to see "how the Yankees did it," he journeyed east to Wesleyan College for his higher education. He chose to obtain a liberal arts background with a major in economics, which sparked him with the idea of becoming a treasurer of a large company. Which company, he didn't know. It was just the first hint of a direction. He envisioned a preliminary career in banking as a shortcut to becoming a corporate treasurer.

After college, he obtained a job as a pension trust department trainee at a major New York City bank, but the career was over sooner than he had expected, for he was called to serve in the Korean War. Recruits rarely climbed the ladder of success, but Wayne was an exception. As the Korean War ended, he found himself sweeping floors in the base PX.

"What's a nice boy like me doing sweeping floors?" he asked himself one day. He persuaded one of his co-workers to allow him to look at the books of the PX, and calling upon his accounting background, he began to find shortages in the accounts. By bringing these shortages to the attention of his superiors, Wayne ended up in charge of that PX, and of two others as well.

Discovering that a person can move up, even in the Army, Wayne took advantage of his aggressiveness and moved into the editorship of the regiment newspaper. But there were still more comforts and conveniences to be found in the office of the regiment colonel. Wayne could only type twenty-three words a minute, which theoretically wouldn't qualify him for the job of secretary to the colonel. But he got the job, learning as he did that it's not just technical skills that count, but the ability to understand another's needs. In this case, the colonel had great difficulty drafting his own letters, and Wayne was able to draft them for him. Although he typed only twenty-three words a minute, Wayne retained the job until he left the Army in December 1955.

He returned to the New York bank, with a salary of $400 per month, $100 higher than his pre-Army salary. He remained there for a year and a half, and realized that in the midst of similarly trained and motivated young men, it would take more education to get one jump ahead of the mob. So it was on to Harvard Business School.

With his credentials and his experience mounting, the challenge of the big New York City bank no longer seemed as intriguing. He was offered, and he accepted, a position with a bank in Denver, heading up the new business department. Under Wayne's direction, the bank went from zero to $33.5 million in deposits in eighteen months. He was now earning $10,000 a year, and had no place to go but up.

And up happened shortly thereafter. Through an ad in the *Wall Street Journal,* Wayne learned that a to-be-formed bank in Portland, Oregon, was looking for a president—not just someone to run the operation, but someone with the background and know-how to assist in getting the charter and the initial investors, and building the operation from scratch. There was no assurance by the promoters of the bank that the charter could be obtained, nor that the necessary financing could be arranged, nor that the other regulatory authorities would give their approval. It could have turned into a year or two of running headlong down a blind alley. But the offer was attractive—Wayne's salary would double—and he took the gamble.

He delivered the goods. The bank was formed, and Wayne was its first president, at the age of 34. He remained there for four years, but personal objectives motivated him to return to Denver. There, another relatively new bank offered him an executive vice-presidency at a salary of $25,000 per year. It was a smaller bank fighting the giants, and the levels of responsibility given to the higher-echelon officials in such institutions are quite extensive. But within a year after Wayne took this position in Denver, the majority stockholders of the bank decided to sell to another group, and Wayne felt that he could not work well with the new owners.

Now, he realized, he had built himself a Frankenstein. He had moved so swiftly up the salary ladder that none of the other local banks could afford him. Those with duties and titles similar to his in the larger banks earned considerably less. And the larger banks simply had no openings that met his salary level. He had, in effect, reached the top too quickly. Where could he go from there?

Wayne surveyed his skills. Economics major, Harvard Business School, ten years in banking, with high-level experience, and a drive that just wouldn't let go. From personal experience, he knew the problems and frustrations of the small businessman. Management consulting! That was it! Starting from scratch, risking everything, but with an abundance of self-confidence, he hung out his shingle as a management consultant. He gave himself no time limit. He simply was going to make it.

But his early days were frustrating, indeed. One of his first ventures was to send out over 6,000 letters of solicitation to local businesses in order to make his services known. He got two deals out of this expensive promotional effort, one of which paid him only $25. But each project led to another contact, and each of those led to other contacts. He lost money during his first year, broke even during his second year.

All was not going well financially, but he was doing what he thought he could do best. As a sideline, he gave politics a try. It couldn't help but aid his self-promotion. He made a run for a seat in the state Senate, and went out beating the bushes for votes. He was successful. But it was, in his words, "the most expensive thing I ever did."

But now, with the political experience, a new dimension had been added, or had surfaced from some subliminal reservoir of talent—public speaking.

Recognizing his skills, acquired, revised, and updated, Wayne now prepared to take another step up the ladder in his activities. He knew the problems of the business person. He could speak effectively and articulately to the public. Why not combine the two and get paid for it?

Again starting from scratch, he developed himself as a fixture on the lecture circuit, specializing in motivational talks to business groups. This endeavor was somewhat akin to a kid who can knock tin cans off a fence with rocks trying to get a pitching job with a major league baseball team. Those who hire lecturers for their businesses and associations are besieged daily with pamphlets and presentations from top-name speakers and high-powered lecture agencies.

But Wayne hustled. "Follow up" was his credo, and he pursued his new career with a vengeance. Where the typical lecture brochure is mailed and forgotten, Wayne followed up with telephone calls, more letters, more calls. He received his first speaking fee, a paltry one, in 1970, but it gave him the opportunity to acquire a good testimonial from the group. He parlayed this with his follow-up procedures into another and another and another engagement.

Today, Wayne is established as a speaker of national repute in his field, earning $500 for a one-hour lecture, and $1,000 for a day-long seminar. Shortly after my interview with him, he was to embark on a tour that would take him from Denver to Des Moines to Memphis to Cleveland to Phoenix to Honolulu and back to Denver in twelve days. During the following summer, he was booked for seminars in London, Amsterdam, Brussels, and Copenhagen.

He has preferred to remain based in Denver, simply because he likes it there. With his management consulting and his lecturing, his financial success is greater than it ever was.

And yet, the restless spirit continues. "I still take things one step at a time. I may be off in a new direction soon. But whatever I do, one thing is for sure—I'll always stay on my own. I've seen too much trouble with the big successes. I've realized that the quality of life is now more important than the quantity of life. Success is truly the bitch goddess. She's never satisfied, no matter what you give her. What profit is there if you gain success, but lose your soul? I forget who said that, but it's true.

"There's no security anymore in the paycheck. Besides, employees have to spend too much of their productive energy and their time convincing others of their decisions, and protecting themselves. It's better to use your productive energy for your own results.

"If there's work to be done, I want to control the work. Most people, especially employees, have their work controlling them."

Since Wayne makes a substantial portion of his living motivating others to work better, I asked him what advice he would have for anyone who wanted to get free and go off on his or her own.

"Anybody can be good enough. But most people don't really want to make the effort. They don't keep trying. They don't follow through, and they get too upset by rejections. Rejections don't necessarily mean that you're not good enough. You might just be trying to sell your product to the wrong party or at the wrong time.

"If you're going to go off on your own, have everything set for you before you leave your current job. Get all the machinery in working order. Don't kill time after you've split trying to get something going.

"When you jump, hit the ground with your feet already running."

# Let Your Ego Work for You, Not Against You

*If you wish in this world to advance,*
*Your merits you're bound to enhance;*
*You must stir it and stump it*
*And blow your own trumpet*
*Or, trust me, you haven't a chance.*

W. S. GILBERT, *Rudigore*

KEN'S STORY: Worried about financial security? Ken was making $900 a month with a real-estate management firm when he decided to get free. Nothing unusual about that? At the time, his infant daughter was in need of open-heart surgery, which would cost in the neighborhood of $5,000. Leaving his job meant giving up his medical insurance. But he went anyway. And everything worked out for the best.

You'd have to call Ken mild-mannered in virtually every respect. He speaks softly, dresses conservatively, lives modestly. Not the characteristics you might expect to see in a successful businessman who embarked on his own in a highly competitive industry (real estate) in one of the nation's fastest-growing cities (Tucson). Just as Wayne carries his lecture-podium flamboyance into his personal demeanor, so Ken carries his calm, deliberate business manner into his discussion of the battle he fought with his own ego.

Ken had a "baby complex." He was the youngest of three children, and was constantly on the short end of the sibling rivalry with his older brothers. "My brother was always knocking me. Even when I was in grade school, I lacked confidence and couldn't make decisions. All my decisions were made for me. I was still being told what kind of shoes to buy when I got into high school. I'll never forget wanting to buy a pair of white bucks, because that's what was popular then. But I was told that wasn't sensible, and I went along.

"I went through high school as an average student. I wasn't involved in any particular activities, and I had no particular career aspirations. I had no pressure from my folks, and unfortunately I didn't have much guidance either. But I did know that I'd need more education in order to have some kind of career. So I went to the University of Arizona.''

Ken's dad, already semiretired by the time Ken started college, was enjoying income from some real-estate investments. A personality clash between Ken's dad and one of his tenants gave Ken his first glimpse of the real-estate field. For reasons that Ken still can't recall, his dad asked him to mediate the argument between himself and the tenant. Though only 18 at the time, and totally unfamiliar with the particulars of the transaction, Ken realized that the difference of opinion was strictly a matter of common sense, and was able to help them negotiate it successfully. This early success stayed in his mind.

While in college, Ken was under no financial pressure to make any career decision, nor, because of his dad's semiretirement, was there any family business that he could easily go into. Ken spent much of college ''trying to find himself.'' His early thoughts on a career direction were focused on law school, because his older brother was an attorney; and on retailing, because he had had some part-time work in sales to help support himself in college. But underlying these specific directions, there was an ego that had to be satisfied.

In the latter years of college, Ken took a course in real-estate law as a part of his general business major, and did more work on some of his dad's buildings.

As college ended and decision time came near, Ken chose to go to law school. This would provide a profession, a career, a direction—even though he had never had any real personal desire to become an attorney. Perhaps he was more motivated by a feeling that the professional credentials of a degree in law would satisfy the churning lack of self-confidence that he had carried with him all these years. As evidence, Ken confesses to a Walter Mitty fantasy that had followed him constantly: ''I wanted to see my name on big buildings. I didn't necessarily associate it with wealth or power, just a kind of ego thing, I guess, to show them that I could be a success. This probably tied in with the little experience I'd had in real estate, and I guess it motivated me to pursue that eventually.''

The ego took another drubbing in law school. Ken flunked out after his first year, but now the failure syndrome prompted a reaction stimulus. He bounced back strongly with a desire to ''show them,'' to prove himself. He had done well in his real-property course in law school. He nurtured his fantasies about seeing his name on big buildings. He had had some experience in the real world of real estate. He knew that he needed more training. He felt that real estate retained some of the aspects and professionalism of law practice. And he was bound and determined to make it now.

(An interesting aside is Ken's analysis of his weakness in law school. Very likely, the weakness prevails in students more today than it did in Ken's day. He discerns the ultimate weakness as his inability to write and express himself, and feels that he had not been trained in high school or college to do these things. "The teachers in high school and college," he says, "give true-false or multiple-choice exams. Sure, they're a lot easier for them to grade, or they can give the exams to a computer to grade. That means less work for them. But the students aren't learning the basic writing skills that they'll need, either in law school or in other endeavors. Thus, the student gets the short end of the stick. Unfortunately, I wasn't aware of this until it was too late. Now, I certainly advocate that all young persons develop their skills in writing and expressing themselves as soon as possible and as fully as possible. If you're ever going to make it, you have to be able to express yourself accurately, interestingly, and succinctly.")

Ken wasn't ready to go out on his own, but he sensed that someday he would. In the meantime, he needed to acquire the background and the skills to make it in real estate, so he took a job selling houses for a major brokerage firm. His ego won a few quick rounds when he passed his real-estate salesman's license exam, and later his brokerage license exam, without having to take the recommended courses. (Since that time, certain instructional courses have become mandatory in Arizona, as well as in other states.) Thus, even though he had done poorly in law school, the skills he had acquired in the real-property course proved to be of use to him.

Ken was going to prove that he could be a success. He was going to reestablish his pride and self-confidence. But his first job left him disillusioned. "Selling residential property wasn't challenging, at least not to me," he told me. "There was no motivation. I was nothing more than a chauffeur. I wasn't selling, I was *shlepping*. There's very little selling to be done. If a wife likes the house, then the husband decides if he can afford it. That's what's critical. The financial details can always be ironed out. But it's an emotional thing. If a woman doesn't like a house, there's no way that a salesman can convince her to like it. Maybe another woman can, but I couldn't."

The residential real-estate job was short-lived, interrupted after nine months by a stint in the Air Force to fulfill his military obligation. During the last months of that job, Ken learned that there was more money to be made and more challenge in getting listings of houses for sale than in actually selling them. "This was where the real selling took place—convincing people that I, or my firm, could sell their house for them better than anyone else could. I could see this ultimately as an activity I'd enjoy doing on my own," Ken said.

After a year in the Air Force, he had to make another decision—to strike out on his own then, or to stay with the company and get more experience. ''I felt then that any success I was ever going to make had to be on my own; any success I could make with a company would be limited. But I still knew that I needed a company to grow with, to get more experience before I tried to go it alone.''

While looking for a job after his Air Force duty, Ken took a course in real-estate appraisal to increase his credentials. But he still wasn't sure which speciality within the very broad field of real estate would suit him best—construction? development? mortgage broking? He remembered a statement from one of his teachers that, particularly in rapidly growing cities, there would be a tremendous demand in real-estate management for professionals who could take care of all of the needs of large buildings for absentee owners.

This struck his fancy, but he found that everybody else had gotten there before him. Jobs were so tight that he had to talk his way into a job as a management trainee with one of the larger local firms, on a thirty-days-without-pay basis. ''They had no open positions. I had to prove myself within thirty days, or I'd be out. If they were satisfied with me, they said they'd offer me a job. Within the thirty days, they fired another man that they had hired just before me, and I took his place. This was in September of 1962, and I started off at $400 a month.''

Ken did his job well. Within three months, his monthly salary was raised to $500, and six months later, it was raised to $750. The firm was large and growing rapidly with the community. He settled in with the firm for what looked to be a long and satisfying career.

He married, and in the interest of conserving capital for an ultimate breakaway, he bought a much more modest house than he could afford at that time.

Then, the traces of handwriting began to appear on the wall. ''I was working on salary. They didn't pay any of their management people commission. This kind of takes away some of the incentives to improve the profitability of the property you're managing, particularly when it comes to leasing the premises. To help create some incentive for myself and the company, I asked them for a percentage of the profits on the buildings I was managing or some form of commission. But they were an old-line company and weren't about to change their ways. They said no. My income level was at the top for the kind of work I was doing, almost equal to what my boss's was. I could see that I was getting into a rut. But I had to stay at that time because my daughter was going through her first heart surgery. Even with the group insurance covering most of that cost, I still had to dip into my savings to keep up our life style.

''Part of anybody's success in breaking loose and going on his own has got to be that you know an opportunity when it presents itself, and when to make the move. My daughter's operation had indefinitely delayed my making the break, but one day a client came in to solicit our company's management of a building he owned. I discussed all the details with him, and the conversation ended up with him offering me a full-time job at a substantial increase over what I was making. My ethics wouldn't allow me to discuss such a job when I was on my employer's time and representing my employer. But the man called me at home later to pursue the matter. I had reservations about his job offer, because it would require extensive travel, and I didn't want to be away from home, particularly with my daughter ill. Then, he said that if I were on my own, running my own management firm, he'd let me take over the management of a local shopping center that he and some others owned."

At this time, Ken was making $900 a month, plus fringe benefits, and had no overhead at the real-estate office. The management offer would have grossed him $600 a month, and he'd have the overhead of his own office and no fringe benefits. But that was the break point. He felt confident that he could keep the account and attract new ones, using the skills and the contacts that he had accumulated over the six and a half years with the large firm. It was then or not at all, even with another $5,000 operation on the horizon.

"I had prepared myself, including getting my Certified Property Management designation, which is the prime credential in that field of real estate. I had about $1,800 in my savings account at the time. We were living fairly modestly. And I just knew I could make it. I had no thought of any failure. At the worst, I knew that I could go out and find another job. So I gave up my job, and with it the insurance that would have paid for almost all of my daughter's heart surgery."

In April 1969, Ken opened his own office. Within nine months, his earnings were back to the level they had been at when he had left the large firm. Today, his income is many times that, and he has three active salespeople working for him, in addition to his basic office staff. Ken attributes his success to a number of things.

"If you've got the basic knowledge and experience, and people know that you're honest and ethical, many of them will go to you to help the new little guy get started, instead of going to the big company. A lot of clients wouldn't have used me when I was with the big company, but they will now because they know they're getting personal service and the personal touch. They know that I'll show them more attention and be more personal than I could have been when I was with the big company. I never solicited any accounts that I had with the big company, nor would I.

"In this kind of business, as in many kinds of businesses, you're handling a lot of other people's money. Their trust in you is the most important thing. I can't afford to behave in any way that would cast any doubts on my honesty and integrity. That's been my code, and I've followed it to the letter.

"One thing I've learned and want to pass along is that regardless of what anyone says, most of the time you create your own good luck. You do this by recognizing opportunity when it comes along and being prepared to take advantage of it. A lot of people have good breaks fall right in front of them, and either they don't see them or they aren't willing to take advantage of them. A lot of people who get caught in a rut are committing the same big mistakes—they're afraid to take a chance and they're afraid of hard work."

Ken was once a person with zero self-esteem. Now he has enough to pass some around to others.

# In Search of Art

*To be nobody but myself—in a world which is doing its best, night and day, to make you everybody else—means to fight the hardest battle which any human being can fight, and never stop fighting.*

E. E. CUMMINGS

LARRY'S STORY: There are three people involved in this segment. First is Larry, the lawyer-turned-haberdasher/clothing designer who made his switch while in the depths of personal depression. Then comes the story of Jay and Helen, a couple who virtually think and act as one, who made their mutual shift while immersed in the counterculture drug scene in New York City. The quest for all three was for the freedom to be creative.

Larry grew up in Buffalo, New York, a member of one of the few Jewish families in a predominantly Gentile neighborhood. He remembers himself as being a roly-poly, fat kid, the youngest in his class, but the number-one student. He was not an athlete in an environment that bestowed praise on athletic skills, and he was a Jew in a community where overt anti-Semitism had to be tolerated. The oldest of four children, Larry often helped his father in their small, corner grocery store, stamping coupons, weighing potatoes and sugar in bulk, and being fascinated with meeting people person-to-person. The mercantile instinct had touched him before puberty did.

"My real interest, ever since I can remember, probably back around the age of 8, was art. I was an avid comic-book reader, and spent all the time I could cartooning and drawing. I never thought of it as a career, it was just something I enjoyed doing. But that was no activity for the typical son of the typical Jewish mother, which I was. Even though my own aptitudes and interests as a kid were toward art and theater and dramatics, my mother was drumming it into my head that I should be a doctor. I know that sounds like an old joke, but it was true in my case. I had no pressure from my dad one way or the other, but my mother was constantly telling me of the security, prestige, and dignity that one could obtain by becoming a doctor."

By early adolescence, then, Larry had three influences working on him—his own inclination toward art, his mother's pressure on him toward medicine, and an unconscious tendency toward the mercantile, gained from exposure in his father's grocery store. Larry was not aware of any conflict. He says that his childhood was happy. But in our ensuing conversation, it became quite apparent that the early childhood influences did create some degree of confusion in his mind, which no doubt led to considerable insecurity as his career developed.

"Looking back, whether my mother was right or wrong, she did at least elevate my taste level. Without that, I probably couldn't be doing the work I'm doing today. And yet, even though I know what's nice, I can live without it. Personally, I don't have any need to possess. When you're defining success, there's quite a difference between the person who has a need to possess and the person who has no need to possess. Everyone should keep that in mind."

High school was Larry's "great glory." It was a 3,500-student melting pot, and he was the first Jewish president ever of the student body. He was a member of the National Honor Society and editor of the school newspaper. He graduated in 1950.

Larry's success in high school earned him entrance into Dartmouth, and packed in his bags was the message from his mother: "You need a profession—be a doctor." Being a doctor, he was told, and he rationalized, meant money, prestige, and helping people. Even though he had no scientific bent and no real desire to pursue medicine, he repressed his mercantile inclinations, and apparently paid no attention to his own artistic desires. He was embarking upon the path he had been programmed to follow.

But college was a traumatic change from high school. "All of a sudden I was among a lot of other high school valedictorians and big-money people. Here was an academic world offering vastly broader choices then I had known in high school. Things like advanced physics and math. I hated them. It was hard work for me and very unpleasant. But these were courses that I needed to become a doctor.''

Larry began to reexamine his career goals. His distaste for the immediate requirements of premed swayed him away from the program. ''If I'd sat down and talked to some doctors about it, I probably would have changed my mind and stayed with it. I would have had a different view. I had only taken the short-term view of getting into med school. Also, at this same time, I became interested in psychology, which led me to an interest in a career in clinical psychology. I was probably rationalizing, but I saw this as a form of medicine, and I didn't have to go to med school in order to achieve it. It could satisfy my parents, and for me, it was a line of least resistance.''

At this point in our conversation, I asked Larry whether or not this was the college student reacting or the roly-poly Jewish kid in the Gentile neighborhood always getting picked on and laughed at for his unathletic tendencies, just wanting to be left alone to do his own thing, to doodle with his cartoons, and to dream about the world of theater.

''I never thought of it quite that way, but perhaps that's it,'' Larry answered. ''Basically, I guess I've always been a noncombatant, and I still am. I didn't like having to confront people or strange circumstances back when I was a kid, and I still tend to avoid them.''

By the second year of college, a romance had started to bloom between Larry and a girl whose father owned a modest discount store in Buffalo. One son-in-law was already in the business with the father, and the father had an obligation to a nephew. Anticipating marriage, Larry's girlfriend suggested that he not bother with college, but just go into her dad's business. By this time, Larry had determined that he really didn't like the basic academic life, even though he was a good student. The appeal of the merchant life surfaced again, and the prospect seemed like a good way to get out of long-haul academia and into the real world.

In the middle of his junior year, fate intervened and sent Larry off on the first of many zigs and zags in his life. His father suddenly became very ill, and needed a serious operation. He'd be out of work for up to three months, so Larry left college to go home and run the business. It seemed as though the chips were falling in the right place. His girlfriend was there, he was constructively at work, and even though he pursued his studies at night school in Buffalo, he was already having serious doubts about continuing into any form of graduate school. Here was a convenient way for him to determine whether or not marriage and going into business with his father-in-law would be the simple, secure solution to a dilemma that he couldn't quite get hold of.

''As it turned out, I realized perhaps a bit too late that my initial romance with the girl was a case of my glands overpowering my brains. When I got back into the home environment and saw the pace of her father's business and its limitations, I knew that I'd always be low man on the totem pole. Just to get a job and be an employee and a son-in-law wouldn't be so hot after all. Thus, my head turned back toward continuing my education. But where and how? I talked to a lot of people about it. Maybe the law. It involved language and communication, and this seemed attractive. I had no deep desire to be a lawyer, but it seemed like something I could do successfully, and it had the prestige and professionalism of medicine. I guess I still wanted to please my parents."

By combining certain credits, Larry was able to commence law school at Syracuse after his final half-year at night school in Buffalo. The love affair was still smoldering, and the girl wanted to get married and accompany him to law school. But Larry's funds were limited, and he didn't want to have to work any more than he would already have to while going to school. He suggested that they wait a year and see what happens.

"You don't love me! I want to get married now! All of my girlfriends are married, and it's about time . . ."

"So we broke off," Larry said. "I cried when we parted, but I guess my brains regained control over my glands. She got married within a year to another guy, and as far as I know she has lived happily ever after."

Larry never really did like law school, but he saw it through. He had part-time jobs selling shoes during his first year, and other retail experience subsequently. In his second year of law school, he met his wife-to-be. She was from Elmira, New York. They were married right after he graduated from law school, and through her father, who was a CPA, Larry obtained a job with a law firm in Elmira, starting at $40 per week, with a $5-a-week raise when he passed the bar. The firm had no speciality—he was involved in general practice.

A few months later, Larry went into the service, attached to the Judge Advocate General's Office. After one year he was offered a commission, which he refused because it would have meant spending an additional year in the Army. "Perhaps I should have taken it—it wasn't all that bad, what with travel, fringe benefits, and so on. But the antiestablishment feelings in me were too strong. The army was not creative, there was no freedom, it was stupid. These were the same feelings that I had probably had about the establishment when I was in grammar school."

The good thing about the Army was that it took Larry to California, where he was able to spend time in the greater Los Angeles area. He had never been to the West before, and while there, he got the idea to stay on in Los Angeles. But that would have meant taking the California bar exam. Besides he had natural situations awaiting him back in New York State, both his and his wife's families were in the East, and so on. Thus, he returned to Elmira after his Army service, but was quickly disenchanted. "I was like a high-priced office girl," Larry said.

About that time, his father-in-law moved into new office quarters, and had an extra room that he offered to Larry at no rent for the first year, plus free telephone and a free secretary to help get him started in his own practice. Larry saw this as the way to go. During his first year, he grossed $6,000, 50 percent more than he had projected. By the second year, he was grossing $8,000, and he bought his first home. He became settled in the community, and as editor of the synagogue's newsletter, he felt that he was satisfying his creative urges.

Thoughts of going back to Buffalo came but didn't last long. He felt he lacked professional contacts there, and Elmira was a smaller and closer community. His attitude toward his parents, still living in Buffalo, had taken a sharper edge, complemented by his wife's dislike for his parents. He now saw his mother as domineering and shortsighted, and too materialistic. He didn't want to be too close to them. It would be better this way. Besides, he was getting along fine with his in-laws and enjoying the challenge of moving up in the smaller community.

He practiced on his own from 1959 to June 1964, by which time he was earning $10,000 a year. It was enough to satisfy his and his family's basic needs. The relationship with his father-in-law flowed nicely, with business being referred back and forth, both ways. His practice varied but was basically business-oriented—corporate, collectons, real estate, estate planning, and probate.

"But still, I didn't really like the practice of law. Why? I really didn't think I was that good a lawyer. I was a loner. I probably felt insecure. I thought maybe I needed a partner. Maybe that would change things. I looked for a partner but couldn't find anybody that seemed right."

Larry's success was superficial. He admitted that by this time he was seething inside with regard to his career, and his marriage was turning sour as well. "Frankly, my marriage would have been bad regardless of how things were going with my career. It just wasn't working out. Some people get gratifications in their career, some people get gratifications in their home life. It's a trade-off. I had neither. But divorce was a stigma. Nice Jewish kids in a small town just didn't do that. So we found ourselves staying together in spite of the obvious troubles we were having."

In the meantime, Larry's sister had moved to Los Angeles and had started to convince Larry to move out there. Larry and his wife decided to take a month off and look around Los Angeles to see what kinds of opportunity and worlds to conquer there might be. He talked to many people and sought a job. He never really got any offers, but he liked the area so well that he decided, "Let's move. I'll find something."

Using the proceeds from the sale of their home in Elmira, Larry and wife and their two children moved across the continent. They had hoped that the move would help their failing marriage and boost his flagging career. "But both of us were being like ostriches," Larry told me.

Within three weeks, he received a position at a personal-injury firm, at less than half the salary he had been earning in his own practice. After passing the California bar, his salary went from $400 a month to $525 a month.

"Something happened that I liked. I was part of a good firm, there was a lot of camaraderie, and we were doing well. But the funny thing was, I always wanted to settle cases and not go to combat. That's not necessarily a good credential for a personal-injury lawyer. Oddly, I was good at settling cases because I so desperately didn't want to go in court. You've got to have the killer instinct to go to court, and I knew at the outset that I didn't. I guess it's the roly-poly little boy in Buffalo again, wanting to be left alone and not go to war."

Within a few years, his salary had tripled and he was a senior associate of the firm. But that was small consolation. His marriage problems had crept back quickly after the move to Los Angeles, and had reached an intolerable situation from both sides.

"That summer, my wife took the two kids back east. I didn't know if she was ever coming back. In spite of my apparent financial success with the law firm, deep down inside I really wasn't happy with it. When you're not happy with either your work or your home life, bad things start to happen. And when you're all alone to boot, it can get even worse. I was drifting lower and lower in spirit. One day I took a ride out into the mountains on a work-related matter. I was driving along at a high speed, and became sort of hypnotized by the sounds and sights of the road in front of me. The sunlight was coming in very warmly on my hands and face, and for a few moments I found myself almost hallucinating that this must be how it feels to be dead. For an instant, I almost slammed my steering wheel hard to the right to plunge myself over the shoulder and into a steep ravine. I guess that's how badly I wanted out of the situation. But I said to myself, after my heart stopped pounding, 'That's the bottom. You're on the floor now. You damned well better do something about it.' "

Larry took some aptitude tests from a psychologist. But nothing seemed to jump out and say, "Do me." The test results were inconclusive. Music teacher? Clergy? Social work? Small business? Nothing seemed right. He was depressed, exhausted, and retreating within himself at every possible moment.

Reenter the glands. Larry's next-door neighbors had been having marital difficulties as well, and the husband left for an extended period. The two lost souls, Larry and the attractive gal from next door, started with a bit of mutual sympathizing, which led to one thing and another. "We had such joy with each other. We were both feeling guilty but happy. My heart was singing, because someone was taking me as I was."

That probably snapped Larry back into reality more than any psychiatrist could have. The affair with the neighbor created a chink in the wall that was building around him, and through that chink came a beam of light—ideas, creativity. He wrote to his wife that they were going to separate, and that he was going to take his own apartment. "She came back, but it was all over. I told her I had to live my own life. In the meantime, my neighbor was divorced, but I wasn't ready to make a full-time commitment to her so quickly, so that romance petered out too. In the meantime, I had hit bottom and bounced back up again. But I still didn't know what I was going to do."

Then, like the man said, a funny thing happened on the way home from a clothing store. The peacock revolution in men's clothing had started to make itself felt, and Los Angeles was the heartland. One day, Larry went to buy a pair of tight-fitting, flared-leg jeans, breaking from his normally ultraconservative mode of dress. He tried them on and liked them, and bought them on the spot. But he found that they were so tight-fitting that he had no place to put his wallet and other things that he normally carried with him without causing unsightly bulges in the pockets of these highly styled jeans. Thus was born in Larry's mind the idea of the "hip kit," a masculine carry-all bag for men that would suit the new style of the peacock generation. The idea swiftly took root in long-fallow but overly fertile soil. As if in a flash, Larry saw a potential new career before him. He talked to friends in the clothing business, and they encouraged him to submit some designs to see if he had the talent to actually create men's clothes that could sell.

Here comes the roly-poly Jewish kid from Buffalo, ready to do his own thing!

"The interest in styling and designing came over me like a wave. I started studying everything there was to study in men's fashions. I borrowed some money from my brother to live on, and, believe me, a jar of peanut butter was a gourmet treat. I started making sketches and showing them around the industry. I got encouragement, but no job offers. The fascinating thing was that there was no tradition to follow. The men's clothing industry had gone off on a wild tangent, and anything and everything was possible. But here I was with no experience and no credentials except that I was once a personal-injury lawyer. That doesn't cut it very much in the men's clothing industry for becoming a designer."

Larry finally decided to take the big plunge. He would open his own store, where he could create and sell his own designs. His father wouldn't lend him any money, but he did lend him stock that Larry could use as security for a loan. On 5,000 borrowed dollars, Larry opened up a tiny, hole-in-the-wall boutique, mostly for men's wear, but a smattering of women's wear as well. He wisely picked a neighborhood that catered to the "swinging singles" crowd, and his newly revived personality, plus some attractive female sales help in see-through blouses, started bringing the business in. After almost a year of trying and groping, he was finally in the black.

After plowing as much as he could back into the business and paying his alimony and support, Larry's net earnings after the first year were about $200 per month. Yet, he managed to live on it. He became a carpenter, a painter, a tailor. "I didn't really know what I was doing, but it had to get done, so I did it. I had never even worked in a clothing store before. But somehow I knew that I was going to make it."

After a little more than a year in the original location, he was doing well enough to move into a swankier location in a higher-priced shopping center. At this point, he was a totally self-taught fashion designer, but he found that the economics of manufacturing his own designs in such limited quanties as he could sell in the local market tended to price the items out of the market. "My main objective was to be a designer, not a haberdasher. But I couldn't quite work it that way. I still get my satisfaction, though, because much of what we sell is custom-created from swatches. When I go on a buying trip to Paris, I use their colors and materials, and basic designs, but the garments are largely created to my own individual specifications. It's not the ideal, but it's a good compromise."

Larry is still competition-shy. After the first few years of the peacock revolution, mass marketers started producing the same goods. What Larry had specialized in exclusively was now available in Sears Roebuck catalogues and on discount-house racks. Rather than fight the competition, Larry jumped up a number of notches in price to the most exclusive lines of men's clothes. There was still abundant clientele for these lines in his location near Beverly Hills, and his store continued to prosper.

Recently remarried, Larry says, "It's the best thing that ever happened to me." His new wife is also his partner in the business, and they complement each other quite successfully. "But I'm still sick at heart over the first marriage. The kids won't see me, and it breaks me up. I promised more in the way of support money than I ever would have legally had to because I just wanted everything to be ended without any bitterness. And, boy, is it costing me. But in a few years, my support obligation will be over, and I suppose I'll have a fresher attitude about things in general. In the meantime, I'm so busy at business that I don't have much time to think about those old things."

Larry does have some reservations about how his business has grown. Starting off as a designer, then finding himself a haberdasher, he's now an administrator of a small business with twelve to fifteen employees. He doesn't get to do the floor work that he enjoyed, or the design work that he was so fond of. "I've got a tiger by the tail now, and I'm afraid to let go, or I'll get bitten by the tiger. As my growth goes up, so do my costs. Sometimes it seems like an endless circle. I'm working six days a week, ten to twelve hours a day. Relatively speaking, I guess I'm successful. But I still don't know for sure. I've risen to the challenge, I like the industry and the people in it. But I'm still playing it by ear. In any event, I'm a lot better off today than I was a few years ago."

Back in the 1940s in Buffalo, New York, there was a roly-poly little Jewish boy who wanted to be left alone to draw his cartoons and dream his dreams of the theater. He was looking for rosebud. Somehow I feel that Larry is still looking for it today. But he's gone a long way toward finding it.

*The artist isn't made by a haberdasher and a left wing editorial. He's made by the explosive in him that bears the label, "beware of uniformity."*

BEN HECHT

We've all read those stories about the advertising-agency owner or the corporate executive or the college president who drops out to raise filberts on a farm in Vermont. It's kinky, harmless, and the media love it. We don't hear much, though, when six months later, the drop-out drops back into his real world—"Raising filberts just didn't have that old excitement that I needed to really feel alive."

Glossed over in the tumult over the acid-rock generation that sprouted in the late 1960s were those people who drew the pictures that connoted the essence of that ilk—the posters, the record-album covers, the magazine-article illustrations. Successes in that esoteric field of illustration were not the button-down-collar types with their briar pipes. More likely they were as acid-soaked as the generation they were illustrating. But if one has a true artistic talent, and he gets gobbled up by that kind of fad, how does he get free to pursue his true creativity? That's the story of Jay and Helen—a couple whom we'll take one at a time until they join forces to get free of a world that was all but consuming them.

JAY'S STORY: "For me it was art since the age of 7. I remember it distinctly. My sense of play was connected with art and drawing. I was very much aware of art, and was drawn more to it than to any other activities. I was in the basement drawing all the time. At 8 or 9, I was doing collages. By the time I was in high school, I knew that this was to be my career. I really had no awareness of fine arts as such, I simply got pleasure out of making pictures. In high school, they called me "Jay, the artist," and I was kind of a weirdo. Frankly, I was totally out of the mainstream. I kept a discreet distance from my peers, and never really saw the point of school. I simply knew, without question, what it was that was going to be my life's activity, and I just wanted to get it in motion."

Jay's tendencies were very obvious to his parents, both the good points and the bad points. His school marks were extremely bad, and he was considered a real rebel. At one point, he ran away from home to a sports-car race in Florida, and although he returned just a few days later, he was led directly to a psychiatrist. That lasted for one session. There was no stopping him.

Perhaps if Jay had not shown any talent, his parents would have torn their hair. But the fact that he exhibited real native talent made them generally sympathetic toward his inclinations. He began a program at the School of Visual Arts in New York City, where grades didn't matter. The school was commercially oriented, not concerned with development toward the fine arts. It specialized in illustration, or as Jay puts it, "translating visions into dollars." It was disciplined, stressing technique and technical skills. His folks supported him totally through four years at the School of Visual Arts.

"Many of my colleagues were out selling Fuller Brushes in order to support their yearning to get into the fine arts. We all knew that it took years of apprenticeship before you could be recognized by even small galleries. I wanted to get right into it, to do my thing, and be able to earn a living at it. The fine arts didn't matter to me at that time. I just wanted to express my instinctive abilities to make pictures. If the fine arts were to come later, they'd come later."

This was in 1965, before the psychedelic generation was making itself felt. Jay hit Madison Avenue and its tributaries, looking for work, and it didn't take long for him to start generating money. His first assignment came from a group of girlie magazines, where he could earn $100 in a few hours, illustrating articles. As he got to know the ropes, he received assignments from major magazines, advertising agencies, and record companies. For over a year, he designed graphics for an audio-visual company, earning upwards of $100 a day on those few days a month when he worked for them. A record-album cover would bring him $600, and ads for trade journals, paperback-book covers, and poster companies were making his bank account healthier every day.

The native rebel, the native free spirit, the native artist took hold of the growing freedom that was represented by the drug culture. Soon his art began to take on a psychedelic look, and so did the money he was making from it. Everything began to fade into a mass of swirling colors, and time itself became meaningless.

"In spite of the drugs and the binges, I was always able to make money when I needed it. I was a totally poor businessman and blew every dollar I ever got. Occasionally, I had to borrow a few bucks from home, but I could always generate new cash. But I only did so because money bought freedom because it bought time. When I was free, I would do art for my own sake. I never kept track of any of the money, but I did the work, living from day to day, with no thought of the next day. I had no thought of where the work was going to go. But little by little, I was building up a portfolio of my own work—work that I did for myself—not for somebody else. This was art for Jay's sake. It was total self-indulgence, but it was totally self-expressive. And it was totally play. I loved it.

"Thank heaven I had a fail-safe wire built into me. I wasn't aware of it, but one day in early 1968, I suddenly became aware of the fact that I was deteriorating physically. I had been awake for ten days at one particular stretch. I was heavy into the drugs. I wasn't taking care of myself. And I was on my way straight down the tubes."

Jay had become a victim of the generation he had helped to create. It supported him, allowed him to afford his habits, and nurtured the habits. And it was all but killing him. Yet, he was able, throughout this, to protect his native instinct to want to draw, as he puts it, to do "art for Jay's sake."

HELEN'S STORY: "I went through twelve years of parochial school in the Bronx. I was basically a straight person. Straight, that is, compared to my peers. A dozen of my friends had died from drug overdoses, mainly heroin, during high school. That turned me off of drugs. That's how I mean I was straight. My family was lower middle class. I had never had the slightest exposure to art. To be a secretary was the level of aspiration that was imposed upon us in school. And I never aspired to anything more than that.

"I always felt that there was something else, but I wasn't sure what. Nobody in our neighborhood lived except from day to day. I was streetwise by the time I was 13, if you know what I mean. Almost half of the girls in our parochial school were. The school created more rebels, because of the residue of guilt, than the church will ever realize."

Helen was a good student throughout high school, and after graduation, she went really straight for a year, and married her high school sweetheart. She achieved the level of aspiration designed for her, and got a job as a secretary in New York City with a large international paper firm. She had no career goals, no desire for or thought of higher education. Her father had wanted her to go to college, and she could have gotten a scholarship through her dad's work. But she didn't want to go to college since none of her peers were going. She just wanted to marry and get off the street. Her father was disappointed, but let the matter drop. Helen's rebelliousness was mainly against the school and the street life that she had been exposed to.

"When those kids played with guns, they were playing with real ones," Helen told me. "I saw more than one game of real Russian roulette. The only way to survive was to stay within the gang."

After two years as a secretary, Helen began to see some career goals emerging. She liked her work, and realized that better earnings would come her way if she could move up the ladder of bosses.

Just as Helen's career goals were beginning to take some shape, her husband's career took a different turn. When they were high school sweethearts, he had been into hard drugs, and she had thought that he had given up the drugs when they were married. He drove a truck for a living and had no aspirations at all, or so she thought. Until the day the police broke down the door of their apartment and busted her husband for dealing, mostly grass and speed. Fortunately for Helen, the house was empty except for a tiny bit of grass, and the judge was lenient and let them both off with probation.

This taught Helen's husband an important lesson: that crime does pay as long as you keep the incriminating evidence out of sight. He continued dealing, bigger and better. He got Helen on grass again, and their marriage stayed together, mainly because she was high most of the time, and therefore unconcerned with the trivial problems of their day-to-day existence.

They were living fairly well. She was now earning $125 a week, plus what he was making from his dealing. A year later, he lost his truck-driving job and fell in with a new and emerging rock group and their acid. He became involved with the band, attempting to get them bookings and managing their affairs. He was earning nothing, and she was supporting both of them from her job. She was not aware at the time how much, if anything, he was making from his drug dealing, or if in fact he was still doing it.

Through it all, Helen still held on to some form of goal. Her general aspiration was to make enough money to buy a house on Long Island. Beyond that, she had no thought of her future. She was happy smoking grass, and still didn't have any idea of the world beyond her immediate boundaries. They both had pie-in-the-sky feelings that the rock band would become a hit, and they would start making enough money to live the way they wanted to.

"Then, believe it or not, the band did hit. They got a contract to do a record album, and they went off on the road. It really looked like our ship was going to come in. That was the summer of 1968. Then the ship suddenly sank. It all blew apart. The group went off to do a gig in Los Angeles, and I stayed behind. When they came back, I learned that the trip had been an orgy of sex and drugs and all the bonds were broken. It really freaked me out and something snapped.

"They got a contract to do a second album, and I went with my husband and the band one day to the record company to meet the guy who was going to design the album cover. It was Jay. That was the beginning."

Since that day, Jay and Helen have been as one. Shortly after they met, she left her husband and moved in with Jay. Jay: "One day we had dropped acid and took a ride on the Staten Island Ferry. Just beyond the ferryboat pier on Staten Island there's a little city dump, and out beyond that little city dump there are some woods and a stream. We wandered over there and just sat looking around at the scenery. It was so pastoral. Living close to nature. We could look back over the water at the New York skyline. Then, bam! It was time to hit the road. I went off the hard drugs and worked hard, twelve hours a day, making good money. I was bogged down in the business world. I could see my peers were making good money, but they weren't really happy at it. I cleaned up my act, and my desire to get back to the fine arts came back to the surface. I had to avoid getting sucked into that New York City rat race."

In April 1969, Jay and Helen prepared to leave New York City with $1,400 as their total stake. They spent $100 of that on Bertha, a 1960 International Harvester panel truck that was to be their home for the next five years, as they traversed the United States, Mexico, Canada, and Alaska.

Helen: "Leaving work really freaked me out. I'd been working for seven years at a regular, steady job, and in spite of the personal problems along the way, it was kind of a security for me. I really didn't know what I would do. But I was willing to try."

Jay: "I really woke her up to art. I took her to museums, crafts shows. I showed her books. And we discussed them long into the night. One day, I put a piece of clay into her hands. She didn't know what to do with it, and I just told her to do whatever came into her mind. She had a natural talent that astounded me."

They decorated Bertha, bought some gear, and by the time they left New York City, they were down to their last $50. They had no direction, but knew that they were California-bound—eventually. They bought a $7 annual pass to the National Park system, and that, living within the confines of Bertha, was the extent of their rent for the next year. They headed first toward New England and found the local hippie district in each city. Jay's curious reputation as a Madison Avenue hippie was an immediate hit with all of the local denizens, many of whom were into the capitalistic endeavors of the hippie generation—running head shops, boutiques, and doing their own arts and crafts thing. Jay, too, was an entrepreneur. He could earn a quick $500 in each of these towns doing posters, advertisements, letterheads, and logos for the various mod business denizens of the hip community.

That was their routine for the next five years, during which they traveled over 150,000 miles, covering forty states and neighboring nations.

"It was quite a life. We'd flip a coin at forks in the road. If you've never tried that, it's really something to do. Most of my artwork was still in the psychedelic style of the sixties. That's what sold. It took us about the first 12,000 miles to come down from the New York City life style. But then we were out into the world, and my art started to become more my own. I was building a portfolio, and I could sell different pieces of it for living money as we went along. But the money to me was still buying time. I suppose I haven't changed to this day. I still don't have much of a business sense, but I know what I like, and I know what I can do."

By the time Jay and Helen got to San Francisco, in 1971, the poster business was big time. Jay met some poster-company people, and got assignments for posters, pulling in $650 for each one. But he knew nothing about royalties, and never knew how much he could have made had he had some sophistication in that area of business.

But the work was steady, and they settled down in a little community outside of Napa Valley. There, the natural art started flowing, and he got wise to the royalty potential in the poster business. He did a few dozen posters to bring in the living money, and concentrated on his own art during the rest of his time. He generated enough in royalties to be able to count on a monthly check of $500 to $600 for the next two years.

Jay began to express his own personal art more and more in the posters and now found an adequate expression for his inner feelings and was getting paid for it, to boot.

For Helen, these were years of experimentation and exploration. Her natural artistic tendencies fell toward woodworking. She became an accomplished cabinetmaker and custom-furniture maker. Then she tried her hand at making frames for Jay's drawings.

"After a time," Jay says in piqued amusement, "the galleries that we visited fell more for Helen's frames than for my drawings."

The poster royalties had started dwindling, and Helen's work started to become their primary support. Meanwhile, Jay continued to work on his own ideas, which now seemed to be concentrated in pencil and ink drawings from nature.

In late 1973, they wearied of the road, and settled in Laguna, California, one of the primary art colonies in the West. They decided to make a home and establish a reputation for themselves as artists. Two years later, struggling through the fallout of the national economy, they finally felt that they had made it. They rented a small house—the first nonmobile dwelling they had had in five years, and even acquired their own telephone and television set. In spite of the money they had made over the years, they had had angels—grants and loans whose payment still remains open-ended—totaling about $4,000. They still consider themselves to be living on a survival level, but they're establishing a reputation and getting shown in better galleries and shows.

Jay: "My goal? I suppose it's to make enough money as an established artist so I don't have to hustle. Slowly but surely, we're building credits, contacts, exposure, and inventory. We never thought of failure. Failure to us would mean starving to death. If I had it to do over again, nothing would change. I'm 33 today and Helen's 30. We still have Bertha, and we intend to keep her. We're still not married. But we're going to get married. It's about time for us to celebrate seven years of what we've accomplished."

To most folks, Jay and Helen's course of action to get free is something beyond comprehension. Physically, perhaps that's true. But mentally, it's possible for anyone to shake off the conventions, however common or weird they may be, that can turn us into robots, however efficient or rebellious they may be.

# Housewife Blacks and Blues

Marriages, good ones and bad ones, can be bruising to the nonworking female. Lisa had everything she desired, four fine children, and an enviable role in her community. But she didn't have a sense of self-fulfillment. So she became—and why not?—a stockbroker. Karen also had four fine kids, but a doomed marriage. Doomed and damned. When the divorce became final and the support monies began to trickle in behind schedule, she found herself with mouths to feed, mortgage payments to make, and not a skill in the world that she knew how to put to profitable use. So she became—and why not?—a successful life-insurance agent.

> *Shun idleness. It is a rust that attaches itself to the most brilliant metals.*
>
> VOLTAIRE

LISA'S STORY: "I'd never really contemplated any career. I was married at 18 and immediately started raising a family. My husband was very active in the business world, and I was often busy as a hostess to his business entertainments. I was full of community obligations—committees, clubs, ladies' auxiliaries—you name it, I was doing it. Because of the early marriage, I never finished college, and outside of my husband's activity, I was limited in my exposure to the real world. Then, as the kids grew up (the youngest is now 12) and became more independent, I started getting a good look at my peers. I saw a scary lack of purpose among them. There's more to life than just sitting around. I could never let myself be part of that tennis/mah-jongg/bridge set.

"I thought of going to work for my husband, doing something in the office, but that wouldn't really be self-fulfilling. Plus, I wanted to get away and do something on my own. A friend of mine told me that if I didn't do it now, it would be that much harder later on."

Lisa's husband, father, brother, and brother-in-law had all been active in the world of business and finance. Their language was sprinkled with talk of stocks and bonds, debts and debentures, equity and equations, deals and deals and more deals. It was partly out of self-defense, partly out of curiosity about this jargon, that Lisa became interested in the workings of the stock market. A very close friend was a broker in a branch of a major Wall Street firm in her home town, and he suggested to her that they form a partnership, within the firm.

"I didn't go into it for financial reasons. I didn't really need the money. It was more a sense of accomplishment, and the hope that I could then teach others. Passing my broker's test alone was a crowning achievement for me. The experience gave me a great sense of self-confidence. When I started in at the brokerage firm, the market was in a horrendous tumble. For the first two years of my career, we were fighting a downhill market. But I wasn't discouraged by it. Fortunately, I didn't have to make a living at it, otherwise I might have felt a little differently.

"I was, and still am, thirsty for any kind of knowledge. I'm now taking courses in taxes and accounting. The initial experience has motivated me intellectually. I've found myself now to be a much more thinking and aware person. I think I'm also a better person. Yes, the satisfactions have been more cerebral than financial. I don't mean to belittle the housewife who doesn't care to work. What's right for her is fine, and I commend her for it. I'm just doing what's right for me."

Lisa has been at it now for about four years, and in that time, she has built up a clientele of her own. She hasn't found that being a woman has been a drawback to her in her chosen business. "Sometimes," she notes, "men will call, asking to speak to any broker, and if I'm the broker of the day, I get the phone calls. They're a little surprised to find themselves talking to a woman, but once they get over the initial shock, they realize that I can give them the same kind of information that a male broker can.

"Perhaps it was easier for me to get my feet on the ground in this business because I knew a lot of people in the community and our own family connections helped to generate some business. But I believe that there is ample opportunity today for women to get into the stock market, particularly for women who are established in life. The financial rewards are there if you want to go after them. My greatest thrill is developing business from people who don't know me from a bale of hay, don't know my family, or anything about me. That's kind of an ego trip. Then I always get a kick out of people who don't do business with me because they're afraid I'm going to find out more than they want me to know about their financial matters, and that I'll give them a hard time when I'm soliciting for one of the local charities."

Getting free wasn't a sudden thing for Lisa. It was a growing process for her, and it came upon her gradually. She doesn't feel she could have done it earlier, and she's glad she didn't do it later. She emphasizes that what was right for her might not be right for other women, but that all women in situations resembling hers should examine their souls and see if some form of getting free wouldn't be good for them. She stresses the importance of considering their age at marriage, the number and age of their children, the growth of their husband's career, their relative degree of "sanity," their own personal needs, and their own financial needs.

"One of the saddest things that keeps housewives from fulfilling themselves is pride—men can hold back their women out of pride, or women themselves will be reluctant to be seen at work because of the pride factor. My work is more on the glamorous side. I imagine that the retail clerk in the department store or discount house may not have the same degree of prestige that a stockbroker has. But then again, in the eyes of many, the stockbroker doesn't have much prestige either if he or she comes up with a wrong bit of advice. I like the business world and the so-called male world. What I'm doing puts me on a more even footing with my husband, and has increased our common bond. The sense of fulfillment and achievement that I've gotten has been worth every minute of the work. I've even made good money at it."

*The gem cannot be polished without friction, nor man perfected without trial.*

CHINESE PROVERB

KAREN'S STORY: Karen is a gem. Her face is one that you might expect to see staring at you from the cover of *Vogue* magazine. And indeed it might have, had she not been whisked into marriage at the age of 18. She had taken some modeling courses shortly before her marriage, but they weren't for professional purposes, rather for self-improvement, poise—the typical reasons that many young ladies indulge in such programs. Aside from a brief stint as a teacher in a religious school at age 14, Karen had no work experience. Her early marriage precluded a normal college education, which might have provided her with some skills for the working world. But, to all appearances, it didn't seem as though she'd ever have to worry about that.

During the first four years of her marriage, while her husband was going to law school, she worked as a dental assistant. But that was strictly a temporary situation, and it stopped when her first child was born, in 1956. From that point, until 1967, Karen devoted herself to the career of being a housewife and mother. Three more children joined the family during those years. There were periodic requests for her to model in charity fashion shows, which she gladly fulfilled. However, she did this not for career purposes, but to get out of the house and continue her activity with the various charities, as many women do. There'd been some suggestions from people in the business that prompted her to seek part-time work, for pay, in the modeling field in 1967. "But it wasn't really for the money, or for any career aspirations. My marriage had started to go bad, and I'd been fighting an ego problem for a number of years. In spite of what people told me, I really didn't know that I was attractive. My husband had put me down, telling me that I wasn't sexy and didn't know how to dress. I had a bad case of the housewife/marriage blues, and was desperate for something to build up my ego. I knew I had some kind of potential for myself, and I had to try to fulfill it."

For the next two years, Karen earned $400 a month working part-time, about three hours a day, at her new-found ego-building career. Part of the work she was expected to do for the agency was "cold-calling." This involved making the rounds of department stores, advertising agencies, and specialty shops, seeking jobs for the agency, and, she hoped, for herself. Models weren't paid for this work, but they were expected to do it. If the cold-calling resulted in a job for the agency, the model would get a credit for it. If the job involved the model herself, she'd get paid accordingly. It wasn't pleasant work, but it was necessary, and Karen found that she was good at it. She had something going for her: a bright mind and an articulate manner. She could talk and, unbeknownst to her, she could sell.

Meanwhile, the marriage had turned from bittersweet to sour, and by 1970, it was at an end. Her husband's own career had faltered, and he was hard pressed to pay even a minimal amount of support. When he did pay, it was often late.

"I was really up against it. My monthly budget was $873, and I had four strapping boys between the ages of 6 and 12. I was earning about $400 a month, and had to make up that difference, and in a hurry. Many were the times that I had to tell my boys that I couldn't afford to buy them a new pair of sneakers, and our food budget was right down to the bare bones. I was totally innocent and unknowledgeable about the world of work. I sought advice from my friends, and they told me that modeling was not secure, and that I should go out and get a "real job." If I had been on my own, I suppose I might have followed my own mind more closely. But with four children to take care of, I listened to the advice I was given.

"The first 'real job' was as a so-called assistant manager at a small ladies' dress shop. Stock clerk was more like it. I worked long hours, and it was very unfulfilling work. And the irony is that I was making $400 a month—the same amount that I had been making as a part-time model, except now I was working forty to fifty hours a week, instead of ten to fifteen hours. But it was a 'real job.' Trying to do that work, run a house, take care of my kids, and run what seemed like hundreds of miles of car pool every week really got me to the end of my rope. I needed something bad, and I needed it fast.

"At that time, I started dating a fellow who was very optimistic about people and their potential. He convinced me that I should leave the dress shop and find a selling job. I'd never sold anything in my life, and my ego told me that I wouldn't be able to do any selling. My friend told me, 'Don't stay home and bake cookies and mope—get out and visit every old friend, and ask each one of them if he knows of any situation that you can better yourself by.' "

Karen did just that. She had acquired many friends over the years, and she visited each and every one of them whom she thought might have some contact with a job that would be suitable for her circumstances. But it was 1970, during the time of a minirecession, and jobs were not abundant. "Even so, looking back on it, that experience of getting out and talking to people, even though they were my friends, helped me break a little bit out of my shell," Karen told me.

She had registered with various employment agencies, and one of them called, offering a job with a life-insurance company in the sales area.

"Life insurance? Yuch! I knew as much about life insurance as I did about nuclear fission. I hadn't the foggiest idea what it was all about, plus I would have to pay a $300 fee to the agency for getting a job. But I went and looked into it. Apparently, I impressed the boss, and he urged me to take the job. I would get a crash training course, and I could get an advance against commissions. My naiveté must have preceded me by a mile. I was to be, in a manner of speaking, bait to get perspective clientele into the office. Unwittingly, and certainly unintentionally, I guess I've always been a bit of a flirt. Once I'd finished the training course, I worked mostly with the boss, and we sold mostly to men. I would call up the prospect and explain that our company, which happens to be a very fine, major life-insurance company, was offering some new ideas in estate planning, and I'd like to visit with him, the prospect, at his office to explain what we had to offer.''

Unlike the typical insurance salesman, with the attaché case and natty tie and fast line of patter, Karen was easily able to get into the inner sanctum of the prospect, if for no other reason than that the prospects were curious to see what an attractive gal like this had to tell them about estate planning. After the first brief introductory call, it was Karen's job to lure the prospect into the office of the insurance agency, where the professional approach by the boss would be applied.

''Let me tell you that I found myself going back to the office in tears many, many times after lunches that the prospects honestly believed had nothing to do with life insurance, but with some other, more personal relationship. You know what I mean? I learned the ropes pretty quickly.''

Karen and the boss made a good team. During her first year, she was selling in the $.5 million area, and earning commissions in the $8,000 to $10,000 range. And that was working roughly twenty-five hours a week. By 1972, she was chosen as ''man'' of the year for her office. She excelled over the ten men in the office, the award being based on sales, attitude, and ambition. She also embarked on the rigorous course of instruction to earn her Chartered Life Underwriter credentials.

The life-insurance career continued successfully until 1975, when Karen remarried. With the drive and the need for money gone, she gradually eased herself out of the insurance business, taking care of existing clients only, and devoting herself again to a happy homelife.

''I was so timid and foolish at the beginning. I didn't know anything about the world I was getting involved in. I didn't learn until much later that that $300 fee that I had paid for the job was unnecessary—I was the only agent who had to pay it. All the others had the company pay it. But what did I know?

''Yes, I guess at first I achieved what I did because of my looks. But as I progressed, I was able to sell out of knowledge and the quality of my work.''

Skills unwittingly acquired in other endeavors often surface again to be put to good use. During her brief modeling career, Karen had been required to do cold-call selling on prospects for the model agency's services. This was the same type of cold-calling she found herself having to do with the life-insurance agency. Cold-calling comes very slowly to the novice, but Karen had had good solid experience. This accelerated her success in the life-insurance field, and she's well aware of the value of having acquired those skills.

''Now, I realize what I'm capable of. I can deal with people. I have a sense of self-fulfillment. I believe in my own opinion, and I voice it. I'm a better listener. I can sell if I have to. But overall, I can walk around with my head up. I went through the wringer, and I came out of it in good shape. At first, I wouldn't have believed that I was capable of achieving anything. I know that a lot of other women feel that way too. But I proved to myself that achievement is possible, and I hope that I can prove it to other women as well.

"Take it from a 'man' of the year."

# I Didn't Work My Way into My New Career . . . I Married into It . . .

*I have seen boys on my baseball team go into slumps and never come out of them, and I have seen others snap right out and come back better than ever. I guess more players lick themselves than are ever licked by an opposing team. The first thing any man has to know is how to handle himself. Training counts. You can't win any game unless you are ready to win.*

CONNIE MACK

BRAD'S STORY: "Before I met her, I didn't even know what a travel agent was."

Brad was a straight-A student in high school in Westchester County, one of New York City's affluent bedroom communities. There was some subtle pressure from his father toward a career in engineering, but Brad seemed more artistically inclined, enjoying writing and creating. His first year in engineering college was a near disaster, and, not seeing a future in engineering, or in the creative arts, he shifted into business school during his second year and majored in advertising and marketing—what seemed like a good compromise between his own urges, his parents' wishes, and reality.

Brad graduated from Indiana University in 1959, and after a brief commitment with the U.S. Army Reserves, he went to work for U.S. Amalgamated, a large conglomerate.

Though his initial work was slightly out of line from his major in advertising and marketing, he found it interesting and enjoyable, and was able to work in many different departments. He edited the house organ, worked on labor negotiations and employee benefits, and became the assistant to the industrial relations director.

"But everything seemed to be without a specific goal—both for myself and for the company. I was living at home with my folks, and on my $9,000-a-year salary, I was able to sock a lot away for the future. But for what purpose? I really wasn't sure at all. The company was growing rapidly, and I was getting good training in all the departments I worked in. But the company didn't seem to know which way it was going to go either. We were getting into the so-called go-go years of the early and middle 1960s, and growth was so rapid that we really couldn't keep pace with it. We got a new president, and he brought in outsiders for the choice jobs and kept all of the existing management in a pretty static position. After a few years, it began to appear that the opportunity to move up or into other divisions was going to be limited by this new philosophy of bringing in outsiders. I was starting to get itchy about it, but was willing to hang in there, because I didn't have anything better at my disposal."

In 1961, Brad married a young lady who was employed at a local travel agency. By 1962, the itch was becoming intolerable, and Brad and his wife discussed the possibility of opening their own travel agency. A skiing accident in January 1963 helped them to do this: Brad broke his leg and spent three months in a cast, during which time his salary was paid by his employer. This gave him time to do the necessary research into the feasibility of opening a travel agency. He and his wife opened their own travel agency in an adjoining community in January 1963. The cost to open the agency was $10,000 in working capital, which Brad was able to raise through a local bank.

For the first year of their business venture, Brad stayed with his employer, feeling that it would be necessary to have this income for living expenses. His salary at that time was $10,500, and the new agency lost $5,000 in its first year on gross income of $9,000. Although they were very inexperienced, they felt they had the basic skills and know-how that eventually would prove successful. Brad left his job and went to travel-agency school to sharpen his skills. He worked nights and weekends at the agency. Business began to pick up, and they felt that it certainly would be able to support them in short order. They broke even during the second year, after taking out $8,000 in salary for themselves. They were living modestly, and were able to get by.

"We were completely confident. We had no thoughts of failure. We knew that if we just stuck with it, we could make out handsomely. I'm not a get-rich sort of guy. I'm fairly content to live modestly if I'm enjoying my work and my family."

By the third year, the money was rolling in satisfactorily, and his wife semiretired until their first child was born. After the birth, his wife went back to the agency for one year, and then left again to give birth one more time. By 1972, their gross income in the agency was $90,000, which netted them $20,000 after all expenses.

But as the agency was becoming more successful financially, their marriage was starting to decay. In the early days, keeping their noses to the grindstone was the first priority of business. But as the agency became more successful, they were able to take more advantage of the so-called familiarization trips that were offered by many resorts, cruise lines, and other pleasure-oriented businesses. Typical familiarization trips are heavily populated with young, swinging, hell-raising travel agents, and a good time is usually had by as many as can possibly work it out that way. Brad and his wife rarely went together on these trips because someone had to stay home and mind the store. As human temptation gives way, it eventually has to affect the marriage. It did. Brad and his wife separated in 1970, even though they remained in business together. The divorce became final in 1972, and in lieu of alimony and support for the children, Brad turned over all of his interest in the business, as well as the house.

"It was really a shame. We were a great business team. We just couldn't hack it being married. Giving up the business as part of the marriage settlement set me back ten years. I would have preferred to keep the business, but the settlement was imposed by the court. Another part of the settlement that really hurt was that I couldn't open up my own agency within ten miles of the old one. In that part of the world, ten miles is like a thousand miles. You've built up all of your contacts within a very small radius and just moving that extra few miles away can make all the difference. I couldn't see staying in Westchester and working for someone else. I did want to be close to my children, but I couldn't envision any kind of successful career unless I moved a good distance away. I was determined to own my own agency again, but I had no money to start one. So I started out in my search to buy an existing agency, looking for a situation where I could put a minimum amount down, and pay the balance over a period of years."

Brad explained some of the difficulties of getting involved in the travel-agency business. "It's virtually impossible," he said, "to make money within the first two years of setting up your own agency. At best, you can break even in the second year, and perhaps be making money by the fourth year. To start a new agency, you need four qualifications in order to get the appointments from the airlines and shipping lines. Without the appointments, you simply don't get commissions, so unless you want to work for nothing, you get your appointments as quickly as you can. The four credentials are: (1) $15,000 worth of capital, (2) two years of experience by the owner or the manager, (3) an accessible location, and (4) the demonstrable ability to sell travel for an unspecified number of months. You don't get commissions on this travel during the trial period, but they are retroactive once you've proven yourself.

"You don't have to go through these steps when you buy an existing agency. There's a transitional approval that's granted, which allows you to eventually pick up the prior owner's appointments.

"I heard about an agency in San Diego, where the owners, a married couple, were basically absentee. My experience in the field had shown me that there's frequently a good purchase opportunity where you have absentee owners. Often, the absentee owners will have gotten into the agency for whatever investment benefits there are, plus the discount travel that they can eventually have access to. But, often, it doesn't turn out as they wish. Being absentee, the agency doesn't run as well as they had hoped, the investment often sours, and the free travel doesn't offset the money they have in it."

Thus, Brad moved across the nation to become an employee of the agency, and wait patiently to see if his hunch played out.

Not only did his hunch play out, but history repeated itself. The owners of the agency became divorced in 1975, and to expedite their own settlement, they put the agency on the block on very attractive terms, and Brad jumped at the deal. As manager of the agency for the three prior years, he had had a chance to build up its clientele and its gross income. He had already built his income back to its former level, despite the earlier setback, and expects to pay off his obligation to the former owners within two years.

"I'm still not a get-rich guy, and travel agencies aren't necessarily a get-rich business unless you have a major firm in a very large city. But it's very pleasant work. In the travel business, virtually all of your clientele are anticipating a happy event, looking forward to using the service you are providing them with. Also, there's no price competition. Everybody pays the same for a given airline ticket, or resort, or cruise, regardless of what travel agent they buy it through. The only competition is in service and personality, and this is where I feel I can excel. And, of course, you can't overlook the travel benefits.

"I came into this business on a fluke, and got bounced out of it on a fluke. Then another fluke allowed me to continue with it, and to succeed."

Brad wonders whether history can repeat itself yet another time. He's currently dating another travel agent and is keeping a close eye on the wheel, which is often known to come full circle.

# A Complete Turnabout . . . Or Is It?

*Experience is not what happens to a man. It is what a man does with what happens to him.*

ALDOUS HUXLEY

MIKE'S STORY: "Back then, when I was an electronics engineer in the early heyday of that industry, if anyone had told me that today I'd be running an automobile repair shop, I'd have told him that he was crazy."

Growing up in Brooklyn in the 1940s, Mike was a putterer. Automobiles, a commodity that the nation was starved for during the war years, suddenly came back in a flood of new makes and models, and what typical teenager didn't become fascinated with these machines? Then, there was the chemistry set, a typical childhood toy for millions of young lads and lasses. Mike wasn't satisfied with the basic directions in the chemistry set, mixing the white stuff with the red stuff to come up with a bubbling beaker of blue stuff. He experimented, to the extent of making small explosives to amuse his neighborhood friends.

"In my family, it was predetermined that I would go to college. I was the only son, with three older sisters. Money was no problem. My dad had felt that I should be an accountant, but he never pressured me that way. He didn't feel that I should work in the family business. He wanted me to have a college education and "be something." Throughout high school, I really had no outside pressures, no specific directions. I suppose the chemistry set motivated me as much as anything. I was very serious and scientific-minded, and decided to go to Brooklyn Polytechnic Institute to get my bachelor's degree in chemical engineering."

After Mike's first year of college, he began to reassess his direction, asking himself whether he should really be in chemical engineering or something else. There really was no something else that he could put his finger on, but he did have some vague inkling that the strict engineering program might not satisfy him. But his college advisor told him that he was doing fine and that there was no reason to change.

After receiving his degree in June 1953, he was drafted. He went into the Navy and immediately enrolled in Officer's Candidate School, from which he was commissioned in the summer of 1954. The armed services, not usually noted for matching talents with available jobs, offered Mike his choice of career. His first choice, mainly because of the glamour and allure, was to become a jet pilot. But he flunked the physical. Thus, he was awarded his second choice: engineering.

His service career gradually weaned him away from chemical engineering and toward electronics engineering. He was put on a team in charge of preparing a new electronic gear-laden ship for commission. Much of the electronic gear was newly developed, and Mike oversaw the installation of radar and sonar equipment that was quite new for the time. He was working largely in a managerial capacity, handling a lot of paper work, working late, and overseeing a large crew of men. Early during his Naval career, he married.

"A lot of men feel that the service is an irksome delay, but I never did. Overall, it was a good experience. My wife and I made friends, and we traveled. It was an opportunity for us to see a lot of the western United States, and that experience embedded itself in our minds. I was only in my early twenties, and the Navy helped me to become independent and self-reliant. Both my wife and I had always lived at home and had never traveled, so this was a great adventure for us. Near the end, I was offered an instructorship at Annapolis. That was quite flattering, since I was so young. I gave it a lot of thought, but my wife and I really were not Navy people."

After the service, Mike and his wife returned to the New York City area, where Mike pounded the pavement looking for a job to suit his skills. He was offered a position with RCA in Harrison, New Jersey, as a process engineer in the vacuum-tube division. This, he felt, was back into his bailiwick, respectably close to chemical engineering. This was in early 1957, and his starting pay was $7,200 a year. During that year, a mild national recession caused Mike to be bumped from his job, but RCA helped place him in another division just a few miles away. Then the feeling began coming back that there was something else that should be done. Mike enrolled at New York University to take his master's degree in business administration, commuting into the city from his home in Somerville, New Jersey, three nights a week. "I felt that I needed some further education, and there was plenty of GI Bill money available. Also, I had a feeling that the real future in engineering would be in management, and I needed some skills along those lines.

"I was fairly happy at RCA during those years. We were on the ground floor of a tremendous, dynamic new industry. It was busting out all over, and the growth was unbelievable. Even though I felt that RCA was a bit conservative within the industry, every time I started feeling antsy, I was able to transfer to another department with raises and new challenges. By 1960, I was making about $10,000 a year. We had kids and our family was growing. There never seemed to be an opportune time to leave, nor enough motivation to leave. I was a company man through and through, and was making all of my changes with a view toward broadening my experience. Sure, every so often a bunch of us guys would get together and talk about starting our own firm. That was common in the industry. Some guys did it successfully, and a lot of others bombed out. I never came up with the right idea or the right people to carry through a good idea, so I just stayed there close to home."

A number of factors fell into place to cause Mike to make what would be the first of two major career redirections.

"In 1965, the antsy feeling was more intense than it had been in the past. Thoughts of moving west had been simmering in our minds for the past few years, and I guess that started bubbling up toward the surface. RCA's growth was not keeping up with what other companies seemed to be doing. Also, I remember vividly an old fellow, in his sixties, who was an engineer with RCA. He was doing the same kind of thing as other fellows in their twenties were doing, and I couldn't see myself continuing along my same line for the rest of my life. Guys like this were the real dyed-in-the-wool company men. They would fall asleep at their desk, and nobody would bother to wake them up. I just couldn't see myself, at that age, in that situation."

That same year, Mike's mother had a stroke, and for the two ensuing years, he gave up much of his otherwise free time to travel into New York City to visit with her. This apparently was putting extra pressures on the contentment valve in Mike's head. When his mother died in 1967, he said to himself, "Spring loose." He realized then that his family had been the major factor in keeping him in the East. "It was my duty as a son when my mother was ill. But now, all the ingredients just seemed to come together. I really wasn't looking for a change in job direction; I just thought I'd do better working for someone else. There was an awful lot of job hopping in the industry, and that was really the best way to get ahead. You could get pigeonholed in one place, and you had to make a move in order to improve yourself and be faced with new challenges. I had reached a dead end with RCA. There were headhunters all around at that time, and the opportunities to make changes seemed endless."

In 1967, Mike left RCA and a $15,000 salary, to move to Universal Semi-conductors in Dallas, at a starting salary of $17,500, in a managerial position. The company was young and dynamic, quite the opposite of RCA. But with the dynamism, there was turmoil. A lot of top management left in one coup, having been pirated away by another, older and larger company. In the following years, politics began to replace skill as a moving force for success.

"I was making more money as time went along, and was stepping up the ladder. I was happy generally, but this political thing started to gnaw at me. It wasn't a matter of your productivity, but of who slept with who, and who went out drinking with who after work each day. When the leadership left, the whole scene began to change, and it made a big difference to me. The company had gone through a period of extremely rapid growth, then there was some contraction. It was all going on around me every day, and I felt that I fitted less and less into this newly emerging mold.

"I had been with Universal almost six years, and I was a rarity in the industry—having worked for only two companies in almost seventeen years. I began to think of moving to another company, but it wasn't all that easy.

"I was near the $30,000-a-year income level, and jobs kind of thin out at that point. Most jobs at that level are from within an existing company. With my family situation and my own level of personal contentment in mind, I wanted to stay in Dallas and not go to the trouble of making a major move. My skills in certain areas weren't as keen as those of some of the younger men. This happens in the industry. Some of your skills are lost, and some of them aren't as current as those of fellows just coming out of school. On the other hand, other new skills are gained, such as mine in management. I was running a $10 million division, but I couldn't sell my skills to another company. The job market had gotten very tight for middle management, and after some interviews with other companies and headhunters, I found that I had priced myself out of the market.

"The ingredients began to fall into place again, just as they had when I moved from the East. Though I was basically content with my work, and certainly with my income, the new politics at the company began to affect the quality of my work. I began to suspect that if things continued, I might get laid off. As a matter of fact, looking back at my attitude then, had I been my own boss, I probably would have laid myself off. As things turned out a few years later, I actually would have lost my job had I not made a move on my own. I had reached a dead end with the company. Also, I had reached the mystic age of 40, or so people refer to it. I realized that if I was going to do something, now was the time to do it. If ever there was going to be a change in my life, I'd better get cracking at it."

Mike expressed his interest in a possible career change to a number of friends, asking them to keep an eye open if a business opportunity came along. In his free time, he explored a variety of business opportunities, and sent out feelers in as many directions as possible.

One day, his accountant mentioned to him that he knew of an automobile-repair shop that was on the market. "Though seat covers and brake linings were a world apart from semiconductors, I knew that I had the basic management skills to run a viable business. When you get right down to it, management skills, if they're sharp enough, can be applied to many different kinds of situations. I'd had no retail experience, but I had skills related to controls, restraints, inventories, personnel, and marketing. Could I put them together successfully in an auto-repair shop?"

Mike studied the situation scrupulously. The numbers seemed right to allow him the kind of salary he was seeking, and the business was big enough to justify his being manager.

"I didn't want to start something at ground zero or try to build up a failing business. It meant a choice between investing what capital I had available, or scrounging. I could either eat off my capital while I was scrounging, or invest the capital wisely and live off the income that it should generate. I studied the past track record of the business, and that, plus my basic skills, convinced me that I could succeed. Confident? I had no alternative plan in the event of failure. I simply felt that I would succeed. If I could master skills successfully in the highly complicated field of electronics, I had no doubt that I could do it with automobiles."

So far, Mike has been right. After three years in the new business, his income level is slightly higher than it was when he left Universal Semi-conductors. And the future looks bright.

"I shouldn't overlook that early restlessness that I felt, even as a kid, that there was something else that I might do. And I guess I somewhat succumbed to the great American dream about the automobile that we had when we were kids. I'd always been fascinated with the automobile, and here was an opportunity to kind of do a second-childhood bit. And even though it may have been insignificant, it was a factor. But with a wife and a growing family and a fairly good life style, you don't play games with second-childhood fantasies. You've got to work hard, you've got to give good service, and particularly in the automobile business, where everyone is looked at as being a son-of-a-bitch, you've got to be the nicest guy in the world even when the customers complain. And do they complain!

"Yes, it was quite a turnabout for me. But, in retrospect, maybe it really wasn't that much of a turnabout. I'm still utilizing the same basic skills that I'd developed over the years, except on a different set of tools. People often overlook this fact. They think that their skills can only be used in one specific area. It's not so. I've proven it. You're as secure as you make yourself, and if you put your past experience to the best possible work, you can make yourself as secure as you want to be."

# Partners from Similar Backgrounds

*Action may not always bring happiness; but there is no happiness without action.*

BENJAMIN DISRAELI

Politics—and going into business for yourself—can make strange bedfellows. Fred and Ted, whose stories follow, have personalities that are at opposite ends of the spectrum. Yet they come from similar backgrounds to form a mutually satisfying partnership. On the other hand, Phil and Woody, whom we'll get to know later, are very similar in personality. Yet they come from backgrounds at opposite ends of the work spectrum to form an equally satisfying partnership.

Fred and Ted have a successful two-man advertising agency in Newport Beach, California. Fred is soft-spoken, modest, conservative. Ted is outgoing, with a tendency toward the flamboyant. Mr. Inside and Mr. Outside.

FRED'S STORY: "I grew up in South Carolina, and graduated high school in 1959. I was in the top ten of my class, and had no career inklings of any kind. Nor did I have any push from my family. Dad worked for the government, so the income was fairly moderate, and our family life was on the restrained side. Even though I had always earned my own spending money as a kid, the family was able to support me and send me to college. That wasn't a problem, at least at that time. I had always intended to go to law school—though I'm not sure why—even though I knew that it would mean a basic liberal arts undergraduate program, which would require some language skills. I almost flunked out of college in my first year. It was my first time away from home, and, frankly, I went wild. I was coming off the restraints of our home life, and was out sowing every wild oat I could. I also learned early on that I had a foreign-language disability, and told myself that if liberal arts and language were needed for success in prelaw, then my desire for law was really not so burning."

After Fred's first year in college, his dad had a heart attack. "That was instant maturity for me. I woke up to my financial responsibility. I knew that because of dad's condition, his support of the family was near an end. So I moved back home, lived with the folks, and transferred to the local college."

Still there was no specific career direction. "I thought I had a little flair, so I went for advertising. That was about as much thought as I gave to any career direction at that time. I went to the business school, working toward a major in advertising and marketing."

Fred helped pay his way through college, working as a bookkeeper in a bank, a cashier for a delivery-service company, and as a receptionist/gopher for a small, local advertising agency. (A gopher, as it's known in the industry, is the young apprentice who, when someone needs something, is told to "go for" it.)

Fred was comfortable in business school, apparently having a knack for understanding the subject matter, and his wild oats out of his system, his grades were exemplary.

Fred graduated in 1964, and married shortly thereafter. At about the same time, his family moved to Anaheim, California. Fred's first job was for a local manufacturer of building materials, where he was an in-house "advertising manager," earning $100 per week. "It was the best offer I had, and it was related to what I'd been studying in college. But it was a terrible bore. Actually, I ended up selling cinder blocks and being a gopher to the boss. I stayed there four months. My wife had a part-time job, and between the two salaries, we were able to live comfortably. I kept my ear to the ground to see what other opportunities might be available."

Through a personal contact, Fred heard of an opening as assistant to the advertising director of a large savings and loan institution. "I was still basically a gopher, but this was a multimedia situation with a big budget and seemingly a lot of opportunity. I started at $435 per month, and within two years, I was staff officer earning $750 per month."

That was in late 1965. Fred's boss was fired suddenly, but Fred didn't have the experience yet to move up into the managerial position. A new man was brought in from the outside, at a salary substantially higher than what Fred's boss had been earning. The new man lasted two years and then left. By this time, Fred had the credentials to take charge of the advertising department, but because he was from within, his salary level was back at what his prior boss had been earning, many thousands of dollars less than the salary the interim advertising manager had earned.

"Even though my desk was only a few feet away from where the old one was, it was a whole different experience for me. I had not been getting much flak before, because I was only the assistant. But now I started getting it all. I was supposed to be doing creative work, but I had to spend an inordinate amount of time protecting my neck. I even had to send memos to myself to ensure that there was something in the file justifying all the decisions that were made, step by step, along the way. I was making $12,000 a year, which we were able to live on quite comfortably, though not high on the hog. But I began to feel that the salary didn't justify the pressure I was under. I suppose that if I'd just been doing the creative and administrative work that the position called for, I would have been happy with the money. But it was those pressures from above that made me start thinking of getting out on my own.

"I guess I was a bit resentful that my predecessor had been earning considerably more than I was for the same work. But at the time, I didn't have enough resentments to just up and leave. There were other rewards that were satisfying. In the first place, I was only 30. That's quite young for a job of that status. And then there was the power. I never considered myself a power-hungry person, but I guess I liked having the authority to make major decisions that could have a very big effect on the overall institution. I did enjoy the role, as well as the adoration of my peers. But after the initial blush wore off, and the flak got heavier, I started to ask myself what I was doing there. I began to feel that it was bad for a thirty-ish junior executive to become completely dependent on the corporation. I've always preached against this since then. I saw myself falling into a trap.

"I started going to night school for my master's degree. I never got it, but it did broaden my perspective. It exposed me to theories that weren't being practiced at the savings and loan institution. Most of my work was with people from advertising agencies, and after observing them for many months, I began to get the feeling that I could do better than most of these people were doing. And I suppose I never got over the gopher syndrome. Maybe it was my imagination, but I always felt that management looked on me as a glorified gopher. After all, I was young, and I came up through the ranks. A new boy coming in from the outside has the advantage of his supposed expertise in a larger city, and is given a freer hand in setting policies and making decisions. I wasn't enjoying that kind of trust from my superiors. All of this started to boil down to a bad attitude on my part. I didn't really have any desire to get into the upper-management levels of the institution—I didn't consider myself a money man, and preferred the more creative work to the supervisory work that the loan officers and administrators got involved in. Within my department, there was only one step up, to the position of director of marketing services, which oversaw the advertising, public relations, and other marketing areas of the savings and loan institution. Any other step up within the institution would mean shifting my emphasis, and I preferred to remain with the advertising.

"I suppose that by that time my attitude was bad enough that I would have been fired if I'd stayed. I don't really know. I was friendly with all the people I worked with, including those above me, and I'm still friendly with them today. I don't bear any grudges, I just think I found myself in the wrong situation after enough time had gone by. There wasn't any particular incident that finally made up my mind for me. It just all fell into place, and the decision was there in front of me."

Fred left the savings and loan institution in early 1972, walking away from a $13,000-a-year salary, with no job in front of him and a wife and two children to support. He risked $3,000 of his own savings, and within three weeks had opened up his own one-man agency. "I had confidence in myself. I'd been living relatively frugally, well below my salary level. I knew that if worse came to worst, I could go out and sell encyclopedias or something. I knew that I could always stay afloat. I didn't set any time limit on this new venture—that is, how long I'd give myself before I went back to a real job. But as it turned out, I didn't have to. Within a few months, my income level was back up to where it had been when I left my savings and loan job. I went out and beat the brush looking for clients, and was able to get them. The contacts I had made over the years at the savings and loan job paid off. I never had to borrow any money to go into this venture, and the moral support I got from my wife and my parents was terrific. That's probably one reason why I was able to do what I did.

"I never could have moved to another city and done this. The contacts that I'd made here in the media were too important to me. Besides, I really didn't want to move. We liked our life here, and I was sure that I could make it."

Running a one-man agency soon proved frustrating for Fred. There were limitations on what he could do, and much of the work had to be farmed out to free-lancers. It was a hip-pocket operation, and he began to feel the need for a partner, someone whose own skills would complement his.

Ted had also recently left his position to form a one-man agency. Fred and Ted had known each other for a number of years; they had kept in touch during the early days of their respective one-man shops. One day, over lunch, one thing led to another, and in January of 1973, less than a year after Fred had left the savings and loan institution, he and Ted formed a partnership. Three years later, Fred's income was double what it had been at his former job.

"I can see the cycle that so many young men fall prey to," Fred said.

"First, there's the lure of power—you have the say over the careers and well-being of other people, and if your decisions are correct, you can put your company into the limelight. After a while, that kind of fades. Unless you have an insatiable desire for power, the thrill goes out of making those kinds of decisions. Then there's a shift in your emphasis from power to money. You're entrenched in your position and earning the maximum becomes the prime attraction. That, too, I learned can be a false goal. When the power and the money don't hold the fascination, then the desire for personal freedom starts to well up in you. Freedom means time—time to do what you wish, whether it's with your family, your hobby, or whatever. I had my choice. I could have bitten the bullet and stayed on with the big institution, and eventually worked my way into a position of considerable power and money. But I chose the freedom route, and I don't regret it for a minute. If I had it to do all over again, I wouldn't change a thing. If, out of the blue, all the money that I ever needed to sustain my family for the duration should suddenly become available to me, I suppose I'd be a bum for about six months, then I'd go back to work doing what I'm doing now.

"The agency is well established today, and I don't really think there are any limits on our growth, except for our own personal desires and energies. But Ted and I both prefer the moderate course. You get too big, and you end up running a big business and not really doing the kind of creative work you want to do. More important, keeping things on an even keel as we are now allows me to spend more time with my family. And that's where my ultimate pleasures really lie. For example, a few months ago we gave up our most lucrative account. We simply told him, 'No more.' It was an automobile dealership, extremely demanding of our time, and starting to put a lot of stress on our partnership. We figured we'd be better off without the account, that we could replace it in short order (which we did), and that our long-range business situation would be better off. We made the right decision. We gave up some bucks, but we retained our sanity and our composure. It was worth it. We'll do the same thing again if the occasion arises."

TED'S STORY: "Since I was a little kid, I've enjoyed being in business. I used to organize and run neighborhood carnivals—you know, where all the kids come in and spend a few pennies to knock over soda bottles with tennis balls. In the summers, I set up fruit stands and juice stands. In the sixth grade, I started a neighborhood newspaper—I wrote all the articles and sold them door-to-door for a dime apiece. During a few winters when we lived in Chicago, I devised a successful snow-shoveling system. I didn't shovel any better than the other kids, but they all went door-to-door asking 50 cents or so for each job. I went door-to-door and told people to pay me what they thought the job was worth. And I always got more than the other kids. I had some kind of success syndrome. I'm not sure why. I just enjoyed it. I was an entrepreneur. By the time I got into high school, I had my own record business. We hired bands and recorded them on 45 rpm records. We weren't very successful—we had five releases and a couple of albums—but I was doing something that gave me great personal pleasure.''

Ted graduated from high school in Long Beach, California, in 1959, with a clear-cut idea that he wanted to get into some aspect of show business. In addition to his record business in high school, he had worked (at no pay) as a disc jockey for a small FM station in the area. ''It was a fun thing, an ego thing,'' Ted said.

College didn't satisfy his energies. After six weeks, he quit to take a job as a disc jockey, earning $37.50 a week, working a 42-hour week. His parents were upset, but Ted stuck with it for five months, until he was fired. He then took a job at a local TV station as an announcer and a clown on a kiddie show, earning $1.25 an hour. But his great enthusiasm soon ran out and, bored, he went back to college in the fall of 1960.

He started out majoring in liberal arts, with an emphasis on broadcasting and journalism, and he held down an announcing job on the side at a local radio station. By this time, Ted had had his fill of the announcing and performing end of the media and decided to shift emphasis: to major in marketing and advertising, a field he felt was allied with the overall broadcasting industry. But he maintained his disc-jockey job, now paying $2.50 an hour, just to pay his rent and give him some spending money. It no longer represented a career goal to him. ''I observed some of the other DJs who were already at the ripe old age of 30. Their days seemed to be meaningless. That wasn't for me, not for the rest of my life.''

Ted got what he considers his first big break on his first job interview after graduating from college in 1965. The break was that he wasn't hired. The interview was with the Los Angeles branch of J. Walter Thompson, one of the nation's largest advertising agencies. His escorts during his tour of the offices were Dwight Chapin and Ron Ziegler, and the reject letter came from one of the Thompson big wigs at the time, H. R. Haldeman. ''Who knows where they all would have taken me had I been hired?'' Ted mused.

Shortly thereafter, a radio station offered Ted a job selling time. He would have no desk or account list, only a locker. This was the bottom of the ladder, but Ted took the job and was successful at it. ''I hustled shoeshine parlors, used clothing stores, anything I could get to buy a minute on the station. Fairly quickly, I was earning between $400 and $500 a month, which in 1965 was pretty good money for a young punk. I stayed there for four months and was offered a better situation at another station. Three years later, I was making $1,000 a month doing the same thing.''

In 1968, there was an opening at a major television station for a time salesman. Ted applied, along with a hundred others, and won the job. ''That's when I really discovered the power of television. I was doing a good job for my clients. They were reaping the success from their advertising, and I was making $40,000 a year before I was 30 years old. I loved it.

It was a great job. Then I did something that really wasn't like me. I started saving. My folks had always spent whatever they took in, and I had always done likewise. But I was making more money than I could spend, and I started stashing it away. My wife influenced me in that area. She had been taught the virtue of thrift, and she prevailed on me to save.

"My job was sales. I wasn't what you'd call a company man. I wasn't concerned with the company overall. Another fellow and I were the top salesmen, and I knew that the other guy would get ahead faster. While I was out beating the bush, he spent a lot of his time courting the boss. So he ended up with the boss's ear, and when a sales-manager job opened up at an affiliated station, he got it.

"I was result-oriented. If I had to, I bent the rules in order to satisfy my clients. I'd bring in material after the deadlines had past, thus making some of the secretaries work late. This meant friction. I was bringing in a lot of billing, but to a lot of people in the station, I was a pain in the ass. But my boss was smart enough to see the bottom line, and he went along with me.

"Then there was a change in bosses. The guy who had understood me left, and a new one came in. He was a bad salesman, and a worse sales manager. He didn't like my tricks of the trade, even though they weren't illegal. He was chastising me constantly, and I couldn't stand it. By this time, I'd built up a nice nest egg, and had had a lot of time to see how other advertising agencies worked. I'd also learned a lot about television, and how it works as a sales medium."

The combination of his dissatisfaction with the station and his growing intrigue with how the television business worked prompted Ted to think of starting his own agency. Some of his clients didn't have their own agencies. Ted was doing much of the work that an agency would normally do, including writing copy and arranging for the time on the station. He took a calculated risk that some of these clients would be willing to use him as an agency if he in fact started one.

"Even though I had no preparation to be on my own, I gave the station two weeks' notice. My hunch worked: two clients immediately came into my fold, and between them, I was making $1,000 a month right away. I felt in my bones that I'd get the business I needed to succeed. Quitting was a fabulous experience. I felt thrilled and completely positive, although my wife was nervous."

Ted's agency began in May 1972, and by November of that year, he was making almost $3,000 a month. Even though this was below what his income at the station had been, he could easily live within it. He had dipped into his kitty for about $2,000 in order to get started. Within a year after he had started, his income was back to its original level.

"All I really knew was television, not print or billboards, or any of the other media. And there was a lot of business to be had. But knowing only television, I was limited. I knew Fred from his days at the savings and loan, and knew that he had a broader agency background than I did. We got together, with the intent being that Fred would do the detail work and run the office, and I would handle the sales and the television end. But, oddly enough, it turned out that Fred wasn't a detail man, and he was a better account executive than I was. So we ended up with our roles kind of reversed. And it worked out well.

"I'm working twelve hours a day, and I love it. It's like being on vacation all the time. But I'd suggest to others not to go into partnerships unless the prospective partners are completely compatible, and that usually means being opposite in temperament. Fred and I are very lucky. We hit it off, and rarely disagree."

Ted and Fred exhibit the same moral values—their families take precedence over making a lot of money, and they both want only moderate growth for their business, in order to maintain their personal lives.

"Advertising is a business like any other, only a bit more creative. It requires the same elements for success as any other business. Creativity alone isn't enough. You have to run an efficient shop, you have to take care of your billings, you have to make sure you're getting good-paying accounts, you have to have good personnel practices, and you have to have people who believe in you. When we first started out, we were hungry, and we'd take almost any account that came our way if it looked like it would pay. But that can get people thinking that you don't have the integrity that they're looking for. Now, we're not hungry any more, and we'll turn down a lot of accounts if we don't feel they fit into our mold.

"We've kind of reached a plateau, and we're leveling off. We could take on twenty more people if we wanted, but we wouldn't necessarily make any more money. It probably wouldn't be worth it. This way, we're in control, and we control our own destiny."

# Partners from Dissimilar Backgrounds

*The vitality of thought is in adventure. Ideas won't keep. Something must be done about them. When the idea is new, its custodians have fervor and live for it.*

ALFRED NORTH WHITEHEAD

Phil and Woody came from diverse backgrounds, and pursued vastly different careers before they embarked on a partnership in a restaurant business. Yet, their personalities seem strikingly similar—mature, contemplative, soft-spoken, and, indeed, they were roommates for a number of years while single.

PHIL'S STORY: "I've been at this for almost seven years now. It's the longest time I've ever stayed in one particular career, and I'm not sure this is it for keeps. Times have been bad in the restaurant business, and we've felt it. We've made some mistakes, too, but if we had it to do all over again, I'd probably stay in the restaurant business and make some adjustments that could avoid some of our current problems."

A successful restaurant operation, particularly in a tourist haven like Honolulu, has to have a certain dramatic flair. Phil acquired his dramatic flair as early as his high school years, where he was working professionally as a technical director for the civic theater in Portland, Oregon. Community theater was very active there at that time, and Phil's early and profitable experience directed him toward seeking a career in the theater. But the Navy interrupted this course for two years, and he found himself doing espionage work. Apparently, his mind was not totally made up regarding the theater, for after two years of espionage work, he decided he wanted to pursue that. But there were no openings at the time, and he chose college instead.

"There were so many exciting things for an eager 20-year-old to do. Maybe there were too many things, which is why I didn't settle down for a long time. I was smitten with the idea of going into business, after taking courses in business management. Then, I took some philosophy courses. That has turned out to be my continuing love, but there's no money in it. But the philosophy courses changed my outlook. I discovered gray. Prior to that, in my more exuberant youth, black and white had been the only options."

When Phil started college, he had no pressure from his family. They were willing to give him whatever money he needed to go through school. But Phil wanted to do it on his own, to become a self-sufficient individual, wanting to set and accomplish his own goals, on his own. "After being exposed to all the facets of the education process, I felt it all boiled down to business management. This seemed to be the best way to incorporate the many directions that I found myself going in. It would be a funnel through which everything else would flow.

"A strange little incident shaped what was to be an active career for me for a number of years. When we had moved to Honolulu, my folks bought a new home that needed some landscaping. On one particular day, I wasn't doing anything, and my dad asked me to go to the nursery and get some plants for the house. I swear that until that day I thought that a nursery was a place that took care of kids. I didn't know that any other kind of nursery existed.

"The local nursery naturally specialized in the tropical kinds of plants. When we lived in Oregon, I had become accustomed to the rain-forest foliage, and during the service, I'd spent some time in the desert and learned about the foliage there. Here was another whole world of things, and I was fascinated. The next thing I knew I had taken a job at the nursery to help pay my college expenses."

At first Phil did the dirty work—carrying bushes, digging holes, cleaning the nursery premises. Soon after, he became a salesman, which led him to thoughts of buying and running his own nursery.

"I realized that if you go through life and never make any decisions, you're going to end up a vegetable. If you make a decision, you've got at least a 50-50 chance of succeeding. I thus decided to concentrate my efforts on making enough money to get my own nursery. I was going to drop out of school at that point. That was my decision. And all this in spite of the fact that I didn't know the first thing about owning or running a nursery, or any other kind of business.

"Just as a safeguard, I took my thoughts to the guidance counselor in college. He quizzed me heavily about why I wanted to leave school and go into business on my own, and I had answers for every question. Apparently, my answers were so good that I convinced the counselor to quit too, and we pooled our money and became partners in buying a nursery. Our two talents blended well, and we were very successful. I had put in $1,000 of my own, and you may find this hard to believe, but within ten weeks after we started, my partner, the ex-guidance counselor, offered to buy me out at ten times my investment, or $10,000.

"And I decided to sell to him. Why? I guess it was the antsy youth in me. My partner promised to pay me out of profits over the next two years, and indeed he did. Then, believe it or not, the very same day I had sold the business, I was approached by the owner of one of the largest nurseries in town, wanting me to run his place for him. I was intoxicated with the idea of someone else wanting me to run his large business, and I took the job. I ran that nursery for a little over a year. Then I was fired. As it turned out, there was no harmony between the owner and myself, and life was nothing but conflicts. On top of that, my mother died, and our family fell into bad times. Life had been a bowl of cherries for me until then, and this was my first come-down. I kind of decided to withdraw myself and let some time go by while I regrouped my thoughts."

Phil then got a job as an apprentice refrigeration mechanic, which lasted for one year. Then came another nursery job, which lasted for a year and a half, until a freeway came through and took the property.

"All this time I really had no goals," Phil said. "I was satisfying urges. If I had any goal, it was to be secure in something by the time I was 30. I was a hard worker and self-sufficient, and I was always able to get jobs that paid well. I was a truck driver for a time, earning $900 a month, and I made more than that in 1961, when I was working as a refrigeration mechanic. I always made much less money working in the nurseries, but I was willing to take less because of the challenge of running the nursery. I guess deep in my heart I wanted to be in some kind of business, probably the nursery business."

By this time, Phil had reached the tender age of 25, and after the few years of jumping from one job to another, he decided to get his landscape contractor's license, and went into business with a friend. "We could earn as much as we needed, enough to satisfy the moment. We were having good times. The whole world belongs to 25-year-olds, in the sense that they can do just what they want to do when they want to do it. I could have earned a lot more money back then, but I was single, having a good time, and I had no need for more money."

Yet Phil couldn't seem to get anything going that lasted. A year after entering the partnership, the partner got married, and his financial demands changed dramatically. No more of the good times for him. The partnership dissolved, with the partner taking the whole thing.

"Then the fun began. I couldn't find a job I wanted right away, so I moved in with some friends and took a job at a local Sears warehouse, doing expediting work. I never realized it, but I found that I had a photographic memory, and the expediting job turned out to be too easy. It was boring, but I stayed at it for two years, then decided to go back to college. I was living really cheap then, paying $30 a month rent for the apartment that we shared.

"Being a good bit older than most of the other college students, and having had more business experience, I saw an opportunity to make money on the whims and desires of these kids. In a total departure from what I'd been doing previously, I opened a coffee house near the university. Eventually, it was a coffee house with booze.

"I don't really like bars—so many of them are sleazy, they smell bad, they're filled with unhappy people. So I opened a nice bar. But I soon learned that happy people don't go to bars, and it didn't work out. I worked my butt off, putting in a hundred hours a week for three months to get it started, then I stuck with it for two and a half years. It was a little bit of show business coming back to me again. Even though it wasn't working financially, I liked it. During this time, I started forming thoughts of the ultimate restaurant that would be successful, that would allow me to mingle with people I'd like to mingle with, and that could throw off a good living to me. As soon as I could, I got out from under the coffee-house business."

It was back to landscaping for Phil, and he thought that he would make this his career, until the right opportunity came along for the ideal restaurant. He soon became involved in a relatively new aspect of landscaping—swimming pool area design. Nobody else was doing it nearby, and the opportunity was unlimited. He free-lanced successfully for a number of years, concentrating on the design of swimming-pool landscapes.

Sooner or later, the restaurant opportunity had to come. It arrived for Phil when he visited a newly opened restaurant in Honolulu that specialized in a very limited menu of steaks, salads, and drinks. With his business-management experience, he quickly assessed the significance of this new type of operation: virtually no waste, minimum of kitchen help, minimal buying problems, and the same price tag per dinner served as with restaurants with a varied and costly-to-maintain menu. He observed the new restaurant for some time, and was astounded by its success.

"Woody and I recognized that the formula was super, and that there was a huge demand for this kind of operation. And we knew that not only would it thrive on the competition, but there was plenty of room for competition. And that was about all we knew about the restaurant business—that this place needed competition. Everybody that was anybody in town frequented the place, and when we announced that we were going to build a competing facility a few blocks away, the money flowed in.

That was rather astonishing. We were completely unknown operators, with no experience whatsoever, and yet we got $15,000 in seed money, based only on some simple drawings and the concept. Now that we look back on it, the money was too easy to come by. A lot of people are fascinated with the restaurant business, probably for the same reasons that we were. There's some kind of glamour to it. There's also a lot of hard work to it. That's what people don't realize.

"There's a lot of creativity in running a restaurant, too. Designing the menus, creating new dishes to serve, establishing the decor and changing it from time to time—all of these things I guess go back to my original show biz urgings."

The restaurant was a great success at first. But then Phil and Woody had to face some of the competitive aspects of this business, particularly in a highly transient and highly competitive city like Honolulu. New restaurants were opening all the time, with new products, new appeals, new ambiance. And the public is fickle. You can be their favorite place for a few months, until the next new favorite place opens up. "There's got to be a constantly developing series of new products, or new ways of packaging the old products. This is a business. It's got to be run like a business. The original good idea in food lasts only as long as people are attracted by it, or until they're attracted away by something else.

"And you've got to be flexible enough to ride out the changes in the economic climate. One of the factories lays off a few hundred people, and our business goes down immediately. These are bad times right now, and we're kind of down in the dumps. But I'm sure that the times will get better again, and if we still own the place, we'll be happy for it then."

WOODY'S STORY: The other half of this partnership, Woody, came to restauranteuring by way of a career in chemical engineering.

"By the time we'd moved to Honolulu I had gone to four different high schools in various parts of the country. I didn't know about Scholastic Aptitude Tests until the night before they were to be given. Yet I was in the National Honor Society and the top 5 percent of my class when I graduated high school."

Woody grew up in the Sputnik age, and not unexpectedly for a kid interested in electronics and rocketry, he embarked on an engineering career. Family financial problems required Woody to work his way through college to support himself, and to do so he had to live in bare, minimal quarters.

"This guy had a little apartment near the university for $30 a month, and I moved in with him. It was Phil. We roomed together for a couple of years during college, and I even helped him out at his coffee shop when he opened it. But I had no more thought of being in the restaurant business than the man in the moon. It was just something fun to do for my buddy."

Early in college, Woody shifted his emphasis from electronics engineering to chemical engineering. Chemistry was definitely a career goal. After graduation, he received his first job as a propellant chemist, making $500 a month. Then he was drafted, joined the Naval Reserves, applied to Officer's Candidate School, and was accepted. He spent the next four years in the Navy as a full lieutenant. He was assigned the post of repair officer in nuclear/biochemical warfare, the area most closely related to his training. He was responsible for the readiness of the ship in a defensive capacity. After the Navy, he took a job as head of a department in charge of manufacturing electronic equipment. "My experience in the Navy was more in a management capacity than as a chemist. I had between fifty and a hundred guys under my command, and the experience really changed my outlook. I moved away from the pure scientific, learning about people and their problems, how to apply yourself, and how to really work. The electronics industry seemed to offer more challenge. Without graduate work in chemistry, I was definitely limited as to how far I could go, and I didn't feel like going back to college."

Still single, Woody moved back in with Phil, who by now had bought a modest house, attractive bachelor's quarters, with his earnings from the landscaping business. Woody remained with the electronics firm for four years, until that challenge also started to fade.

"Living with Phil again, the talk often turned to running a restaurant. We were single, and we liked to cook and entertain a lot. We put on some fancy dinners for our friends, and found the experience very satisfying. I guess I just slipped along into the idea of opening up a restaurant. We'd sit around drinking beer, playing cards, and talking about the restaurant, and the idea just kind of grew. I envisioned a place with really super, custom food, and got caught up in the idea that there was really no good restaurant in town.

"Then along came that steak place, and Phil thought we could compete with it. I was more interested in trying to improve on their formula. I guess I had always wanted to be my own boss, and the job at the electronics firm was turning sour. As it turned out, if I had stayed with them, I would have crashed and burned. They were near the end of their rope, and I got out just in time.

"Phil was more of a business man. He saw our venture as growing into a number of restaurants. But I saw it more as a specialized, personal place. It may sound odd, but I'm using principles of management that I learned in the Navy and electronics in the operation of a restaurant. You have to maintain a certain level of quality in the food business, just as you do in any other business. Where the owner is involved, you can maintain the quality you're looking for. It's the absentee-owner restaurants that usually run into trouble, because nobody really concerned is there to maintain the level of quality.

"I'm a frustrated artist, too, in a way. I always enjoyed drawing when I was a kid, but a high school advisor said that my aptitude was for science. So I canned the artistic desires. Now I get my kicks drafting the menus for the restaurant."

Woody married a few years ago, and has long since moved out of his bachelor's quarters with Phil. "In spite of the turn-down in business, I'm not really unsatisfied. If I had it to do over again, I wouldn't change a thing, including the Navy experience. I wanted to be my own boss, but I never cared much about seeing my name in lights. Security is less important than being in control and being creative. I really believe that. So far, it's been working."

# If You Can't Design Them, Sell Them

*Truth is tough. It will not break, like a bubble, at a touch. Nay, you may kick it around all day, like a football, and it will be round and full at evening.*

OLIVER WENDELL HOLMES

RAY'S STORY: "I didn't really have a choice. There I was being laid off as a result of the recession, and it seemed like all I knew were these electronic widgets. If I couldn't make them any longer, I'd have to try to sell them. I'd just been divorced, had no job, was deep in debt, and had a chronic case of shyness. I had to get over that, and I finally did. If everyone got over their fear of selling, we'd be hip deep in salesmen."

Ray embarked on an engineering career during the tremendous technical revolution of the 1950s and 1960s. The world seemed to be the oyster for these talented, studious youths who were willing to devote their career to the technical side of mankind. As Ray recalls it, at one of his numerous jobs, "Everything there was on fire. Kingdoms were being created daily. Creative energies were well satisfied. We were the fastest-growing company in the fastest-growing industry in the world."

Many still toil in the vineyards, some happy, some not so. Others, like Mike and Woody, have gone into auto-repair, restaurant, and a variety of other businesses. Ray is typical of yet another large group—those who got caught in the seemingly endless upward growth curve of the industry. And like a tidal wave, when it came crashing down, the effects were felt all across the land. From childhood, Ray seemed to have the resilience to pull through a crisis and reestablish a good life for himself.

"I was an only child, probably overprotected, and I watched my folks make it on a hand-to-mouth basis. Dad was a salesman for a pharmaceutical firm, and we only saw him on weekends. Mom ran a beauty parlor in the house, six days a week for twelve hours a day. When I was a kid, I used to help her in the shop, sweeping up the hair, washing the sinks. Things like that. I remember the work ethic from my earliest years—you'll be a bum if you don't work hard, and I was bound and determined not to be a bum. And

I also saw my folks working hard, and they barely made more than peanuts. I never thought that I could make big money, but I always wanted to try."

By the time he got to high school, Ray was already fascinated with technical things, and had become a voracious reader. His experimentation with a chemistry set resulted in an explosion that left him partially deaf in his left ear. "The local high school had a broad selection of courses, such as calculus, chemistry, and physics. This wasn't all that common back in 1949. So I got a good beginning. We had no money for college. It cost less to go to the local college than away to school, and though I would have preferred going to Purdue for an engineering program, I had to stay home and work my way through college."

Following college, Ray climbed the typical ladder of success. At his first job, in 1954, he earned $342 per month. Job number two, in 1957, found him earning $500 per month. Another job that same year took him to $600 per month. Within a decade, his monthly income was nearing the $1,500 range.

Like many of his peers, Ray frequently had thoughts of branching off on his own to do it "the better way." When he got the closest he'd ever come—to a new way of developing a tantalum capacitor—he learned, to his dismay, that someone else had succeeded in doing the same thing just three months earlier. Ray's job hopping, typical in the industry, had him crisscrossing the country until he settled with a medium-sized firm based in Houston, where he was head of reliability in the tantalum capacitor section.

"Then, along came the great electronics depression, and everybody started to get squeezed. The company was hurting badly, and the corporate politics got pretty vicious. I was inclined to try to get into marketing and sales, rather than stay in research and development, because my days certainly seemed numbered where I was. Just as I was about to make the move, I was canned. Nevertheless, I felt that I could make it in the marketing end better than the guys that were there. Whenever they had a question out in the field, they'd have to call me for the answers. I was the chief hell-catcher, and I was doing most of their job for them. Except for my overpowering shyness, I felt I could do a better job than most of the regular marketing reps, and they were making a lot more money than I was, to boot. As a matter of fact, I learned that engineers were being had, compared to what could be made in marketing. But it all boiled down to their innate fear of the public. I suppose when you go into a profession like that, where you work pretty much on your own, not having to deal with the public, you do so because of a basic desire to stay away from the public.

"It was a rotten time to become a representative. The economy, at least in our industry, was going from bad to worse, and there was no sign of a turnaround.

"I remembered one lesson that someone had taught me—make your mistakes on the other guy's money. With that in mind, I set out to become a swimming-pool salesman—about as far from the work that I had been doing as I could possibly get. But it forced me to go out and sell, to speak to the public, to get involved in the give and take of the sales pitch. I learned when to shut up. I learned how to close a deal. I learned how to organize my time. I learned how to be on my own. In short, I put together a structure: how to weigh the priorities that had to be faced in this kind of work. I also learned how to cope with factories and delivery schedules, subcontractors and the weather. I didn't really intend to stay with swimming pools—I wasn't making that much money at it, because the bad economy was hurting the pool business as much as it was the electronics business. As soon as things seemed to be turning up a bit, I shifted my gears and went back into electronics, working as a rep for a large firm. I stayed there for about a year, learning what I felt I had to know to go off on my own.

"Now, a salesman can't be a salesman until he has something to sell, and back then there were a lot more salesmen than there were lines. A lot of guys like myself who'd been busted out of the industry were trying to make a living peddling the goods. I scraped around for lines to sell, and finally decided to risk what little money I had and bought a line from the firm I had been working with. After a while, my salary and commission with that firm were bringing me in better income than I'd had when I'd been canned from the electronics laboratory. But I was determined to go out on my own, and I did in September of 1974. I had remarried in the intervening years, and my wife was working. Without her income, we couldn't have made it, because from September 1974 until February 1975, I had zero income. I don't think I would have tried it without my wife's income, but I had such a heavy obligation for support and alimony to my first wife that I knew I had to become successful.

"Now I've got it made. I have no thought in my mind of working for anybody again.

"There are no secrets, just hard work. I knew my lines, I knew my customers, and it's just like the old saying—find a need and fill it. That's what I set out to do. I function far better on my own than I ever did as an employee. There's no power structure to contend with. I'm totally responsible for myself, and that's the way I like it. My dealings are basically simple, one-on-one. I know if I'm doing a good job, because my books show it.

"In a corporation, you can create the illusion of a good job. You can get so involved in protecting your own ass, and spend such an inordinate amount of time on that, that 60 percent of your productive energy can get siphoned away. Sooner or later, the illusion of a job well done is seen through by somebody. But you've been trapped. You had to create the illusion because you couldn't actually get the work done because of the corporate structure. It's like a vicious circle. A catch-22.

"Independent people can produce more effective results toward a set goal when they're not playing at appearances. I've always believed that independence is a basic cornerstone of our society, and I'm living independently now."

# The Career Women

*To create anything at all in any field, and especially anything of outstanding worth, requires non-conformity, or want of satisfaction with things as they are.*

BEN SHAHN

Sandy, Pris, and Liz are essentially career women: literary agent, real-estate saleswoman, and publicist. All went from situations of being employed in similar fields into individual entrepreneurships. They broke away and went on their own, and have been as successful as any of the men discussed in these case histories. They all had marriages and divorces along the way, but the marriage careers didn't seem to have a bearing on their working careers. It could be said, of course, that the working careers had an effect on the marriage careers, perhaps a deleterious one. But I have concentrated solely on their working career, for each seemed to stand on its own as an example of how a motivated woman can get free.

A personal note now about the ratio of men to women in these case histories. I haven't discussed more men than women because I'm sexist or anti Women's Liberation. It's simply a fact that there are still many more male breadwinners than female breadwinners. Perhaps in time the ratio of men to women will become more equal. But until then, I hope the examples of females getting free that I've included here will be representative enough and encouraging enough to supply the needed motivation for any woman looking for a reason to go off on her own.

SANDY'S STORY: Sandy graduated college in 1963, an art history major. Although her family could have supported her, she wanted to work and make her own living. Her first job was starting a small art gallery. She was hired to design and set up the gallery, and within six months, it was successfully under way, and she was let go. Then, through an ad in the newspaper, she found a position as assistant to the public relations chief in a medium-sized publishing house. Her first experience in the world of art left her feeling that it was a dead-end career, so she took the publicity job, starting in 1964 at $75 a week. She stayed at the same job, and at the same level, for two years, working her salary up to $135 per week.

Then an opportunity presented itself for her to become an associate publicist at one of the nation's largest publishing firms. She took the job, starting with a yearly salary of $10,000, and eight years later, when she left, she was earning $20,000 a year, and had the title of publicity manager, and a staff of seven under her.

"During my career there, I often had thoughts of starting my own publishing firm. Publicity is fascinating, but in the publishing business, it's at the end of the process. All the work has already been done. The book is manufactured, and the dust jacket, good or bad, has been designed. You really have no control over the product until it's put in your hands. Then, if it's not a success, you can get blamed for it.

"At one point, a group of four of us thought seriously about leaving to start our own firm, but as it turned out, we didn't have enough confidence in ourselves as a group, even though we had enough confidence in ourselves as individuals. Interestingly enough, of the four of us, one stayed on with the same firm, another is now the head of trade publishing with another major firm, one is a senior editor at a major women's magazine, and I'm the fourth one.

"I guess I was getting weary of being at the end of the publishing process, and I wanted to find something a little more creative and earlier in the whole publishing procedure. After we disbanded our plans to form our own firm, I took a leave of absence during the summer of 1973. During that time, through the many contacts I had built up, I was offered a job as a literary agent with one of the biggest talent agencies in the country. Even though I had had no agenting experience, they felt my knowledge of the publishing business warranted their paying me a higher salary than I had had with the publishing firm.

"The good part was that I was going from the rear end of publishing to the front end—getting the talent together, working with the author to consummate a deal with the publisher, seeing the project to its completion, and then working toward its ultimate success. I had plenty of contacts in the business, and I knew that I could make use of them. This was an opportunity for me to learn a new area, one that I'd been intrigued with. I didn't see the job as a long pull, and if I hadn't gotten a job there, I probably would have sought out work as an agent with a smaller firm.

"There was also a rather strange and unfortunate thing that happened when I started with the agency. You could call it stupid. I'd been offered the job without anyone talking to the "elder," a sort of guru at the company without whose opinion very little happened. I don't know how I was hired without her approval, but I was. I wasn't even aware of her existence until after I had started the job. Also, the younger people at the agency—my contemporaries—had not been consulted, and there was quite a bit of resentment at the money I was making. I wasn't exactly welcomed with open arms, and within six months, I felt quite unhappy about the personal side of my job. This was in early 1974, and I decided to stay as long as I could stand it, to learn as much as I could, and then split."

Sandy stayed for one more year, learning the business at a company through which filtered some of the top names in the literary field. Then, in June 1975, things began to fall into place to motivate her to break loose. Others had been encouraging her to go on her own, and one woman, for whom she had a great deal of respect, gave her an ultimate push. Another curious thing happened: one of the clients she had had while she was still with the large agency had proposed to write a book that Sandy took to a small but prestigious publishing firm. The firm was interested in the book, and asked to meet the author for an extended discussion of the proposed project. Sandy went with the author to the meeting, and listened while the author and the chief editor discussed the project for close to two hours. A deal was made between the author and the publisher, and the project went into the contract stage. Two weeks later, Sandy called the author to tell him that the discussion with the editor that she had attended had helped to motivate her to leave her current job and go off on her own, and she wanted to know whether the author would remain with her. The author agreed to do so. The title of the book was *Getting Free—How to Profit Most Out of Working for Yourself.*

Sandy had some good breaks that helped her to get off on her own. One was that the former employer let her take her existing clients with her, and released certain incomes to her on projects that she had been involved in. She also had a form of modest financial backing that took some of the pressure off her: she had no rent or overhead worries for the apartment that doubled as both her home and office.

"I risked about $5,000 of my own money to get started, and I knew that I could get by with a minimum income until things started to develop. I didn't set any deadlines for myself, but now I kind of see a three- to five-year span in which I'm either going to make it or not. The rent subsidy has allowed me to be choosy in the kind of material I deal with. I've been extremely selective, taking only top-grade stuff. I can afford it now. Without the subsidy, I'd probably have to take some junk stuff and probably wouldn't like it. But I could get by.

"Things are starting to develop really well now. You have to understand, though, that there's a terribly long span between the acquisition of work and the reward for it. From the time I start working with an author, it may take a few months until a contract is signed. There may be some advance money upon the signing, but usually the full advance isn't paid until the book is partly or completely accepted by the publisher. The really big money, if it's going to come at all, comes after publication, when paperback rights, movie rights, book-club rights are sold. Thus, it could be as much as two years from the time the deal is struck until the big money comes in. It's hard to budget around that kind of phenomenon, but once you get your business rolling, it can take care of itself.

"Sure, I want to make money, but that's not my prime motivation. Terrific things can happen in this business—the people that you meet, the excitement that occurs when you hit a winner. I'm glad to be away from a regimented office and all the problems that go with it. I work better when there's no strict routine. My time is my own now, and I don't have to worry about punching a clock, or seeming to be daydreaming when I'm really trying to be creative.

"Sometimes I have a wish to work with others, to share the excitement and the confusion. Some old friends help out when I have a particularly vexing problem, or some enthusiasm to share. But I still have something to prove by being on my own. Even if the right person came along today, I don't think I'd affiliate with him or her right now. The need is there, but it's not that strong.

"Everybody should do this at least once. I have a new definition of security now, and I'm very happy about the way it all turned out."

PRIS'S STORY: Pris doesn't really have to work, for anyone else, or on her own. She received a substantial inheritance many years ago, but preferred to invest it and make her way in the world of work.

Pris was raised on a farm outside a small town in Florida. Through childhood, and high school, from which she graduated in 1956, she had a yen to be a veterinarian. "I was accepted at veterinary college and then had a dumb fight with my folks. At the time, it was the most important thing in the world to me, but looking back it was so silly as not to be believed. We fought over whether I should specialize in large animals or small animals. I wanted to work on large animals, since we had a dairy farm. But my folks thought there was more money in small animals—house pets—and I was afraid that I'd get too emotionally involved in caring for small animals. We couldn't resolve our differences, and even though I'd been dreaming of becoming a veterinarian for years, that fight made me give up the idea altogether. Call it what you will—spite, rebelliousness, I don't know. I was having a very trying time at home between the ages of 15 and 17, and I guess I just wanted my own way too much. But I have a dream today—some day I'd like to start my own wildlife park. It probably goes back to those experiences as a kid. I don't know if I ever will or not, but I daydream about it quite a lot."

Pris is attractive, bright, articulate. The kind of girl who could just sit back and wait for Mr. Right to come along. But she didn't see it that way. She started college in a liberal arts program, but in her second year transferred to business, specializing in real estate. Though she had no specific career goals, this seemed like a practical course of study to her. The family was extremely comfortable financially, and she had anything she wanted. There was no backlash that she remembers over her abandonment of becoming a veterinarian. She graduated college and enrolled in law school, where she remained for two years. But an unrequited love affair and disillusionment with the possibility of a law career prompted her to drop out.

"Frankly, I was scared to death of the real world. My alternative was to go home and wait until I married, but my mother was of an advanced age, and my being around her would have been distressing to her. So I moved to Miami and went out to find myself a job. My sole aim was to get a job and have a salary that I could live on. It didn't matter what I was doing. I had no goals. This was in 1962. I was 23 years old. The shame of my quitting law school was evident from the fact that in the law-school aptitude tests I came out in the top 3 percent in the entire country.

"I always had money from Dad's estate. For a short time I depended on it, but then I started investing it. I must admit that having this cushion has affected my long-term thinking. I've never really been that hungry. Still, I was motivated to work and be self-sufficient. It was a matter of pride. I was going to show my family that I could make it on my own. Sure, I had offers to be set up in any business that I wanted. All I had to do was ask. But I was going to do it myself."

Pris's first job in Miami was as a typist for a title-insurance company, earning $300 a month. "This wasn't a come-down. I was told I had a good future, and could move up in the company and earn a lot more money. I felt confident of my ability, and at the time, I felt that I'd stay with the company forever. I was promoted within two weeks, and six months later, I had my own secretary and office. I was an escrow officer, the first female escrow officer in Miami, and I was earning $500 a month. My background in law and real estate had helped me. I was making it on my own."

Pris stayed at the title company for three years, and eventually became a branch manager. She was pushy, young, and wanted more. There were five men above her in the company, and she was told that there was no way that she'd ever break into top management. "They told me that I was a woman, and that I could make more money, but I wouldn't move any higher in the hierarchy. This was in 1965. I believed them. And I wasn't going to fight a losing battle. I decided then to go off on my own."

Technically, Pris is now an employee of a large real-estate firm specializing in residential sales. But this type of occupation meets the criteria of getting free: Pris draws no salary; she works on her own time, strictly on a commission basis. In short, she is a free-lancer, but is provided with an office and access to funds for advertising her properties. All of her expenses as a saleswoman come out of her own pocket. The firm is aggressive and successful, and salespersons who don't meet the quota level twice a year are tossed out like so much dead wood.

"I had known the owner of the brokerage firm through my work at the title company, and he'd been urging me to come with him. I knew that I'd be starting out at zero income, but I wanted to see what I could do with that challenge."

After three years of active selling and ninety hours of class work plus an examination, Pris became a full-fledged broker. Her time is largely her own, except for a thirty-minute sales meeting once a week, plus a two- to three-hour tour of new listings each week. In addition, each agent at the firm has to spend twelve hours a week hosting an open house, plus a few hours a week of floor time at the brokerage firm. The floor time at the brokerage firm is actually a plum, given only to the top half of the producers within the firm. It's the floor brokers who have the privilege of latching onto clients who call the firm, seeking either a listing or a house to buy. Though income levels will differ from city to city, and will fluctuate with the changes in the nation's economy and the community's economy, brokers with firms like Pris's can average $10,000 to $15,000 a year. Twenty percent of the agents net $20,000 a year, and perhaps 5 percent have incomes of $35,000 a year. "It all depends on how much you want to work. I'm working fifty to sixty hours a week, but I can take off any time I like. Usually I take off three to four months per year. It means earning a little bit less, but enjoying life all the more.

"Shortly after my marriage broke up, I decided to stop working, and I stayed home for five months. I nearly went out of my mind. I really didn't know how much I enjoyed my work until I tried not doing it. The fact that I have an inheritance doesn't really change my life style at all. I don't live it up that much, and I don't think I ever will. I don't have any thoughts of remarrying at this time, because I enjoy my career and my social life as they are. If I had it to do all over again, I wouldn't change a thing. And if I had all the money in the world, I wouldn't change a thing, either. I'd still be working just the way I am now. The challenge is always exciting: working with people, making the deals, watching people embark on new lives as they acquire a new property.

"There are definite advantages for a woman in the real-estate sales business. I can't promise how much any woman will ever make because salaries vary from place to place and from time to time. But your life is your own, and you can shape your own career. Most of the decisions in buying houses are made by women, and they respect the intuition, judgment, and expertise of a female salesperson. Even men, I've found, appreciate dealing with me more than they might with other men. I think they feel I have a good rapport with their wives and that makes their own job easier. My experience in law school, particularly in the real-estate course, had a large part in motivating me to seek out this career. But it's not all that complicated for anyone who wants to devote the necessary study time. It can be rewarding in so many ways, and you're free to be yourself. You can't beat that."

LIZ'S STORY: "I was $25,000 in debt. I had hocked my jewels and refinanced my house. I took that to get my back to the wall, and when it was, I came out fighting. And I made it." Liz *is* public relations. An entire wall of her swank office waiting room is a mural of her pixyish face. It's not offensive. It's just there to tell you where you're at. And you know right away. If you can't toot your own horn, you can't toot anyone else's. That's what the PR game is all about, and Liz does it masterfully. But it took a brush with financial disaster to get her where she is today.

"I graduated high school in 1962, and even though I had been strictly groomed for college, I didn't go. Why not? I was a bright student, and I could have done well. But I was in love with a guy, and I wanted to be close to him. So I stayed home and got a job as a secretary at a local radio station. I was earning $275 a month. My goals were strictly short-term. I didn't even try to define them. I wanted to have fun and to do something worthwhile. The love affair cooled, but I stayed at the station, and soon a better job opened up. I found that I was very upwardly mobile, and I looked for every chance I could find to grow and learn. I had three jobs in the first two years, always moving upward, always broadening my experience base. But I still had no goals. I found that I could master things very rapidly, and I quickly became bored and was always looking for new challenges.

"One challenge that came along then was marriage. I chose to keep working, even though I could have gotten by without it. I also felt that I had learned all I could within the confines of radio, and didn't know where to go. One of the major advertising agencies in town offered me a job as secretary to the president. I took it, even though it wasn't me. I was bored to death. I couldn't fix a good martini, and I wouldn't make it with the boss, but they knew that I was bright. I stayed for about a year and saw my income rise to about $550 a month.

"Then, in early 1967, I had an offer from a small agency—four or five people—where I'd have a chance to work in all phases of advertising, not be pigeonholed into one specialized area. I took the job, at the same salary I had been making, and gained incredible experience in all of the various media. Unfortunately, the agency ran into its own financial difficulties and closed down. Then I got a job in another small agency—seven people—in charge of buying all media. Even though I had had no formal education in advertising, my on-the-job experience began to lead me to certain theories about how to effectively produce the service that our relatively small clients were seeking. The theories weren't exotic—just opening up lines of communications between the account executives, the creative director, and the media director that had otherwise been shut down by hierarchy, tradition, or what have you. I like to believe that my theories, put into action, helped the agency prosper. Within a year and a half, we had grown to a staff of twenty-three, had a branch office, with another on the way. Then, in the middle of 1969, I became pregnant and had to leave. Motherhood became my new career. Up to that time, I had lived only for the challenges that hit me at the moment."

For the next two and a half years, motherhood became all to Liz. She stopped working, and starting reevaluating her marriage, which by that time was on the rocks. In late 1971, Liz went back to work, in anticipation of a divorce, which followed soon thereafter. Her need now was financial, for she knew that there wouldn't be adequate support.

"I'd been working for almost ten years, and the thought of going out on my own had never entered my mind. Right at this time what I needed was another job and the security that came with it. I'd been out of the market for two and a half years, and a lot of contacts that I had built up had faded. I went back to the last agency that I had been with as their director of public relations. This was a whole new ball game to me, and for two years, I was thriving at it. Then it all seemed to start crumbling. My creativity was being frustrated. The firm had grown large, and I was having to spend most of my time selling the boss my ideas before I could go out and sell the clients on my ideas. All of my peers seemed to go along with this routine, but I couldn't. I had reestablished a lot of my prior contacts, and I naively thought that I could make it on my own. So I made the break."

For the first year and a half, all of Liz's referrals came from old contacts. She had no specific aim other than to try to generate a living. Her initial work was a grab bag of everything related to promotion—public relations, representing talent, marketing, publicity, and advertising.

"I had $5,500 available to get myself started. That went for the first few months' rent on the office, the equipment I needed, and payroll. I realized very quickly that I knew nothing at all about operating a business. But I figured that the worst that could happen was that I could always marry money. I never really set myself a make-or-break deadline, and I vowed that I'd never close down. It was a matter of pride and belief in my theories. I guess it was somewhat of a testimonial to myself that I was able to borrow as much as I could to keep meeting my expenses. At one point, I was into the banks for $25,000, and had hocked my jewels and refinanced my house. Why the bank carried me all that time, I'm still not sure. After two and a half years, during the summer of 1975, my back was really against the wall. Something clicked inside of me, and I suddenly became more aggressive—desperate may be a better word. I pitched five advertising accounts all in one fell swoop and closed five out of five of them. That made the difference. My billings started to climb after that, and my gross profits along with them.

"Why didn't I start fighting right at the beginning? Because I hadn't been threatened. But when I was, I knew what to do. Call it instinct. I was probably two years premature in going off on my own, but it was worth the aggravation. There's no substitute for the ordeal by fire, and I'd do the same thing all over again. I learned by doing—not just the basics of publicity and advertising, but dealings with the bank, collecting receivables, the basic business acumen that has to be applied no matter what your service or product. I always could have asked my parents for some financial help, but I didn't until the going got so terribly tough that I had no other choice. Then I asked them for a loan of $3,000, and I repaid it in thirty days plus interest. They'd always been on my side, but that transaction helped our relationship immensely. They had a new respect for me and a sense of pride.

"A lot of women feel as I do—they're looking for a way to identify. Well, I found that you can identify through achievement, either professional or personal. There are growers and there are nongrowers. I guess I'm a grower, and I just acted that way. I was starving for a time, but through it all, I kept my cool, because you have to have the appearance of success in this business." Shortly before I talked to Liz, she had received an offer from a major advertising agency to buy her out. She was offered a position as senior vice-president and a $25,000-a-year salary, plus a piece of the action. But she had said no. "The offer came just as I had turned the corner myself. Maybe I was a fool, but again my pride told me what was right.

"I'm not really sure where all this is headed. I'll stay flexible, and I won't commit myself for too long. When my own personal growth becomes stymied, then I'll resist and do something about it. I suppose I still want marriage. I'm not meant to be a business tycoon—I'd like to level off and maintain a little more private life. But a lot has certainly happened that I don't regret. And I've got a lot to look forward to. After all, I'm only 32."

# The Franchise Experience

*The busy world shoves angrily aside the man who stands with arms akimbo until occasion tells him what to do; and he who waits to have his tasks marked out shall die and leave his errand unfulfilled.*

JAMES RUSSELL LOWELL

HAL'S STORY: Perhaps you have an image in your head of the typical person who has gotten free and gone off on his or her own. Might it be a rather aggressive, outspoken, forceful individual? Would you feel that he or she would dominate a conversation? Would be sought after for wisdom and counsel? Would be a person who has "self-made" emblazoned on his or her forehead?

If that's your image, then Hal would destroy it instantly. Hal is as mild-mannered and unassuming a person as you might ever meet—probably the kind that would fit your image of a person who falls into a rut early in his career and is very content to stay there, without question, without daring, without caring.

"By the time I was ready for college, I had no goals of my own. But my folks had goals for me. They wanted me to be a doctor, but I didn't like the idea at all. They would have paid my way all through premed and med school, but when I told them that I didn't want that, the matter dropped very suddenly. I don't remember if anything specific was said, but I ended up paying my own way through college. The subject never came up again between my folks and me. Dad's now 80, living in Forida, and we have very little communication. I suppose there was some resentment on my part, but I never expressed it as such. I guess I kept my feelings bottled up, but some kind of seed of rebellion was planted."

Hal got his BA in psychology in 1949, and started on a series of jobs, first as a personnel manager at a large company in New Orleans, then to a small manufacturing plant as personnel manager, then to a travel agency in Cleveland, where he remained for five years until 1960.

"For almost a decade, I was floundering, still having no goals. The work was interesting, particularly the travel agency, where I found myself learning to communicate better with people. I did fairly well, and was happy with the firm, but wanted to return to New Orleans. By this time I was married, and my wife and I wanted to get back to our home. But I still had no goals. I was making $8,000 a year when I left the travel firm, and had two children. My father-in-law was a very successful businessman, earning over $100,000 a year. He gave us some gifts now and then, which helped make the difference between getting by and hurting. My wife was an only child, and her dad was always more than willing to help, even without being asked."

Hal got a job in sales with Burroughs Corporation. "I was still thinking short-term. My primary motivation for this job was a few more dollars. I had absolutely no idea of going out on my own at that time. Because of the help from my father-in-law, we had never felt the wolf at the door; I could always have asked him for the money to go off on my own if I needed to."

Hal started at Burroughs at $9,000 a year, which included a guarantee of $600 a month, plus commissions. After seven years, his earnings were up to $20,000, and he was able to put some money away into savings.

"But by 1967, I was starting to get restless, starting to look for other opportunities. The company was cutting my territory and my income potential, and I was offered management positions with them but at a cut in pay, although with a better long-term potential. But they wanted me to move to a smaller city, and neither my wife nor I liked that.

"By this time, I was closing in on 40, and my kids were nearly grown. One influence that motivated us to start going off on our own was that most of our friends were all either professionals or in business for themselves, and they were making considerably more money than I was. I looked at them as an example of how to make money, and wondered why I wasn't able to.

"Then came the happenstance. I was traveling with my family through the West on vacation, and we had stopped at a laundromat outside of Salt Lake City. I was waiting for the wash cycle to end and was reading that day's *Wall Street Journal,* when I saw an ad for an instant-printing franchise. The legendary light went on in my head, and I responded to the ad. A few days later, I was instructed to fly out to California for a briefing session. Actually, I guess you could call it a sales presentation. My wife and I had fallen in love with the area, and although instant printing was quite a bit different from the sales work I had been doing with Burroughs, I somehow felt that there was a tie-in—working with printed forms, printing, dealing with the public. I just felt instinctively that I had an aptitude for this kind of work. The instant-printing concept was new, the potential seemed rosy, the price was right, and the timing was perfect. I felt that I could utilize the tools that I had learned in selling to the public, and my wife, who had never worked before, said she'd be willing to work to help keep us out of financial difficulty."

Within two months after Hal had read that ad in the *Wall Street Journal,* he had sold his house in New Orleans and moved the entire family to Salt Lake City. And that included a three-week training program at the home office of the franchise. He realized a profit of $25,000 on the sale of his house in New Orleans, and put virtually all of it into the business. The business was in the right place at the right time, and it boomed from the start. Within four months, he had bought the area rights to the entire state of Utah for another $10,000 in cash. And within a few years after that, he had sold subfranchises to a number of successful operators throughout the state.

Hal may have survived a greater risk than he was aware of at the time. The franchise boom busted soon after that as thousands of "mom and pop" operations around the country found themselves possessed of a business for which they had paid enormously, surrounded by competitors of not just other firms, but of their own firm as well.

Aside from luck, hard work certainly made a difference in Hal's new career. On any given day, his wife and two children can be found working at the shop, and the shop has grown from the instant-printing concept of 100 copies for $3.49 to a full-fledged commercial printing operation that does everything but bookbinding. The business has grown to a staff of fifteen, their floor space has grown by eight times, and there's no end in sight. The franchise name means little anymore. Hal has established his reputation by diligence and customer satisfaction.

Impulsiveness rarely pays off. In Hal's case, it did. Had I been advising him prior to his ultimate decision, I probably would have told him that he was crazy, that the project needed months of study and careful analysis before he embarked on it.

But, then, if he had been advising me before I made my decision, he would have called me crazy too. And we both would have been right.

# Making It in the Ego Industry

*Progress has not followed a straight ascending line, but a spiral with rhythms of progress and retrogression, of evolution and dissolution.*

JOHANN WOLFGANG VON GOETHE

RICHARD'S STORY: Richard represents what I call the ego industry. Yet you might say he's a misfit.

The ego industry is a group of diverse businesses that develop products for sale to the public based on a sole criterion: that the developer of the product likes it. The developer—or a committee of developers—simply believes that his taste, his judgment, his discretion, and his ability will turn out a product that the public-at-large will accept. This may seem like a rather unusual endeavor to be discussed in an otherwise practical book. But it is the ego industry that a great many people aspire to when they think of breaking loose from their existing career and embarking on a new adventure.

The ego industry, in the main, consists of publishing (books, magazines, newspapers, records) and many fields within the fine arts, such as painting, sculpture, and even extending to handicrafts. How many millions of us nurture in our souls an unspoken desire to become a writer, a composer, an artist? And how many millions more have spoken of these aspirations, yet have remained paralyzed to do anything about it?

Jules Feiffer once aptly mocked this syndrome in a cartoon that depicted an obviously successful artist standing at his easel bemoaning his fate: What had destiny done to him? He hadn't really intended to be a successful artist. He just picked it up after graduating college because it seemed like something to do. He'd just stick with it until the right opening came along in his chosen career. Then all of a sudden he was in the public spotlight, receiving accolades from the critics, and selling his canvases at undreamed-of prices. His fame and fortune grew in spite of himself. And there seemed to be no end in sight. But deep down inside, carefully hidden from the public eye, was a very unhappy man. Cruel fate had prevented him from following his chosen path. The world would be shocked if it were to know, but all he ever really wanted, the only idea he ever really cherished, was to be a shoe salesman.

The main ingredient for success in the ego industry is just that: ego. Plus perhaps the bravado of a musketeer, the gut instincts of a professional gambler, and the luck of a leprechaun. Certainly, skill plays a role too. But it's a hard role to pin down. The skilled artisan who lacks the ego, the bravado, the guts, the luck may never be able to bring his fine work to the public's attention. On the other hand, the entrepreneur who lacks the subtle skills may, by dint of his flair, be able to sell the public the sizzle, if not the steak.

The great and obvious danger in the ego industry is that your own individual taste, judgment, discretion will not be welcomed by the public. Whether you're writing novels, sculpting marble, or weaving macramé potholders, ultimately you need public acceptance of your work if you view these endeavors as a means to a livelihood. The only public acceptance that counts ultimately is that expressed in terms of money. Not good reviews from the critics. Not praise from your friends and relatives. Not the satisfaction of knowing that you've done a good job. Money. (If these activities provide you with a satisfying hobby, then forget the money issue. We're talking about them now as a means of earning a livelihood.)

Isn't this a rather calloused way to look at such lofty endeavors? After all, what about art for art's sake, and all that? Yes, indeed, it's a calloused way of looking at art. But it's a realistic one. The only realistic one. If nobody's willing to buy what you've got to sell, you'd better get back to the drawing board.

I remarked earlier that Richard seemed to be a misfit for the ego industry. Perhaps that's why he has been successful. He's self-effacing, has about as much bravado as a tree stump, would shy away from a nickel slot machine even if his pockets were loaded, and his story indicates that while there were some strokes of luck, they were no substitute for hard work and determination. Richard succeeded in the book-publishing field by taking a tack opposite to what many would-be ego-industry aspirants do, which is acting on impulse, almost out of a sense that the world has been breathlessly awaiting their arrival.

Richard, on the other hand, once he awakened to his own capabilities, proceeded with caution, with cunning, and with sound business principles, usually so lacking in ego industrialists.

At the beginning, Richard seemed almost not to care at all. The son of a well-to-do family, Richard went to a fine prep school near his San Francisco home, where he was programmed for an eventual college career. At Stanford, he majored in English, had no career goals, was not aware of any family pressure in any particular direction, and was generally ruling out those careers that seemed too demanding, such as law, medicine, finance. He had no need to work for income during college, and was more active in lacrosse, squash, and poker than he was in his school work. He almost flunked out during his first semester.

His college career was not one of high aspirations. Perhaps not even one of aspirations at all. In his senior year, when the job interview sessions came around, he paid them no heed. His first job after graduation, which he just happened to "drift into" was with a local magazine, doing a variety of glorified copyboy tasks. There followed brief periods as a copyboy at a local newspaper, and as a clerk in a local bookstore. After a six-month stint with the Army, he took a job with a trade-magazine publisher, which lasted a year. "I wasn't a writer. I had no talent in that direction. I didn't want sales either. I really wasn't trained for anything. All I could say was that publishing felt good. I had never really thought of a career, I was just letting one thing follow another."

Poor boy, you may be saying. Didn't really have to work. Didn't really have to worry. Mom and Pop would take care of him if the going got tough. It's hard to think much of a person like that.

That's exactly what Richard felt, too. Gradually he began to realize that his self-esteem was of the lowest order. A correction came with his next job, which seemed to break him out of his lethargy and apathy, and give him a sense of personal value. He went to work for the West Coast division of a firm that published the so-called continuity premiums—the encyclopedias and other series of books that you find in supermarkets: the first week is free, then 49 cents a week thereafter gets you a complete set of *Animals of the World,* and so on. This was a pounding-the-pavement kind of activity, and while not mentally challenging to Richard, it did give him the challenge of being able to translate his energies into specific dollars on a day-by-day basis, which was something he had never done before.

"I gradually began to realize that I could achieve, that I could accomplish, that I could do something that came from me. I still didn't have any clear-cut goals, but I was becoming aware that publishing was probably my field. I'd been accumulating a variety of skills that one needs for that activity, albeit accidently, and I knew that I didn't feel comfortable with large companies. It was all starting to fall into place."

After a few years in the continuity-premium business, Richard and a friend decided that they could do it better than the big New York publishing firm, and formed a partnership to develop continuity-premium properties on their own, primarily for West Coast distribution. "We knew our markets better. We could do it our own way and not have to answer to others," Richard said.

In addition to book series, they dabbled with record albums and other items. Their searching for good properties led them to investigate many hard-cover books that had not been successful. Often, the paperback rights to these books can be picked up for a song, and Richard and his partner speculated on some of those rights, feeling that if the properties were properly packaged and promoted, they could be turned into successes as mass paperback books. This is where the luck of a leprechaun came in—two of the titles that they had obtained turned into best-selling paperbacks, and threw enough money into Richard's coffers to finance the start of a full-fledged publishing firm.

But still he floundered. "After about four years, we dissolved our partnership. It just wasn't working out satisfactorily. I decided to go it alone as a publisher. I didn't have any master design. It was more a case of survival. Frankly, I never was really confident of making a lot of money. I was driven by the challenge and the fun that you can have, and the psychic rewards that come from seeing an intellectual process being packaged and sold to the public. We had the cushion from the paperback sales, which helped us to get along, because we weren't really making much money. I had never considered giving it up at any time. It was kind of an ego thing."

All this time, Richard was really not his own man, so to speak. He was packaging the book properties and then seeking out other, larger firms to distribute the books for him. It was still kind of a lazy man's way to try to make a buck, because the real energies in getting the product to the marketplace were relinquished by Richard to these other distributors. He was only half a publisher, turning out grade-B material and tossing it out to the big boys to sell.

Richard got free when he decided to do his own distribution. "I realized that we really weren't getting anywhere, just grinding out the pulp and letting others handle it for us. I began to get a sense of the kind of books that I wanted to have my publishing imprint on, and I knew that the big distributors might not want to handle something as individualized as what I had in mind. I knew that I would have to do the distribution myself. That meant getting back to selling, to pounding the pavements. I decided that I would market three of my own titles that first season, and once I had made that decision, everything seemed to just flow. All my previous experience came together, and I instinctively grasped all of the steps needed to take my projects to full fruition.

"I've been at it for five years now, and our list has grown to seven or eight titles per season (there are two publishing seasons each year). This is a strange field. I've always felt that if you do your work well, if you strive for personal satisfaction, and if you have the expertise, the money's going to come to you. Maybe not an awful lot, but there's a tremendous amount of ego satisfaction to be gained. Right now, I'm concentrating on quality.

When I look at a manuscript for publication, I ask myself whether it feels right for me. I've turned down an awful lot of stuff that's perfectly marketable, but just not right for my operation. It's got to suit my personal taste, and my marketing and editorial judgment. Others may make a bundle on it, but if it's not right for me, I can't become involved in it. I can't put my heart into it.

"As your judgment proves right in the marketplace, you build your self-confidence. I exercise complete control over our product, and as a result my ratio of success is probably far better than the typical publisher, large or small, in the industry.

"Am I successful? That's hard to say. I'm achieving what I wanted to achieve. I'm always looking for a better way to do what I'm doing. I want to do better books, not more books. I've got to be constantly improving and growing, or I start wasting away. With each small step I take, I want to master the necessary skill and art. When I've mastered it, then I can take the next step and grow from there.

"I'm always going to work solo. That's the way I work best. I've got to be the sole master of my destiny. I don't think anything of working seventy to eighty hours a week. But you can't do that in a corporate sense."

Richard's story illustrates a facet of a world of work that deserves the attention of anyone seeking greater success in his or her present career, or a successful transition into a new career. That is, that the sum total of any worthwhile venture is made up of many segments: the original inspiration, the design of the new product or service, the actual manufacturing of the product or service, the market testing, the marketing, the selling, and all of the "back office" work that are a necessary part of commerce. We can get so pigeonholed into one of these aspects that we neglect to properly acquaint ourselves with all of the other intertwining elements of the work we're involved in.

To achieve, we must make ourselves familiar with all of these other elements, which we either depend on or which depend upon us. We can't exist in a vacuum. It's not enough to know how to put words on paper, or paint on canvas. You have to familiarize yourself with the business aspects of any endeavor—how the product is brought to the public's attention, how it's sold, why it doesn't sell if it doesn't, and how it's paid for. It takes time and experience to become aware of the rhythms of progress and retrogression, of evolution and dissolution, but you must be aware at the outset that these rhythms do exist, and you must make it your business to know what causes them.

# You're Never Too Old

*A man has to live with himself, and he should see to it that he always has good company.*

CHARLES EVANS HUGHES

BARRY'S STORY: Barry was 52 when he left his career as an industrial engineer to open up a small shop, making and selling, of all things, bola ties. When I interviewed him, he had only been at his new venture for eighteen months, but he was confident that his targets were being reached, and that he'd be able to achieve his goals.

For more than thirty years, Barry was deeply immersed in his engineering career. It had started early in high school, when his fascination with math and electronics surfaced. He received his Bachelor of Science Degree in electrical engineering in 1942, and went right into the service as an electronics maintenance officer with the Navy. After the war, he became a product-development engineer with an electronics firm in Ohio. "I had to devise the tools and the methods to put a given design into production. I was responsible for the budgeting, the capital requirements, the cost factors, the accounting."

In 1958, Barry was laid off due to a recession. "I got a full year's pay and decided to do some looking around. My wife and I had always liked the West, so we took a trip and decided to resettle in the Tucson area. My kids were 12 and 8 at the time, young enough so that the move wouldn't affect them adversely. The aerospace industry was in its relative infancy, but I landed with a company that, unfortunately, wasn't keeping pace with the times. There was too big a hierarchy, and individual initiative was stifled. I guess this was the beginning of my dissatisfaction with the kind of work I was doing. I felt that I wanted to do it my way, and I was being frustrated."

After a year and a half, Barry moved to a larger corporation and became the manager of the industrial-engineering department. In 1961, he had eight men under him, and by the time he left in 1974, he had fifty men under him, and was earning $22,000 a year.

"But again, the discouragement level was bothering me. The company was so big that it was impossible to tell if decisions that you made were successful or not. There were so many other influences on a given project that you couldn't tell whether you were doing a good job or a bad job. I was itching to get out, but I had a financial responsibility to my family. I had put away very little money in previous years, because we lived high. I had to send my kids to college, and had to look out for our well-being when retirement rolled around."

Shortly after his move to Arizona in 1959, Barry became fascinated with a strange little device called a bola tie. It's also called a string tie, and you may recall seeing them around the necks of the ranchers and the town folk in western movies. It's simply a piece of string, held together by a slide that rests over the top button of the shirt. "I became fascinated with these things and decided to do a little research on them. Everybody probably thinks that they date back to the pioneer days. But from all of my research, I was able to find that the darn things didn't seem to exist before 1949. The story, as I've been able to gather it, indicates that the bola tie came into being in a little town called Payson, Arizona, in 1949. A rancher was on the range looking after his cattle, and as he rode under a low-hanging branch his hat was knocked off. Unlike most hats, which have a broad band around the crown, this hat had simply a piece of string with some decorative knobs tied to each end of the string. The string came off the hat, and on the spur of the moment, the rancher looped the string around his neck instead of putting it back on the hat. When he rode back into town, a friend remarked as to the interesting kind of tie the rancher had on. With the little knobs, or tips, on the ends of the string, it looked like a miniature bola that Argentinian cowboys used to corral their cattle. The rancher became fascinated with the idea and began to experiment with other versions of what he called a bola tie. The idea caught on, and the rancher's inventory soon found its way into the major Arizona cities, Phoenix and Tucson, where tourists and locals alike began to buy the ties in huge quantities."

Barry's fascination with this unique ornament started him on a collection, and then into some tinkering in his home workshop, and making his own. "Pretty soon, friends would be asking me to make them for them, and I could see that my hobby had a business potential. At first, it was a pipe dream—maybe at or near retirement age I'd set up a little shop and make these bola ties. Over the years, I watched the progress of the bola-tie industry, and it grew phenomenally. According to best estimates, by the mid-sixties, there were a half-million dollars' worth of bola ties being sold throughout the state. In 1971, it was named as the official neckwear of the state of Arizona. I'd venture to say that today there are $5 million worth of these ties being sold each year in the state, at an average price of about $18 to $20. That's probably divided up 50-50 between the residents and the tourists."

Around 1970, Barry's itch started to become more than he could bear. "The maverick in me had surfaced with a vengeance. I just couldn't put up with bucking the hierarchy anymore, and it was beginning to have a physical effect on me. I wasn't a kid anymore. I was treated for hypertension, and every Sunday afternoon, as the weekend neared its close, I became a changed man—all knotted up inside and full of anxiety over having to go back to work the next morning. I was about 50 at the time and still concerned about my financial obligations. I said that when I reached 55, instead of 65, I would leave my job and go into business for myself. But then the kids had grown up and left, and my wife said, 'Why wait?' So at 52, I up and did it. It was my wife's urging mostly that helped me to do it.

"I had had some business experience, but only in the academic sense. I'd taken courses in marketing, accounting, and sales. But my managerial experience at work was what sustained me."

It cost Barry $1,800 to open his small shop, plus an inventory that cost him $5,000 and that had a retail value of $9,000. After a few months of losing money, sales started to pick up, and his projected targets were being met. "It's been a struggle, especially for my wife. But she backs me 100 percent. We wouldn't have done it otherwise. We don't have a cent, but we're happier than we ever were. We can't vacation, and we can't do even small things that we used to take for granted, like buying magazines. But we have a whole new value now for the dollar. We'll get by. This is going to be successful for me. I put all negative thoughts out of my mind. Sure, if I had it to do over again, I would have done it much sooner. But now I'm 55, and I know that when I reach 60 I can draw a government pension from the service, and then my Social Security. So we're going to make out all right, no matter what."

Barry's little shop is a veritable treasure chest of bola ties, those that he has made himself, and those that he has on consignment from other craftsmen. He sells only bola ties, and his fame has spread across the country. Barry's bolas are no longer simply string with beads on the ends. His cords are made from lambskin leather, steer hide, plastic, and vinyl. The tips, usually formed from sheet metal or wood, come in a wide variety of designs. The slides are the most fascinating and artistic elements of the ties. There are woods (redwood, myrtlewood, sagewood, ironwood); there are stones (tiger-eye, peridot, garnet, turquoise, jade, and agate); there are painted rocks, copper, beads, and coins. Commemorative slides abound for states, cities, organizations, and even corporate logos. Among his Indian handicrafts are slides from the Blackfoot, Pima, Hopi, Zuñi, Navajo, and Apache tribes.

"Even though the business was totally new, I applied the basic skills that I had gathered over my years in industry. But the skill that really thrilled me the most was the skill of using my own hands to create satisfaction for myself and my customers. I was never really aware that I had this skill until I went ahead and tried using it. The satisfaction of doing something like this with your hands, particularly when you never knew you had it in you, can't be evaluated. My income went from over $20,000 a year down to around $5,000 a year. We learned to live on it. Anybody can if he really wants to. And it's been worth every minute of it."

# From a Common Bond

*We grow great by dreams. All great men are dreamers. They see things in the soft haze of a spring day or in the red fire of a long winter's evening. Some of us let these great dreams die. But others nourish and protect them, nurse them through bad days till they bring them to the sunshine and light which come always to those who sincerely hope that their dreams will come true.*

WOODROW WILSON

Could the urge to get free be inherited? Following are the stories of Allen, Ben, and Bob. They are first cousins, grandsons of the lady you read about in the Introduction. They're all the same age, and grew up together with close family ties in upstate New York. Not only did all three leave an entrenched situation to go off on their own—but they did it at almost the same time. They had been bred on a steady diet of self-sufficiency and independence, originating from the tribulations of the young immigrant widow for whom survival was the primary goal. Being close friends as well as family, they no doubt influenced each other. And their common bond has been intensified as a result of their mutual experiences of getting free.

ALLEN'S STORY: Allen's father and his father's brother-in-law were partners in a low- to medium-priced furniture store. By the time Allen reached high school age, the partner's children, who were older, had already departed for careers in law and medicine. Allen was the heir apparent to the furniture store. "But when I was a kid, it never really interested me. I was always a little bit of a miser, a hustler. I always had to make a buck for myself. When I was 9 years old, I sold seeds. You know the kind, the ads you see in the comic books. But most kids get the packet of seeds, sell one or two, and give it up. I really sold seeds. Then it was Christmas cards. When I was 12, I was setting up pins in a bowling alley. That was back in the days when you had to set them by hand. There were no machines. And I swept the floors at a local clothing store for a couple of years. I think part of this drive may have been family-oriented. One of my uncles was quite well to do, and I'd heard a lot of talk about him in my own home. I guess subconsciously I vowed that I was going to prove that I could do as well as he could.

"When I was about 15, my mother had me buy a few shares of stock. She wanted me to become familiar with the stock market. I remember that old brokerage firm. It was the only one in town, and it looked more like a horse betting parlor than a high-level business enterprise. The old men with green eye shades making chalk marks on that enormous board, the mumbling and muttering around the room every time new numbers went up, I'll never forget it. I guess that was the beginning of my fascination with the stock market.

"By the time I was finishing high school, I knew that I had to get into some endeavor where I could make good money. I didn't see the furniture store as offering that kind of opportunity. It seemed too limited."

Allen was accepted at Harvard, and he majored in business. His career thoughts fluctuated between business, finance, and law, and by his senior year, he had decided to go to law school.

"After I'd been accepted at law school, I got a summer job working with a brokerage firm in Boston. Then my plans ran into a bit of a snag. You know how college guys can be when the end is almost in sight. The partying, the gallivanting, the restless youth expressing itself. One day, we got a little carried away and ran into a rather stern disciplinary problem at college. It was right near the end of the semester, and fortunately, it didn't affect our graduation or my law-school admission. But the brokerage firm learned about it, and I lost my summer job. It really wasn't anything that serious, but they were rather uptight and ultraconservative, so I just let it pass. Or so I thought.

"I started law school the next fall, with every intention of completing it and going into a career in the law. But during the first year, my dad's partner had a heart attack. Dad was too young to retire, but too old to run the business on his own. I had been somewhat disappointed with those first few months in law school, and I saw this as an opportunity to run a business on my own. I figured that if it didn't work out, we could sell the business or bring someone else in to run it, and I could always go back to law school. There was also a sense of security, going back to the home town in a business that I knew, and in a business that might have more potential with a younger and more aggressive man in charge. Dad and his partner were in their sixties, and they'd be the first to admit that their energies weren't what mine probably were. So I went back.''

For the next eight years, Allen was a furniture-store proprietor with his dad. They worked well together, and business indeed picked up. ''But there was always that restlessness inside of me. I could look back at my impetuous action of years before and realize that I had compromised. I had given up my desires for the business world and the stock market without ever really trying them.

''Now the conflict was really starting to gnaw at me. On the one hand, I had my own going business, a family, and the sense of security that comes with a family-owned business. On the other hand, I knew that there were things out there that I had to try. Oddly, that little incident back in college discouraged me. It was probably foolish, but I thought that if I ever applied for a job with a brokerage firm, they'd find out about that incident, and I'd be turned down. Others told me how foolish I was being, but there was some peculiar sense of pride that held me back for those many years.

''Then some outside factors started to influence me. Our city was embarked on an ambitious urban renewal project, and the early plans indicated that our building would be taken for the project. That would have provided me with a perfect opportunity not only to break loose, but to break loose with a good chunk of cash in hand to help me over the transition. But I still held back. As a matter of fact, I went out looking for other locations for the furniture store once our building had been bought. One particular building was appealing, and I went so far as to make an offer on it, and gave a substantial deposit. I was committed to staying in the furniture business, and no doubt would have. But our offer to buy the building was turned down. That was sort of an act of fate that helped me change my mind. At about that same time, my cousin Bob was making a major change himself, moving from the lap of security to a job with a bank in Arizona.

''I remember him telling me, 'You only get a one-way ticket and there are no do-overs,' so I finally said what the hell, I'm not going to let any old skeletons in my closet worry me any longer. I made application to a local brokerage firm, and a few months later, I was behind my new desk, starting my new career. The urban renewal project demolished our store shortly thereafter, and my dad was able to find work with another firm. The slate was wiped clean, and I was starting from scratch at something I'd always wanted to do.''

Very shortly after the move, Allen's income level was substantially ahead of where it had been in the furniture store. Today, he's not only the top producer in his office, but one of the top producers for the firm in the country. "My income and my net worth have risen considerably. It's hard work, but I love it. I set out with a specific challenge in mind, and I think I've achieved what I was seeking. And yet, I now find myself asking whether or not there isn't still another venture out there for me. I'm not sure what, but I'm open-minded. I guess I'll never stop asking or wondering."

Sometimes the maverick spirit never subsides.

BEN'S STORY: "I had no specific direction after finishing college and the Army. I had majored in sociology, which doesn't really prepare you for anything specific. I had some job offers come my way, but none seemed too intriguing. Then my uncle invited me to come in with him. He had a successful law firm and was also active in real-estate investment and development. It seemed like a natural. There was security, good opportunity, and it was family. It would also give me an opportunity to work with my cousin, who was just finishing up law school and was ready to come in with his dad. My original thinking was that I would clerk for the law. At that time, you could substitute formal law school classes with clerking in a firm and qualify to take the bar exam. I don't know how serious I was about becoming a lawyer, but it seemed like a path that couldn't lead anywhere but up.

"But I soon found myself drifting toward real estate. I enjoyed working with people, seeing a deal through from beginning to end, watching buildings go up, and planning new developments. It seemed unlimited, and I enjoyed it immensely. I was cutting my teeth on virtually every phase of real estate.

"In 1967, my cousin left the firm, and this prompted my uncle to start cutting back in his activity. The security and opportunity were still there, but I started asking myself where I might be ten years from now. I was beginning to wonder if I wouldn't be better off on my own, with greater potential, and more of a chance for self-satisfaction.

"I got along beautifully with my uncle, but I wanted to express my own abilities, not merely carry out his general instructions. I guess my age was a big factor, too. I was just turning 30, and felt that now was the time, if ever, to go off on my own. My decision was helped along by the fact that my younger brother, who had been working with IBM, was interested in going in with me if I decided to break loose. Even though he'd had no experience in real estate, his general activity in sales would be helpful, since he could translate that experience into what we'd be doing.

"But I got pressure from my family. Why did I want to leave? Why did I want to turn down security for something completely unknown. The pressure ranged from moderate to heavy, between my wife and our parents.

"I carefully planned a six-month transition period with my brother. He left IBM and began to set up our office. Our initial aim was in the development area, but we had to start off in brokerage because there was more money to be made more readily in that kind of activity.

"When the time came for the split, I did a quick evaluation: I had a wife and a family, a nice home, and a reliable paycheck. I was jumping off into the unknown, and even though I was sure I could always go back in with my uncle, I never really envisioned that happening. It never entered my mind that I wouldn't make it. I guess you could say that I had big balls. We borrowed furniture, rented an office, and got started. I had about $2,000 in commissions coming to me from prior deals, and I knew that could carry me for thirty to sixty days.

"I'd been making between $12,000 and $15,000 a year with my uncle, and I hardly missed a beat with my income level. Our activity was vigorous right from the start, and my income climbed steadily, probably faster than it would have had I remained an employee. Right after I split, the pressure from the family eased up. I never asked them for any help. It simply wasn't an option. Pride was probably my biggest driving factor. I wasn't going to be defeated. I wasn't going to go back.

"We continued concentrating on brokerage, and within a few years, we had seven full-time salesmen working for us. The money was good, and the sense of personal satisfaction was second to none. But there was that old restlessness starting to surface again. I had accomplished what I had set out to do and was looking for bigger and better challenges to conquer.

"Thus, I was susceptible to an offer that everybody around me thought was crazy. One of the major hotels in town had fallen on bad times and was up for sale. A fellow I'd known for a long time approached me and suggested that we buy the hotel and convert it into a home for the elderly. He felt that he could generate the money that would be needed, and I'd handle the rentals and administration of the project. A third partner, a contractor, would take care of the needed renovations.

"Until this time, our deals were in the tens of thousands of dollars. All of a sudden, I found myself intrigued with a deal that would get up into the millions of dollars, and a business venture that was as remote from real-estate brokerage as astronautics was. Who knew anything about running a home for the elderly? Certainly not I.

"Perhaps I had already gotten too entrenched in the brokerage business. Maybe I was feeling the urge to get free again and go off in another direction. In any event, I went along with the deal. We raised the money, bought the building, and renovated it. Then came the grueling task of filling it up with paying occupants. For about a year, things were pretty grim. We had abandoned our brokerage activity to concentrate on this new project, and our income had slowed to a trickle. I had to dig deeply into my nest egg in order to keep the family afloat for the year. But I knew we were going to make it. We worked our butts off. Slowly but surely, the building began to fill up, and we began to see the light at the end of the tunnel. As things started to improve, we made plans to build another similar facility in another community, and to buy an existing one in yet a third city.

"I wouldn't want to go through another year like that one, but now it's proven to have been worth it. Our income is good, and should get much better in the future, as we get the other homes into a more profitable situation.

"If somebody asked me today what I do for a living, I guess I'd tell them that I'm an administrator and part owner of a chain of homes for the elderly. Not a real-estate broker anymore. I take great pride in what we've accomplished in building these facilities, but when the right buyer comes along with the right price, I'm not going to shy away from selling them.

"I'll get into something else, though I'm not sure what. But it won't be quite as demanding on my energies as this last go-around was. I've set as much fire as I want to set, now I want to sit back a while and watch it smolder and be able to take the time to enjoy my children while they're still growing up. That's the way I feel today. Until something else challenging comes along, that is."

Sometimes the maverick spirit never dies away.

BOB'S STORY: "Mollie Schreiber, wherever you are, I thank you. I think."

When Bob was entering the seventh grade, his school's curriculum offered a choice between the normal English class and an English class that was supplemented by journalism instruction. As an adjunct to the class, the members produced a quarterly newspaper for the junior high school. "Mollie Schreiber, our journalism teacher, put the first bug into my head. It was my first exposure to journalism, but, perhaps more important, it was the first chance I ever had to express what must be the innate writer in me. Getting yourself published regularly when you're 12 or 13 years old probably has a spoiling effect for the would-be professional writer. I particularly remember one little piece that I had written for an issue that came out around Easter time. I had manufactured my own "Easter bonnet" out of a variety of absurd things, and accompanied by a photo of myself wearing the bonnet, the article made a youthful attempt to satirize the fashion trends of the day. I was a celebrity. I had made my peers laugh, and the ego satisfaction made me feel warm and mellow."

Throughout his high school and college years, Bob leaned heavily toward writing, developing his craft as he went along. At summer camp, he wrote for and edited the camp weekly newspaper. In prep school, he was an editor of the newspaper, and at Yale, he became managing editor of the monthly humor magazine. He majored in English, with an emphasis on creative writing, and took all the courses in that area that the university had to offer.

One of the unique courses that he took was referred to as "daily themes." The requirement was that each day of the week, the students had to turn in approximately 300 words of original fiction. The material had to be in the professor's office by nine o'clock each morning, Monday through Friday, for twenty weeks. Failure to deliver the theme, except for a good reason, would mean dismissal from the course. This was a craft-building, discipline-building regimen that stayed with him throughout his professional career.

By his junior year, Bob was firmly committed to a career in some phase of communications. He was going to be a writer, though he knew not yet for whom, or of what.

His first job after college was with CBS, in their so-called executive training program. This meant the mail room, and Bob delivered messages from one end of the New York City CBS facilities to the other, for $37.50 a week. This was the ground floor from which future presidents emerged. The theory was that as job openings within the company occurred, they would filter down the pyramid and whatever was left by the time they got to the mail room would be available to the mail-room clerks.

"After about four months of this, with no vice-presidencies being offered to me, I decided I'd had enough. A good friend of mine and I had generated some ideas about creating television shows, and we decided to leave CBS and go into partnership to become television producers. It was as simple as that. We were simply going to do it, even though we hadn't the foggiest notion of what went into putting a television show together. My family, who was subsidizing me, expressed their feelings that I was nuts, but they went along with me. There had been some gentle hints, but never any pressure, that I go to law school and embark on a legal career with my dad's firm. But I would have none of it, for I had to prove myself in my chosen profession.

"My career with my partner lasted only a few months. The nuttiness of New York City started to get to me, and I really didn't feel that I could be expressing myself by trying to create cooking shows for obese housewives—which was our first project, affectionately referred to as Kalorie Kitchen. By November 1957, just five months out of college, I decided that if I was going to be a writer, I'd better do nothing else but sit down and write. Shunning the oncoming winter, I took off for Miami Beach and rented a tiny room in a rundown little motel. That was the closest thing I could afford to the romantic image of the Hemingways and Faulkners and Fitzgeralds that had intrigued me during my college years. For three full weeks, I sat in that little motel room, clean paper in my typewriter, waiting for something to happen. Then the realization came to me: I was 21 years old, had lived a relatively sheltered but happy life, and I simply had nothing to write about.

After all, if a writer has nothing to say, how can he proceed? Perhaps my dream was reaching fruition early. Maybe it was time to pack it away and go on about something else until I did have something to say.''

Basically a prudent person, Bob heard the sounds of security ringing out of his home town. In addition to his law and real-estate activities, Bob's father had become involved in a small local bank, first as attorney for the bank, and eventually as a part owner of the bank. Through his father's connections, Bob was able to get a job as a trainee at a small bank in Miami. ''I really had no ambition or desire to become a banker, but I figured that it was a good way to get some basic knowledge about the family business that I seemed to be gravitating toward, and was also a good way to stay in the warm weather through the winter. I figured I would give it a few months and then see which way the wind was blowing. During the next five months, I worked at the bank, and learned everything that there was to be learned, from printing checkbooks to working a teller's window to the installment-loan department. To my surprise, I found myself taking to it rather naturally.''

In the spring of 1958, Bob returned to his home and started to become active in the real-estate business with his dad. ''I was a total novice. My dad was an excellent teacher, but I knew there was something lacking in my ability to handle the work. Being an attorney, my dad understood everything about leases and mortgages and contracts and deeds. It was Greek to me. Then things happened all at once. I realized that in order to keep up with the pace in the real-estate activity, I'd have to get some law school under my belt. Also, I met the girl who was to become my wife, and she was going to be starting undergraduate work at Syracuse University, where, conveniently, there was a law school close by. And third, I had received my greetings from the draft board, and knew that to avoid Army service I'd have to be enrolled in graduate school. Thus, three things in one swoop: getting the education I needed, being near my lady fair, and staying out of the Army, at least temporarily.

''We were married after our first year in Syracuse. I really never envisioned myself becoming actively involved in the practice of law. I enjoyed the intellectual exercise of the law and felt that it would be of use to me in my real-estate activity, which was more intriguing than law practice. Nonetheless, I did fairly well in my studies, and realized that my writing ambition had been pushed to the distant background.

''During my senior year in law school, two other fortuitous things happened. My wife became pregnant, which eliminated the requirement for me to serve in the Army, and my dad made a major decision to acquire controlling interest in the bank and become active as its president. Thus, as I neared my graduation, I was free of any military obligation, and had my choice of any one or more of three possible careers: law, real estate, or banking.

"I chose all three. I guess I was basically so restless that no one of the three would satisfy me completely. I found something in each of them that I enjoyed. Most of the real-estate activity was in conjunction with my cousin Ben, who was in our office. I'd generate the deals, and he'd carry them out. I always had a sense of satisfaction in making a good deal, but I never really had the patience to stick with it through the detailed execution. Thus, Ben and I worked together very nicely.

"My legal activity was largely confined to our own real-estate activities and the bank. I'd draw the leases, the mortgages, the construction contracts for the real-estate deals; and for the bank, I'd work on legal matters required by the governing authorities, as well as on leases and construction contracts for our branch activities and the ultimate moving of our main office. Within the bank, I confined myself at first to the advertising and public relations end. Here was an opportunity for me to express my writing urges, and I was relatively satisfied for a couple of years. But, looking back, I think that the real creative satisfaction came from my work on buildings that we were doing: finding a piece of land, generating a tenant, working on the design of the building, and then the actual construction itself. It was a whole life process that never ceased to amaze me.

"After about two years of this, I was drawn more deeply into the banking activity, by a rather weird incident. The staff of the bank was small (about twenty to twenty-five) and very closely knit. There was little turnover; they had all worked together for many years. One day, on a routine audit, some irregularities appeared. The immediate reaction of the staff was that one of the loan officers had been writing fictitious loans to himself and was pulling off a blatant embezzlement. That particular loan officer had been out sick for the previous two weeks, and all suspicion was immediately cast in his direction. My dad was out of town at the time, and the rest of the staff was so shocked and flustered by the incident that there seemed to be nobody with a cool head who could pull the whole matter together. I found myself instantly involved in the situation, and, as it turned out, mine was the cool head."

The embezzlement turned out to be relatively modest in amount, and with the dismissal of the loan officer, Bob found himself playing an active day-to-day role, filling in at that ex-officer's desk. He learned the routines of making loans, and the basic operational aspects of banking. "I found myself becoming quite committed to banking. We were far and away the smallest bank in town, yet I knew that there was abundant opportunity for growth. We were tucked away on a little side street, with very poor parking, and our facility was dingy and drab, to boot. One of my fondest accomplishments, as I recall, was to bring about a complete renovation of our main office in the course of one weekend. From the time we closed on Friday, until the time we opened on Monday morning, we had completely redone the premises, including painting the walls, hanging a new ceiling, installing carpeting, and putting in new tellers' counters and furniture in the officers' area. The looks on people's faces on Monday morning were of utter astonishment. Actually, we had to do it this way so that we wouldn't interrupt the normal flow of business. It was a fascinating challenge, and it satisfied my latent creative energies.

"In the ensuing years, I became an active member of the community. While still keeping busy in the law practice, the real-estate development, and the banking, I also became a member of the board of trustees of various organizations, slightly active in local politics, and very active in amateur theater groups. In retrospect, I realize that many of these outside activities were not necessarily to satisfy my civic duties, but were a form of escape for me from work routines that were becoming less and less challenging. Also, my mother was terminally ill during this period, and the escapes provided me with some release for the personal pressure valves.

"As the everyday work became less and less fascinating, I found myself going from challenge to challenge, almost creating them in order to satisfy my energies. Two ultimate challenges then came along that occupied almost two full years.

"Our family had always been involved in the local Jewish Community Center, which was a nonreligious organization designed to provide recreational services to the members of the Jewish community, and anyone else who cared to join. Over the decades, the organization had struggled along in a ramshackle old house that a member of the previous generation had donated. Now, the Jewish population of the community was burgeoning, and the long-spoken-of need for a new building captured the imagination of a handful of active community members. My dad's generation had made a valiant effort to get such a new building built, but it had never succeeded. Now, the gauntlet was thrown down to the new generation, and I became one of the nucleus to spearhead the new building project.

"It was a labor of love, but it was labor. We worked to get the initial commitments from the handful of big givers; we scouted locations; we interviewed architects; we organized the fund-raising program; we worked to increase our membership base (and thus our base of potential donors); and we beat the drum incessantly. With a lot of pushing and pulling, everything eventually fell into place. The project was a success.

"At almost the same time, just two years after we had renovated our original banking quarters, the local urban renewal project got under way, and our banking facility was slated to be taken down for a new municipal parking-lot site. Thus, I began the quest for a new location for our bank, and on finding it and getting the blessings of the state banking authorities, proceeded to work with the contractor in the renovation of an eight-story building and a main banking facility that would be considered as the outstanding architectural accomplishment in the community.

"The community-center project started in 1964, the bank project in 1965. I was working on both of them simultaneously, grabbing what time I could to enjoy my family, and continuing actively in my three professions. I was keeping myself intensely busy so that I wouldn't have time to think of an underlying dissatisfaction that was starting to get the best of me. It began to appear to me that I was achieving all that there was to achieve in this modest community. It wasn't my urge to write that was surfacing. It was my belief that soon I would have reached the end of my rope in this community, and there would be nothing left to look forward to. My life was totally secure, and totally predictable. I could envision exactly where I'd be five, ten, twenty years hence. It began to frighten me.

"On various vacations we had taken, I had always been enamored of the warm climate in the southern United States and in the Caribbean islands, and although the winter weather never bothered me that much, I began deliberating that if you have to live somewhere, why not do it where the sun is shining all the time? Through my real-estate activities and civic involvements, I began to see the handwriting on the wall with regard to the city's future: it was going downhill. The major industry had long since fallen into a state of shambles, real-estate taxes were rapidly zooming upward as the citizens demanded more services and tax-paying buildings were being demolished by the urban renewal project."

The pieces of the jigsaw puzzle started to fill in for Bob. He began to yearn for a move to a more dynamic and growing community, one that wouldn't run out of challenges. One night, he ran into a friend who had just returned from a vacation in Phoenix, Arizona. The friend was wide-eyed from his experience in Phoenix, and he told Bob, "I've just seen the city of the future. It's fantastic."

"I guess that was the spark that got me started. I was restless and unhappy, and the thought of moving gave me some sustenance. I discussed it with my wife, who at first thought I was kidding, but gradually knew that I was dead serious. The move would mean leaving not only the security of my career, but virtually all of our family—parents, sisters, brothers, aunts, uncles, close friends. We kept it to ourselves while I did some investigating. I literally took out a map of the United States and drew a line across it, separating the winter climates from the warm climates. I eliminated Florida, mainly because I had lived there for a time and couldn't see it as a place where I would want to raise my family. I guess it was basic prejudice that made me eliminate the Deep South and Texas, and I found myself looking at the Southwest, primarily New Mexico, Arizona, and Southern California. I started some research on the major communities in that area, such as Phoenix, Tucson, Albuquerque, San Diego, and a few others. I was determined to get free."

In October 1966, Bob represented his bank at the annual American Bankers Association convention, being held that year in San Francisco. Only his wife knew that this trip was not for general convention purposes. He had made inquiries of bankers in the Phoenix area as to potential openings, and he planned to meet with some of them at the San Francisco convention. Following the convention, he and his wife would go to Phoenix, supposedly for a week's vacation but, in reality, for a scouting tour of the community.

"I had arranged to meet Alan at the convention. He was the president of a small bank in Phoenix, and we hit it off beautifully. He looked forward to my visiting with him in Phoenix, and I knew that I had an opportunity to go in with him. The Phoenix area was growing so rapidly that banks and other institutions were hard pressed to find good talent to keep up with the growth. Within an hour after our plane had landed in Phoenix, I knew that this was the community I was looking for. Impulsive? Sure. But I was reacting to a tied-up situation, and I suppose anything would have looked good. Phoenix had the feeling of dynamism, newness, and growth. It appealed to me right off the bat.

"During our stay there, I had numerous meetings with Alan at the bank, and a tentative offer was extended, subject to approval of the board of directors. It wasn't until the following April that the offer was finalized—I was made a vice-president of the bank, at a salary substantially higher than I had been earning in our own family institution. My wife and I flew out there a few weeks later to look for a house, and on July 1, 1967, just eight months after my first visit there, we had completed the entire transition.

"I wasn't really seeking a redirection in my career. I was going to remain in banking, and was to have become house counsel for the bank, but had to wait until I could take the Arizona bar, there not being any reciprocity between the New York bar and the Arizona bar. I was really looking to get away from a confining situation and into a more dynamic situation. I suppose, too, that I wanted to prove something to my family—that I could make it on my own outside the security of the sheltering wing. Even though I had proven myself substantially while living at home and embarking on those projects, there was still some other demand in me that had to be satisfied. An awful lot of people thought I was crazy to make the move. But after they had a chance to visit us in Phoenix, they realized that the life style there was much more pleasant than what we had known previously.

"Another underlying motivation for my move was the urge to write. It had been resurfacing during my last months at home, and I felt that I could never really break away from the work and civic obligations I had there to get the time I wanted to write. If I moved to a strange community, I could fulfill whatever career obligations I felt necessary, and then break away without any constraints. I looked forward to a long and happy career with the bank in Phoenix, and entertained vague thoughts that maybe after ten or twenty years, I'd be able to begin my writing career, albeit late.''

Little did Bob suspect that within nine months he'd be giving his notice to the bank and starting his writing career. Shortly after starting with the bank, he discovered that it had some serious underlying problems. The major stockholders of the bank had bought it only two years previously from a group who had filled the loan portfolio with some very undesirable situations. The new owners, not being bankers, had neglected to adequately explore the quality of their loan portfolio, and shortly after they had taken over, things began exploding all around them. ''I envisioned that in my first five or ten years with the bank, I'd be little more than a garbage man—cleaning up a lot of bad loans and trying to raise the image of the bank, to one of top quality. But I seemed to be fighting a losing battle. Banking in the wild, woolly West at that time was a far cry from what I'd been used to in the conservative East. While I was trying to clean up a portfolio of bad loans, the bank kept on making new bad loans, despite my objections. The bank was paying no dividends to its stockholders, and the majority stockholder was crying for a return on his investment. The quickest way to do this was to generate high-interest loans, and in order to do that, you had to take a lot of risks that a prudent banker wouldn't normally take.

''Still with no firm thought in mind of breaking away, I started dabbling in some free-lance writing for local publications, just to test the marketplace and my own abilities. I would probably have been content to earn a few hundred dollars here and there with my free-lancing, had the career at the bank been going along more positively.

''The big change came so suddenly, that I don't really recall any one incident that sparked it. I remember sitting in my den one Sunday evening late in January 1968, reading the newspaper. It was as if a voice came down from above and spoke to me, commanding me, 'Tomorrow, you're going to give notice at the bank, and you're going to once and for all do what you've always wanted to do—write.' I sat in amazement at these thoughts that had just come pounding through my head, but I recognized that they were right. It wasn't even as if I had made up my mind. My mind had been made up for me. I ran into the bedroom where my wife was sewing, to tell her. She smiled broadly and said, 'Thank heavens, it's about time.'

''I waited a few days before giving my notice to allow all of these thoughts to settle down and take a more positive shape. Over the years, I had developed enough of a nest egg so that I could afford to live for perhaps two years, assuming I received no income at all from my writing. I was willing to risk it all to see if I could make it. By this time, I was accustomed to having people call me crazy, or, as was now the case, gutsy. Although I was confident that I could succeed, I knew that I could always fall back on banking, law, or real estate and make an adequate living for myself.

"To me, the decision to get free was an absolute one. Actually, I probably should have had my head examined, for the chances of success in free-lance writing are indeed remote.

"I planned to keep my overhead at a minimum and just set up a simple office in the house. A bout with the flu a few days later taught me otherwise. I hadn't spent any time at home during the normal work week in many years, and the comings and goings of the children, the ringing of the telephone and the doorbell, the rumble of the washing machine, and all the other homebound activities quickly convinced me that I'd go crazy trying to work there. I had always been accustomed to an office environment, so I went out looking for simple quarters. I found a tiny room in a nearby office building that I was able to rent for $25 a month, with the understanding that I'd get out on two weeks' notice if the landlord found a better-paying tenant. For another $40, I stocked my office with an Army-surplus desk, chair, and filing cabinet. One week after my fourth child was born, I went to my new office for the first time, sat down at my desk, put a piece of paper into the typewriter, and said to myself, 'Okay, fellow, you're a writer. Now, what are you going to write about?'

"My earlier free-lancing with the local publications had paid off, and at the outset, I had a little money coming in. But it was only a fraction of what my previous salary had been. The rest of our living expenses came out of the nest egg. I really had no idea of which direction I should pursue, but I was willing to try anything. I was groping. I tried television, children's books, articles for the ladies' magazines, and short stories for the men's magazines. My file of rejection slips was growing at a predictable pace, but I wasn't discouraged. I pursued all the local sources I could, including copywriting for some advertising agencies, and I was convinced that I could do the job and only needed some breaks to get into the big time.

"I envisioned that a New York literary agent would provide me with that break, and I went off in pursuit of one. On the strength of my unsold children's-book manuscripts, a one-man agency agreed to take me on to try to market those products. He was unsuccessful after the first few months of trying, and then told me that if I really wanted to make it, I'd sooner or later have to write a novel. Sooner would be better. Little did I realize at the time that his specialty was novels. Indeed, that most small agencies specialize in particular fields—they've gotten to know the editors and publishers who need that kind of material, and willingly or not, they fall into limited spheres of activity.

"Well, I didn't have any novel inside of me burning to get out, but if my guru, the New York literary agent, felt that that was the way to success, then I'd damned well better do what he said. I fabricated a plot, and set to work creating my contribution to American culture. But it wasn't my work. I was doing somebody else's work, and it didn't work. I struggled in vain with the plot, with the characters, with the dialogue. I finally finished a few hundred typewritten pages, which ultimately might have been a third of the novel, and sent it off to the agent for his reactions. I was looking at him as an English teacher, not as a business associate.

"I was devastated when he informed me that 'it just wasn't any good.' I was now about one year into my new career, and was watching my nest egg dwindle rapidly. Something had to gel soon, or it was back to the salt mines for me.

"Then, perhaps a bit late, I remembered the ultimate lesson that had been taught me, and every other aspiring writer, in my creative writing classes: write what you know. What I knew and knew well was personal financial counseling, having dealt with it as a banker, and a lawyer, and a real-estate developer. In the course of those careers, I had covered virtually every facet of personal financial matters, from buying and selling houses to writing wills to getting loans to dealing with swindlers to budgeting to insurance, and onward. Because of my training and temperament, I felt more comfortable with a short form of writing such as a newspaper column or magazine article as opposed to the lengthy demands of a book.

"After some research on existing competition, I proposed to my agent that I create and he sell a syndicated newspaper column on family financial problems. He laughed at me. 'You don't just up and sell a newspaper column. You either have to labor in the field for years until you develop your expertise and polish, or you're a big celebrity and they come seeking you out, or you inherit one.'

"Undaunted, I created a package of sample columns and asked the agent to submit them to the various syndicates for me. At the same time, I presented my package to the local newspapers. Let joy be unconfined: one of the local newspapers bought it right away, and within a week my agent informed me that a small syndicate on Long Island had agreed to take on my column. This is where I learned one of the most important lessons: that of all the elements that make a career, such as talent, patience, contacts, energy and drive, none is quite as important as being in the right place at the right time. On the very day that my material was presented to the syndicate, it had terminated another family-finance column and was looking for a replacement. I had the right professional credentials, and enough ability to put words in the proper order to satisfy their needs. We signed a contract, and the column started in national syndication.

"The income was still far from what I needed to survive, and the nest egg was nearing bottom. But the big break had come in, and things started to happen soon after. A publisher read one of my columns and proposed that I expand it into a book, which I did. The book led to other book contracts, and with these credentials behind me, it became increasingly easier to sell my material for good prices to major magazines.

"I had to call on my business acumen to make my new career really pay off. I realized early on that a writer can't subsist by selling his material only once and forgetting it. Each bit of research, each bit of new thinking, can be shaped into many different salable packages. Thus, my newspaper column became the source of scripts for a syndicated radio show. Chapters of a book were broken down into newspaper columns, and newspaper columns were restructured into chapters of a book. Both provided the source for lecture material, and the lecture trips put me into situations that developed new sources for material. Every credit and every credential that I could muster was used to sell yet a bigger magazine at yet a better price. The nest egg had just about dwindled to nothing when the income picked up enough to make up the difference. By my third year into the career, I was flying on my own and was even able to start replenishing the nest egg.

"I had opted for the unpredictable, and I certainly had it. I didn't know from one month to the next what kind of activity this career would take me into. One of my books captured the attention of Johnny Carson, and I found myself commuting to Los Angeles almost monthly to appear on his show. Regular appearances on the "Tonight!" show attracted the attention of other television producers, and I spent the better part of a year traveling the country doing network and local television shows, all the time sharpening my presentation on the issues of personal financial advice. Television had become one of my major sources of income, and it began to intrigue me away from the printed word. I was offered a regular spot on ABC television's new morning show (in early 1975), "AM America." I found myself commuting to New York City from Phoenix about every three weeks to do a five-part series on various issues of money management. Although still a bit shy of 40, I found that this constant travel was wearing me down unnecessarily. While the money was good, the physical deterioration simply wasn't worth the effort. Late in the year, the show went off the air, and I retreated back to my office to concentrate on a number of book contracts that had come to me.

"My current involvement is a book designed to help people break loose from confining work situations and become the master of their own soul. It's called *Getting Free—How to Profit Most Out of Working for Yourself.*

"As impulsive and foolhardy as I was to begin this career, I quickly replaced those shortcomings with a business sense and an awareness of the pitfalls that I faced. I was able to achieve considerable success—probably as much success, short of the popular novelists, as a free-lance writer could hope for: a good income, awards, the glamour of national television exposure, the so-called glamour of the actually grinding and grueling lecture circuit, and the respect of my peers. And, oddly enough, one of the things that I never figured I'd have to contend with was success: after you've climbed all the mountains, where do you go? That same old restlessness still prevails. I can see myself falling into a rut, and I don't know where I'll go when I get out of it. I suppose the best way to describe the frustration is that I still don't know what I want to be when I grow up."

Sometimes the maverick spirit never subsides. Perhaps it runs in the blood.

> *Call nothing thy own except thy soul. Love not what thou art, but only what thou might become. Do not pursue pleasure, for thou may have the misfortune to overtake it. Look always forward; in last year's nest there are no birds this year.*
>
> DALE WASSERMAN, *Man of La Mancha*

Part Three

# Doing It

# If You Want to Pick the Pretty Roses, You've Got to Watch Out for the Thorns

*You can always go out and make more money. But you can never go out and make more time.*

ROBERT ROSEFSKY

Okay, now we've seen how others have done it. In varying degrees, they were all in ruts, they all faced obstacles, they all took risks, they all worked hard, and they all achieved a level of self-satisfaction. Nothing that you can't do yourself.

Then, why is it that so many people who venture forth on their own fail? And why didn't I present case histories of failures? It's easy to fail. You don't need any lessons or examples from me. The simple path to failure—and that most frequently taken by those who do indeed fail—is the route of impetuousness, characterized especially by a failure to do the necessary planning, a failure to generate the necessary discipline, a failure to evaluate and prepare for the risks that will be faced.

Make no mistake: success comes hard. It's a tough world out there. You need patience and restraint, planning and knowledge, discipline and hard work, guts and luck. You'll face an uncaring public, tough and well-entrenched competition, and your own self-doubts, which will invariably surface as you start along the bumpy road of being free. But if you want to make it badly enough, you can do it, provided that you have the right motivation, the right professional help, and the right amount of energy.

The professional help and guidance can be obtained easily enough. This book is your starting point. But the personal motivation and energy ultimately reside, or do not reside, within you.

I was chatting with a friend who owns a specialty shop in Scottsdale, Arizona, and a simple question, "How's business?" prompted a fascinating discussion.

Business had been on the slow side lately, he told me (I was almost sorry I had asked), and prospects for the coming months were shaky. He speculated that perhaps he should start thinking of moving to a new location, or taking other major steps that would improve his prospects for the future. On probing a bit into his obvious sense of dissatisfaction, I came across a curious factor that seemed to be bugging him. He had just recently taken a drive through a very high priced residential area in the suburbs, one in which houses costing hundreds of thousands of dollars seemed to sprout like mushrooms. "Where in hell do guys get the money to build houses like that?" he asked me. "Are they that much smarter than I am, or that much better in business than I am?"

"Not necessarily," I replied. "Some of them have inherited the money, others have stolen it, and still others are just putting up a front that may last for a year or two before the whole facade crumbles. But then there are others who have been motivated to work hard for it, because that's what they wanted. They wanted it badly enough, and they went out and worked for it. The big house or the big car may not be everybody's idea of success, but if it's theirs, and they achieve it, so much the better for them."

"Perhaps you're right," my friend said. "Maybe I just don't want it badly enough."

"Then why let it bug you?" I asked.

As water seeks its own level, so do our own personal energies and motivations. We can set or aspire to fancy goals, but if it's just not within us to achieve those goals, we're not going to. Perhaps disappointment will set in as a result of not meeting the unrealistic goals. Then again, perhaps an awareness will set in that you have reached the level for which you're best suited. If you can find contentment at that level, does it make sense to aspire to more, at the possible expense of your own sense of well-being and contentment?

Before we start discussing some of the guidelines that you will use to help create your plans, let's take a closer look at some of the other psychological factors that can be hazardous for the person aspiring to get free.

## Anticipation

Each seed that's planted germinates at its own rate. The rapidity of growth depends on the quality of the seed, and the amount of water, sunshine, and fertilizer it's given. The seed of your new freedom may have been planted deep in the dark recesses of your mind. There, it may be slow to germinate and take root. In fact, it may never do so. Or the seed may be planted near the surface, where it's readily exposed to factors that will cause it to sprout promptly. Your prime moving force may be a burning desire to get rid of something that's troubling you. Or the prime moving force may be the desire to embark on your new venture. Or it may be a combination of the two.

In any case, you eventually become aware of the struggle of the tiny shoot to break through the surface. This is the phase of anticipation. Specific plans may not have been deliberated upon or evaluated as yet. But there's that new life within you that's surging toward reality, and the thrill of it all can create many distortions in your normal thinking processes. There grows the magic beanstalk that will swiftly elevate you to the land of the golden goose and the singing harp, and the giant be damned. Beware. The aspirations that can easily be shaped during this anticipatory period can easily be warped. In the rosy glow that something great is about to happen, we can easily take leave of our common sense. Yes, it takes dreams and aspirations to lead us to reach our fullest potential, but they must be observed in their proper perspective. It's during this early stage of excitement that we should begin the specific tasks of planning and shaping our goals, and of mapping out the route to reach those goals. Yet, human nature being what it is, it is during this anticipatory stage that our excitement deters us from that hard work. If we daydream too much over what a wonderful beanstalk this is going to be, we can too easily neglect to give it the proper feeding. All too often, the result is a deficient plant that fails to deliver as we had hoped it would.

## Exhilaration

The seedling breaks through the surface! This is it! You're on your way! Without exception, everyone I've ever spoken to who has broken away from the old confines has experienced a sense of exhilaration that can only be compared, in human terms, with the legendary multiple simultaneous orgasm. Indeed, it's something not to be missed by any human being. But these first few days and weeks of your new endeavor are exceptionally critical, and we can't afford to allow the blinding glow of exhilaration to deter us from the hard work needed at these beginning moments. But, again, human nature being what it is, that's what happens all too frequently. This is a time when rigid discipline must be firmly established and followed. Yet, the afterglow of the breaking away, as with a multiple simultaneous orgasm, is, regrettably, not conducive to setting new disciplines for oneself. Savor the moment, but quickly get it under control, lest it deceive you. The initial experience of exhilaration is not going to continue and it's not going to recur. It's a one-time thing, certainly to be enjoyed, but also to be handled with caution and quickly stashed away where you can later relish the memory of it.

## Enthusiasm

The sprout begins to grow, and you're admiring it, boasting about it to your friends, and envisioning all the fruit you'll be plucking from it. But are you tending it properly? Enthusiasm is essential, but an excess of it can be hazardous. Some personal examples may illustrate this best.

I was counseling some gentlemen who were embarking on a new business venture. They had developed a new device to be used in a certain manufacturing process. Not being an engineer, I had to take them at face value when they told me that the gismo would do what they claimed it would do.

They had just shown their invention to a large manufacturing firm that had expressed considerable interest in the product. They had come to see me to discuss the financial ramifications of building and selling their own item at the highest possible profit. As a result of their conversation with the manufacturing firm, their enthusiasm was unbounded, to a point of being almost ludicrous. If the hoped-for order did, in fact, come through, their profits would be considerable. They could hardly contain themselves, and their conversation was redolent of talk of new cars, new houses, sumptuous vacations, based on the profits that they were anticipating.

Then I asked a simple question. "Where's the contract?"

They all but laughed, indicating that getting the contract was as certain as the sunrise the following morning. It was all I could do to convince them not to spend the money yet that they were hoping to make on the deal. "First comes the contract," I cautioned. "Then you've got to perform profitably within the confines of the contract, and you won't know whether or not you can do that until you actually embark upon it. Then, if and when you receive the contract, and if you've been able to perform profitably under the contract, you'll have to reach a determination as to whether you want to spend those profits, or whether it would be wiser for you to pump them back into the business, where they might in turn be able to generate still bigger profits."

They were a bit taken aback, for they had come to see me to help them fulfill their aspirations, not to squelch them. I tried simply to express my view that it was inadvisable to spend money before you made it, particularly in view of the fact that you might never make it.

I began to sense that I would not convince them that there was a valid need for some conservative thinking about their venture. I wished them luck, and we parted friends. The contract did come in later, but on a much smaller scale than they had anticipated. This in itself helped to bring them back to reality, and though I've lost contact with them, I believe that they did succeed, albeit on a much more modest level than they had expected.

The experience recalled an incident that had occurred to me many years earlier, which probably activated the conservative vein deep within me. While it may be anti-enthusiasm, it's valid and it does work:

I was in my twenties, full of youthful vigor, and about to start work with my dad, concentrating in real estate. I was a rank novice, and didn't know a lease from a mortgage, but I had enthusiasm to burn.

I was to become involved in buying older houses, usually distressed and run down, which would then be renovated, refinanced, and, I hoped, sold at a profit. My first piece of inventory was a woeful old clunker that must have been built before the turn of the century. The previous owner had long since skipped town, leaving the house a shambles. It was being sold at foreclosure auction, and we were the successful bidders. We spruced it up, arranged for a new mortgage, and put it up for sale. If we got our asking price, my share of the profit would be $500—a veritable bonanza for me. I began formulating plans on how I'd spend it.

After showing the house to a few curiosity seekers, I finally found a "live one." He looked it over top to bottom and said to me, "You've got a deal." We shook hands on it, and I all but started writing the checks that would be backed by my all-but-in-the-bag profit.

The next morning I walked into my dad's office, and I must have had a "cat that swallowed the canary" look on my face. "I sold the Buchanan Street property!" I proudly announced.

Dad looked up at me without a trace of emotion and said, "Fine. Where's the check?"

"No, seriously," I protested. "I really did sell it. The buyer will be in this afternoon to give me his down payment and sign all the papers."

"That's fine," repeated my dad. "Let me know when you have the check."

What a come-down! Is that any way to treat an enthusiastic, energetic, and aspiring son? You bet it is.

The afternoon came and went, and the buyer never showed. When I called him, he told me that he had changed his mind and was sorry if he had inconvenienced me. Back to the beat. A few days later, I caught another live one. But this one was really a live one. He promised three times that he'd be in my office the following afternoon to sign the papers. Now I could really taste that profit in my checking account.

Next morning. Back into dad's office. "Sold the Buchanan house for real this time."

"Where's the check?"

"He'll be in at two o'clock this afternoon with the money. Honest. He promised three times."

"Fine. Let me know when you get the check."

Two o'clock. Three o'clock. Four o'clock. No sale. Back to the beat.

Now I was hardened. Now I was canny. Now I knew not to spend my money until I had the check in hand. Patience. Perseverance. Finally, here comes the buyer.

This time, I said nothing to my dad. I waited until the afternoon appointment following the showing of the house, and lo and behold, the buyer and his wife came in, signed the papers, and gave me their down payment check. We had a deal!

Into dad's office. Trying hard to suppress a smile. "Sold the Buchanan house!"

"Fine. Where's the check?"

My heart pounding, my spirit filled with glee, I produced the check from my file and showed it to him. He looked up and glanced at it, and with a wry smile on his face said to me, "That's fine. Now let me know when it clears the bank."

A superb teacher and a superb lesson well learned. It has paid for itself many times over during the years, and I hope that it will be of benefit to you as well. (The check, by the way, did clear.)

## Execution

The seed has taken root and has begun to grow. In the early days, you take great pride in it, feeding and caring for it as best you can. You've put your initial anticipation, exhilaration, and enthusiasm into proper control, and now you're at work at your lifelong dream. This is the execution stage. Suddenly, you find that with the initial thrill abated, you're really back at work again. It's not as exciting as you had thought it would be. It's work. It has its up moments and its down moments. Its dull moments and its intriguing moments. The spark has faded. The luster has dimmed. Your energies and your motivations fade, and you begin to ask whether the abandonment of your previous career was worth it. Your effectiveness lessens, and your zest goes flat. You find yourself back in a rut, one of your own making.

This process may take weeks, months, years. It may never happen. It's not necessarily a result of lack of planning; it may simply be the nature of the work and the nature of the individual doing the work that eventually cease to complement each other. Be forewarned that this can and will happen. It may be the result of overinflated expectations. It may be the result of a lack of early awareness as to the ultimate routine that you'd find yourself involved in. Whatever the cause, whenever it happens, you have to be able to ride with it. If you let it get you down prematurely, it can doom a venture that might otherwise have been successful. All human routine involves ebbs and flows of energy. There are high points and low points. If you're perceptive enough, you can begin to predict the timing and cause of the low points, and thus cope with them that much better when they occur. In effect, you can level out the low points, without taking away from the high points. It's a matter of balance within yourself, and you have to know that this issue must be confronted at the very beginning of your venture.

## The Tools

In the remaining sections of this book, we'll be examining some of the tools you'll use to create your new future successfully. The first of these is an invention of my own making, dubbed simply the "goal finder." It's a very important tool, for you can't achieve a level of success, whatever your level happens to be, without having a goal by which you can define the success. Very likely, you wouldn't be considering leaving your current situation if it offered you goals worth striving for or goals actually attainable by you. You're thinking of leaving because there's something else out there that you want, but perhaps you haven't defined it yet. I'm asking you to put a label on that uncertain something, and you can use the "goal-finding machine" to do so. All you need is a mirror with which to look yourself straight in the eye, the willingness to ask five simple questions, and the ability to answer them to your own satisfaction.

After the use of the goal-finding machine, we'll explore the various routes you can take to get free, their potentials and their pitfalls. Then we'll consider many specific elements of embarking on a business, including financial and capital needs, marketing, establishing a location, tax considerations, management, and so on. We'll wrap it up with perhaps the most important question of all, "But what if . . . ?"

To the extent possible, I've designed this catalogue of tools to apply to virtually any type of endeavor you might be thinking of. Space prohibits specific rundowns of all of the possible business activities that are open to you. But in the Appendix, you'll find a listing of source materials that can lead you to virtually any kind of specific information regarding virtually any kind of endeavor that you'll need to suit all of your homework requirements.

# The Goal-Finding Machine—Looking Yourself Straight in the Eye and Asking Who? What? Why? When? and Where?

Who? What? Why? When? and Where? are the five simple, yet potentially perplexing, questions that every professional journalist is supposed to answer in the opening paragraph of all of his stories. "Chicago, a Midwestern City Near the Southern End of Lake Michigan, Burned Last Night. A Cow is Being Held on Arson Charges." Or "I, Joe Smith, Am Going to Open My Own Hobby Shop Three Weeks from Today, at the Corner of Fourth and Main, Because This Is What I Truly Feel Will Fulfill Me." Seem simple enough? Try it out on yourself.

## Who?

Do you have what it takes, as a self-employed individual, to be both boss and employee? As boss, you have to provide the motivational force and the hustle to generate income-producing opportunity. As the employee, you have to follow through on the detail work, the leg work, and whatever else is involved to execute the orders that the boss has put on your desk.

If you'll be working alone, do you have the capacity to function well in solitude, often loneliness, making your own decisions, without the benefit of counsel, following through without the benefit of encouragement, completing a job without the accompaniment of praise?

If you'll be working with others, either as a partner or as an employer, have you developed the needed diplomatic skills to get along with them in those respective capacities, without interfering with the efficiency and productivity of those others or of yourself? Do the personalities mesh or clash? Are the personalities flexible enough to withstand and adjust to changes in the personalities of others with whom you'll be working? Will you and your partners be compatible with respect to work hours, remuneration, goals? Have you discussed these matters with your would-be partner(s)? Are you willing to constantly communicate on such matters with your partners, for if not, incompatibility is likely to grow, and a destructive force is liable to enter into your relationship.

Whether you'll be working alone or with others, have you calculated the effect of your new venture on those especially close to you, particularly your family? If your new venture causes you to vacillate between elation and depression, as often happens, how might this affect your relationship with your wife, your husband, your children, your lover? Have you communicated with them all of the various effects that they might have to expect? Are you willing to continue to communicate on such matters, knowing that failure to do so can cause deep scars and pain?

The "who" that is going to get free is the one who has asked and answered satisfactorily the above questions.

## What?

What will it be—something old, something new, or something vaguely similar to what you're now doing, except in a different setting? And how do you know if it will be your cup of tea? If a career redirection is prompted primarily by a dislike for what you're now doing, and you have no clear-cut goal as to what you do want to involve yourself in, you're going to be in danger. If you do have a clear-cut idea of what path you want to pursue, but aren't adequately prepared for it, you could be in equal difficulty.

One of the biggest and most frequent mistakes made in a new business venture is that the venturer gets into a situation about which he knows too little. Consider the successful electronics engineer who knows everything there is to know about di-hetero-flammicrons. He knows so much about them, in fact, that he has designed a new, solid state, super-di-hetero-flammicron. He decides to go on his own and manufacture and market this new generation of di-hetero-flammicrons.

But he soon discovers that in the world of manufacturing and marketing, as opposed to the world of designing and engineering, he doesn't know an invoice from a W-2 form, he's terrible at handling employees, he signs a ridiculously expensive lease for his premises, and learns that he really can't stand dealing with people on a buy/sell level. Soon, he's back at his old stand, trying to convince his former boss that his super-di-hetero-flammicron should be manufactured by the original company. Now he's hopeful that he'll get a royalty or bonus out of the deal. His lesson was sharp and brutal, and he isn't likely to make the same mistake again.

He who searches wisely for a new business opportunity will concentrate on the fields in which he has a degree of expertise, or in which he's willing to spend perhaps six to twelve months working for someone else in order to gain the necessary expertise. Such a trial run can prove invaluable in helping anyone determine whether the enterprise is suited to his own temperament, whether the capital needs of such a venture are within his grasp, and whether the pace and activity of such a venture would be compatible with his own style.

The answer to "what?" may seem simple on the surface; but if impulse prompts you to answer it incorrectly, you may have blown your chances for another try. Don't let that happen to you.

## Why?

Why are you making this change? For money? ego satisfaction? self-fulfillment? freedom? peace of mind? Going into business for oneself is a whopping challenge. One of the most perplexing aspects of the challenge is to know when you've reached a point called "success." Is it when you hit a certain income level? Is it when you've maintained a certain income level for a certain period of time? Is it when you can sell out at a profit and go on to something else? Is it when you've reached a level of personal freedom, regardless of income? Go to work on the fine-tuning knob of your goal-finding machine. Here's a question that, if left unanswered, can leave you as floundering and as aimless as you may now be. If you venture forth without a clear-cut answer to "Why am I doing this?" you may soon be asking yourself, "Why did I do that?"

## When?

Shall I do it now, or shall I wait until the economy gets better? Shall I do it now, or shall I wait until I have more money stashed away? Shall I do it now, or shall I wait until my children are older? Shall I do it now, or shall I wait until I'm in a home for the aged and have a lot of time on my hands?

All valid questions, particularly the last one. Probably as many new careers floundered because the individual waited too long as because the individual started too early. It simply doesn't do to fly off the handle and make a change as the spirit moves you. The question of "when?" has to be examined carefully, and with the aid of your financial advisor—particularly your banker, who is well equipped to counsel you on the specific current economic factors that may affect your potential for success.

The goal of when you should make your change will begin to come clear as you do your private studying of the subject matter that you'll be tackling, as you test your own motivations and goals (financial and personal), and as you begin to accumulate the facts that you'll need regarding financing, location, and market potential. If you gather that information first, the "when?" will begin to fall into place realistically and easily. If you make your move, and then start to explore those questions, it may have already been too soon or too late.

## Where?

*"You can't run away from trouble."*
UNCLE REMUS

Very often a change in career will be accompanied by a change in location. Something in your life is troubling you; you figure it's your career, and if you make a change, you can get rid of what's troubling you. But it doesn't always work out that way. If the trouble really isn't with your work, but with some other aspect of your personal life, the trouble is going to stay with you, no matter what kind of new work you embark upon, and no matter where you embark upon it. If you stay put in the same city, if you move to a new city, or if you devise a combination of the two that has you traveling on the road periodically and at home periodically, it's all going to be for nought if, in fact, the trouble lies somewhere other than with your current work. Before you settle on the answer to "where," you have to determine for yourself if it's really the work or if it's something else that's at the root of your discontent. If the problem is really with your current work, then the answer to "where?" can be obtained with much more freedom and flexibility. If the trouble spot is not at work then your change could well be in vain, and you'll regret it soon enough.

Who? What? Why? When? Where? Let your goal-finding machine explore all of the little nooks and crannies of these questions, and you'll shape a tangible and realizable level of achievement for yourself. Answer these questions fairly and honestly, and your chances of success are immensely enhanced. If you avoid the truth, you'll only be kidding yourself, and very likely will be wasting your time, your money, and your energy, and risking the dejection that comes with defeat.

# Routes to Getting Free—Potentials and Pitfalls

I've projected seven primary routes that one can take to get free, ranging from the most conservative to the most speculative. Each provides its own levels of independence and responsibility. Obviously, each of these routes has minor variations that you may wish to explore on your own. These are the basic routes:

1. Continuing what you're doing, but as an independent contractor.
2. Switching from a salaried basis to a commissioned basis.
3. Running someone else's business.
4. Buying an existing business.
5. Buying a "new" business: the franchise route.
6. Starting from scratch with an existing product or service.
7. Starting from scratch with a totally new product or service.

The level of risk increases as we proceed down the list. As we examine each of the items separately, you'd do well to bear in mind the essential principle regarding the ratio of potential return and potential risk. This is, quite simply, the higher the potential of return, the greater the risk. And vice versa. Don't limit yourself to reading about the route that seems most appealing to you. It would be better to explore all of them, so that you'll have a broader range of alternatives to evaluate.

## 1. Continuing What You're Doing, But As an Independent Contractor

This is probably the most modest route to getting free, yet it offers intriguing possibilities for people in the right kind of situation. It would probably be least applicable in a large industrial situation, and most applicable in a relatively small business environment, where the individual involved has specialized skills that he or she is putting on the marketplace.

In the large industrial situation, and particularly if unions are involved, the opportunity to switch from employee to independent contractor would likely be stymied by the sheer vastness of the ongoing system: "We've got 3,000 employees, and all of their vital data, including fringe benefits, Social Security payments, withholding, etc., are all built into the computer. If we made one exception, it would throw everything into chaos." While this attitude on the part of management can be discouraging in terms of making such a change, there's no reason why you can't at least explore it.

In the smaller business environment, persons offering specialized skills to a particular user of those skills might have a much better chance of succeeding with this kind of program. The main objective would be to free the worker from the politics and the procedures of the corporate hierarchy, so as to enable him to pursue his given tasks more productively. In theory, at least, this would be to the benefit of the corporation, since it could expand productivity without necessarily increasing costs.

The concept can be applied to many occupations—for example, the engineer working on a particular design or a family of designs; the editor engaged in work on a specific book or segments of a periodical; the advertising copywriter, account executive, and/or artist specializing in the work of a specific client or clients; the radio/television/movie producer/director/technician who concentrates his efforts in one particular area; the banker who spends the majority or all of his time concentrating on one particular account, or in one particular phase of the institution's business; likewise the clothing designer, the publicist, the personnel specialist, the construction foreman, the sales manager, the chef. Many professionals, such as lawyers, doctors, accountants, architects, and so on, might find this approach to their work more fruitful than the normal affiliation with a firm of colleagues. The concept might easily extend to various kinds of service personnel, such as building maintenance, property management, landscape contracting, food service, delivery service, printing and reproduction services, messenger service, equipment repair service, and a variety of hospitality services (parking-lot operation at restaurants, hotels, clubs; valets, bellmen, concierges, laundering, sommelier, and maître d's).

The concept, simply put, is that "I am no longer your employee. I'm an independent subcontractor working for you on a contractual basis. You have the right to my services for a specified amount of time, and at a specified amount of pay. When the contract is over, I'm a free agent. If you want to continue with my services, we'll negotiate at that time."

What are the potentials and pitfalls? You're assured of a continuing source of income as long as you continue to perform the agreed-upon services. You'll probably experience a psychological uplift as a result of eliminating the confines of the blind alley that you might otherwise have felt yourself trapped in. As a self-employed individual, assuming that your agreement firmly establishes you as such, you will be able to take advantage of certain income-tax breaks, particularly lower contributions for Social Security, the possibility of deducting certain of your work-related expenses, and the ability to take advantage of the provisions of the Individual Retirement Act—do-it-yourself pensions made possible under the Pension Reform Law of 1974. These tax advantages will be discussed in more detail in the later section.

As for the possible pitfalls, you may not be entitled to the fringe benefits, especially those insurance-related ones, that you would have as an employee. Thus, you'd have to find the necessary health insurance and life insurance on your own, very likely at individual rates that are far less attractive than standard group rates. You're putting a question mark in your future with regard to the completion of the contract. It's up to you to evaluate whether that question mark is any bigger than the ones that are there anyway, when you evaluate the company's future. You may have to forgo certain vested interests in pensions and profit-sharing plans. But perhaps you can salvage these benefits if your former employer will allow you to "roll over" the accumulated benefits into an Individual Retirement Account or Keogh plan, the various kinds of do-it-yourself pension plans (discussed later, in the section on taxes).

How does it look on balance? Your change may bring you a sense of independence and freedom from the corporate rigmarole that will allow you to be more self-fulfilled and productive. Increased productivity and efficiency could be translated into higher earnings at some future date. The specific pluses and minuses with regard to the dollars involved—the fringe benefits, the pension benefits, and so on—you'll have to work out with the aid of your personnel officer and your own accountant. Assuming that one washes out the other, or even that there may be a slight financial disadvantage to you at the outset, do the potential benefits outweigh this possible initial financial setback? If you have the spirit to get free and realize your own human potential to the fullest, you're probably making a smart gamble by pursuing this route. Granted, it's unorthodox and unexpected. It's rarely been done. But part of the purpose of examining this whole concept of getting free is to see if we can't create some new alternatives that can open up horizons previously invisible to us. Note Rosefsky's Rule Number 738B: You don't ask, you don't get.

## 2. Switching from a Salaried Basis to a Commissioned Basis

This mode of getting free could satisfy the heretofore unscratchable itch in many people. Myriad opportunities exist in a number of fields, and the financial gains can easily surpass those of the salaried employee. Basically, it's a sales-oriented mode of getting free, which may scare some off. But it shouldn't. At least not until you've given it a try.

"But I don't like selling. I don't like hassling with people." How do you know? Because you tried selling one product or service, and found it not to your liking? How about switching to a different product or service, one that might provide greater financial and/or psychological rewards. Maybe you've never tried it, but you know people who do it, and you find their work routine distasteful. That's kind of a silly attitude, isn't it? Why should you allow someone else's work style to influence what's best or what's right for you? You shouldn't. Or perhaps you're just an introvert, and would rather not expose yourself to the open marketplace and all of its presumed frustrations. Your choice then is to remain withdrawn, and you're likely to become even more so, or open yourself up to a whole new world of contacts and communications and experiences and challenges. You can't win if you don't place your bet.

You may already be in a selling situation, but with your income completely, or predominantly, based on salary; you may have a high degree of familiarity with the product or service, but have never tried selling it; or you may already be in a commissioned-sales endeavor, but one that, because of the product, the company, or the working conditions, doesn't give you the satisfaction you're seeking. Any of these situations can lead quite naturally and easily into a new commissioned-sales opportunity. And the commissioned-sales situation can readily become a stepping stone to other opportunities—sales management, administration, marketing, and public relations.

All work activity can be broken down into two major areas: the inside and the outside. Those who work on the inside, the insiders, develop and service a given product or service. The "outsiders" sell the product or service. Although the insiders create the product, it's the commissioned salesperson who creates the action, and who owns a piece of it. And while the insider's ingenuity can be stymied by poor salespersons, the salesperson need not be stymied if the insider offers him a poor product to sell: he can simply move on to find a product more to his liking. The insider is not nearly as flexible.

Probably the most visible and common commissioned-sales opportunities are in insurance, real estate, stock brokerage, and time and space sales for the media. Opportunities abound in every community, and no specialized advance skills are needed. However, it may be necessary and advisable to take courses, particularly in the insurance, real-estate, and brokerage fields. If a firm feels that you have good potential, it may provide the needed training at its own expense, and often will also offer an advance payment against future commissions to help see you through the training period.

The pros and cons? You're trading off a fixed and known paycheck for a variable and unknown commission check. You're freeing yourself from the nine-to-five routine, and your income should be in direct proportion to your energies and expertise. Your own productivity determines your success. Either you sell your product or you don't. There's no committee that passes judgment on your ideas, and there's no hierarchy to battle in order to achieve your goals. While in most of these types of endeavors you are technically still an employee, and as such you may have certain requirements and quotas to fulfill, you can largely determine your own hours while still retaining the fringe benefits that accrue to employees.

You may be able to develop opportunities that combine this mode of getting free with the previous one, the independent contractor. For example, many travel agencies will retain outside salespeople to generate business, paying them on a commissioned basis; furniture stores have designer/salespeople who work on their own outside of the store. Many avenues may be open to you along these lines, offering either full-time or part-time work. It may take some pavement-pounding to find the right situation, but the effort certainly should be rewarding.

## 3. Running Someone Else's Business

Now we're getting more into the entrepreneurial phases of getting free. If you've ever had any thoughts of running your own business, consider the wisdom of first running someone else's business as a form of trial run for what you have in mind yourself. You'll probably want to restrict yourself to circumstances with which you are familiar. But this isn't absolutely necessary, for basic business operations are similar, regardless of the product or service you are selling.

There can be some distinct advantages to this particular route to getting free. With little or no investment, you can determine whether or not this kind of activity is suited to you. If it isn't, you can back out, with nothing lost except some time, but with perhaps a very valuable lesson learned. If it is for you, you should be able to structure a buy-out agreement with the owner, which would enable you to move right into a situation that is partly of your own making.

Many different arrangements are possible along this route. You could remain strictly as an employee of the business, on a salary basis, enjoying the fringe benefits that are available to you. At the other end of the spectrum, you could hire yourself out as an independent contractor and take home a share of the profits in lieu of salary. Or some combination of these forms might be agreed upon, such as a guaranteed minimum salary plus a percentage of profits. Obviously, there's a greater risk involved in taking the percentage course, for if the business proves unprofitable under your direction, you could end up with an empty bank account. And it may be not as a result of your own energies. There may have been a basic flaw in the business that you weren't aware of, which prevented the hoped-for profits from materializing. Perhaps the most desirable arrangement would be to start off on a salaried basis to assure you of a level of income, and then to gradually shift over to the percentage basis, as you become more familiar with the operation and intricacies of the business.

Finding an opportunity of this sort probably won't be easy, but because of the no-investment features, it might be worth your efforts to do some searching around. Much, of course, will depend on your own level of experience, and upon the level of trust that a business owner will have in you. You may find situations that you can walk right into and take over, and you may find situations that call for an extended period of working along with the existing owner until he hands you the reins.

Opportunities may exist where an owner is nearing retirement, has fallen ill, or has become otherwise disabled, or where an owner has no succession program of his own for someone to take over or is having difficulties in the profit column because of shortcomings of his own that you may be able to compensate for.

In any of these situations, the owner will more likely be interested in selling out than in having you take over his operation. Indeed, an owner who wishes to sell might be a bit daffy to consider letting someone else run the business on the chance that the new boss would not buy it after a certain amount of time had elapsed. But you might be able to strike a bargain. For example, let's say that you enter into an arrangement to run a retail store for two years, at the end of which time, you have the option to buy the business at a figure pegged to the then-profitability of the business. The owner is planning to retire. At the end of the two-year period, you decide that you don't want to buy it. The owner might welcome the opportunity to abandon his retirement (many do) and become involved in his business again. Or, if you've done a good job, the business might bring a higher selling price at that time than it would have originally. Of course, the owner will be concerned that you'll run the business into the ground, and that at the end of two years, he'll have nothing worth selling if you don't buy it. This is an obvious risk that both parties run, but the owner's risk can be minimized by the proper financial arrangements at the outset.

Let's put ourselves in the owner's shoes for a moment. His business has been paying him a salary of $20,000 a year, and after all expenses are paid, including his salary, the business has been showing an annual profit of $5,000. An investor looking for a good return on his money might set a price of $50,000 to buy out the existing business. This would allow him to realize a return on his investment of 10 percent (the $5,000 profit), plus a salary for himself, if he wishes to run the business, or a salary for a manager should he wish to be an absentee owner. So the business goes on the block with a $50,000 price tag.

Chances are that the owner will sell on the following basis: a stipulated down payment, with the balance to be paid over a period of years, with perhaps a litle kicker on a percentage basis should the profitability improve. It's unlikely that he'll get his entire amount in cash. Should the business fail, the original owner is likely to be left holding the bag. Should the business continue to do well, he'll eventually get his full $50,000. But until he does get the remainder of his payments, he has only a relatively small percentage of the total price in cash at the beginning. If he received a 20 percent down payment, or $10,000, he could invest that conservatively and reap $600 per year on the invested down payment. Each year, as the remaining payments come in, he can either invest them or spend them as he sees fit, but all he's going to get is the $50,000, plus whatever interest he earns on the money he invests.

Even if he receives the full $50,000 in cash on the closing of the deal, his return on investing that money will probably not exceed $3,000 to $5,000 per year, assuming a fairly conservative investment program.

Now, you approach the owner with a deal that will allow you to run the business for two years, with the right to buy him out at the end of that time. You'll probably have to sweeten the pot a bit, but it shouldn't hurt you if you are as successful as you think you can be. Say that you sweeten the pot to a $60,000 price tag. Remember, you're not obliged to pay it if you decide not to exercise your option. If you have enough faith in yourself, you may be willing to take a lesser salary in return for a piece of the profits. With the business as it has been, you have $25,000 a year to play with—the $20,000 salary for the owner/manager and the $5,000 profit. You propose to the owner that you split that $25,000 down the middle, $12,500 for him and $12,500 for you. But you will receive 100 percent of profits in excess of that first $5,000. Thus, the owner is getting $12,500 cash in hand each year, and he still has the opportunity to sell the business to you, or to someone else, for the full $60,000, should you not exercise your option. That's far more than he would be getting if he sold it outright at the outset.

You, on the other hand, are taking a little less money up front for the opportunity to reap a larger profit down the road, and you haven't put a penny of your own money into it as yet. If and when you do buy out the original owner, you should be in a position where the profits from the business will contribute substantially to buying him out. I've painted an ideal picture here for illustrative purposes. All deals won't work out this way, but this kind of formula should give you the means to proceed with flexible negotiations that can satisfy both parties.

How do you go about finding situations like this? By keeping your eyes open, by asking around, by listening, and by knocking on doors. Approach owners who have put their businesses up for sale, and make your pitch. Many will reject you right at the beginning, but many may also be interested in hearing you out. Friends, relatives, co-workers may know of individuals who would welcome an outsider to come in and run their business. Keep a sharp eye out for businesses that appear to be in distress. They may be ripe targets for a "takeover," particularly if you can convince the owner that your particular skills can revive the business and turn it around. Look for "going out of business" advertising—the owner may have many personal reasons for giving up his enterprise, and may welcome an opportunity to see it continue, with him playing a sideline role to the younger and more energetic newcomer. Again, follow Rosefsky's Rule Number 738B: You don't ask, you don't get.

## 4. Buying an Existing Business

I recall a story told me, with great amusement, by a business broker. He was representing a gentleman who had just moved into town and was interested in buying a tavern. The broker went to great lengths to obtain a list of all taverns that were for sale, and attempted to get as complete a picture of the respective profit and loss statements as he could. He chauffeured his buyer around hour after hour, day after day, with no luck. The buyer just didn't see anything that he liked. Finally, after almost a week of fruitless searching, the buyer spotted a tavern that was for sale, and that suited his fancy. The broker thereupon made arrangements for the buyer and the seller to meet at the tavern to go over the books.

The broker and his buyer showed up at the appointed time, but there were no books in sight. "Where are the books?" the broker asked. The seller of the tavern pointed to a calendar hanging on the wall behind the bar. On some of the dates there was a large red X.

"Those are the books," said the seller. "Each day that's marked with an X is a day I ordered another keg of beer. That's all there is."

Moments later, the seller and the buyer shook hands. To the astonishment of the broker, they had made a deal. The buyer, a former tavern owner himself, was apparently so impressed with the volume of beer that the tavern was selling that he immediately made his decision to buy.

I saw the broker a year later, and he told me that the deal had worked out fine for all concerned, and the new tavern owner was doing the business he had expected to do.

Call it what you will, a stroke of genius or a stroke of dumb luck, I certainly don't recommend that anyone pursue such a course in obtaining a business. Buying into your own business, either partly or totally, is an enterprise fraught with danger and requiring diligence and hard work. If you pursue the matter properly, you can assure yourself of a good investment and a satisfying career. But if you don't pay heed to the basic rules, it's like walking blindfolded across a mine field.

Here is a guide to the location of the most dangerous mines:

• Why is the business being sold? Is it a genuine case of retirement, disability, or lack of a successor within the existing business? Or is there some problem that may not be visible on the surface? If you prepare yourself for the worst, you won't be disappointed. With the help of your accountant, you should examine at least three years of the business's operating statements, as well as three years of its federal and state tax returns. Five years' worth would be even better. Trace the flow of income and expenses to see whether you can spot any trends that might spell disaster for you. Obtain a credit report on the business and the principal owners. This can be arranged through your local credit bureau at a modest fee. Such credit reports would reveal the manner in which the business and/or its owners have been meeting their obligations. A Dun & Bradstreet report might also be helpful, but often the information in those reports is obtained directly from the business people themselves, and thus it might be self-serving and possibly misleading.

Check with suppliers to determine whether accounts have been paid promptly. If the business occupies leased premises, check with the landlord to determine whether the rent has been paid promptly; if the building is owned, check with the tax assessor and utility companies as to the promptness with which tax and utility bills have been paid. If you begin to spot any pattern of delinquency in the business's meeting its obligations, you might be looking at a danger sign. The pattern might indicate, for example, that the owner has been subsidizing the business out of his own pocket, and these subsidies might not show up in the business's operating statement. The owner may have considered such transactions to be private loans to himself, and he may never have entered them in the books. While you as a buyer would not necessarily have to repay those loans, you would find, in short order, that the business was not capable of maintaining itself without further subsidy from yourself. It is best to know this before you get involved.

Other reasons for selling a business might include the threat of future competition. The owner may be aware of plans for development of a major shopping center near his retail outlet and want to sell out while the selling is good, rather than risk being run into the ground by the competition. Check with local realtors who are familiar with the area in order to determine whether any developments in the foreseeable future could have an adverse effect on your own situation. In addition to added competition, other developments might include: changes in highway routings that could be disadvantageous, nearby major construction projects whose noise and dirt could be troublesome to you for an extended period of time, and zoning changes that might permit uses of land and buildings near your premises that would be incompatible with your kind of business.

Especially if you are going into a retail business, find out whether the owner has been relying on any particular brand or product that may no longer be available, or whose price is expected to rise substantially. Are there any claims or lawsuits pending against the business, such as tax liens, claims for refunds, lawsuits arising out of unpaid bills, or damages suffered by persons where insurance doesn't cover the costs?

Has the business maintained a good record with the local Better Business Bureau and any other consumer protection agencies in the community? You'll have to check with those agencies yourself to find this out. A bad record could be a sign that the business has a bad public image, which you'd have to spend considerable time and probably a considerable amount of money to correct.

Has the business met all of its federal, state, and local government obligations? This would include the proper payment of withholding taxes, unemployment insurance taxes, workmen's-compensation insurance premiums, and all necessary filings with regard to its business status with all appropriate agencies.

Does the business offer any service or product on an exclusive basis, and how secure is that exclusivity? If the exclusivity is important to the business, and there has been a threat that you might lose it within your market area, this could prove disastrous.

• If you're satisfied with the seller's reason for selling, you then have to determine how much of the business's success is dependent on the seller himself. Many small businesses and professional practices are successful largely because of the following that the owner or principal has developed. In evaluating the worth of any business opportunity, you have to try to determine the value of the principal, and the cost of losing him. This, at best, has to be called an intangible. It's related to "good will." You really don't know the present owner's value until you've replaced him and seen what the replacement does to the flow of traffic.

On the other hand, many small businesses begin to fail because of the owner's personality and/or diminution of energies. If you can see that this is the case, you may find yourself in an advantageous position. A new infusion of energy can restore a flagging enterprise. The answer to some of these intangible questions may be obtained by interviewing some of the customers or clientele of the business, and by chatting with competition in order to get their impressions. None of this can be relied on totally, of course, but your investigations will help you to determine whether your purchase has the underlying value that you're seeking, or whether it is all going with the former owner when he leaves for his cabin in the woods.

• Unless you're going to do business in your house or in your car, you're going to have to determine what arrangements exist on the premises. If the current owner owns both the business and the building, is he selling you both or only the business? Or are the premises leased? Either of these situations will require you to examine the lease, be it existing or proposed. This can be vital to any business that depends on its location for its success.

How well protected are you, as the tenant, by the lease? How long does the lease run, and what kind of renewal options do you have? What provisions are there for increases in rent? What provisions are there that would require you to pay all or a portion of utilities, taxes, and maintenance costs? To what extent will you be responsible for repairs, ranging from the minor internal ones to major structural ones? Will there be any requirement that you pay a certain percentage of your volume to the landlord as additional rent? If a landlord owns any additional space, for example, in a shopping center, do you have any rights to expand into such space should you so desire, and if so, at what cost? If a lease is nearing expiration, can you negotiate a renewal now, before you commit yourself to buy the business? If not, what assurances do you have that you won't be evicted shortly after committing your capital to this venture?

We'll take a closer look at some of the problems of location later, in the section on creating your plan and making it work.

• How much should you pay for the business? The answer to this lies in the basic law of supply and demand. How badly do you want in, how badly does the current owner want out, and what's the market like with respect to other possible buyers and sellers? There simply isn't any rule of thumb that can be relied upon in the valuation of a business, for the supply and demand factors change from day to day and week to week, from community to community, and from recession to recovery and back again. In many larger communities, there are business brokers and appraisers who can assist you in arriving at a reasonable price. It may be well worth paying their fee to be satisfied that you are getting fair value for your money. Some of the factors that have to be considered in determining the value include the location, the nature and quality of the inventory, the nature and quality of any fixtures or equipment necessary for use in the business, the lease, and that old intangible "good will."

One way to begin an appraisal procedure is to evaluate how much it would cost you to set up a similar operation at a similar location, starting from scratch. On top of the basic costs, you "guesstimate" a good-will figure and add it to the original sum. Another method is the investment approach: how much, after all expenses, including your own salary, will the business return on your invested capital? The average return on invested capital for the companies in the Fortune 500 list ranges between 10 and 15 percent, depending on the state of the economy. If your return is much lower than that, you may be better off investing your money in a savings account and letting it compound over the years. If you're getting much more than that, there may be particular risk factors that you do not know about and should look for before you make your decision.

And what of good will? How can you figure it? Naturally, the seller is going to inflate the value of good will, and you as the buyer are going to deflate it. Good will is made up of so many different personal things that there really is no precise definition of it. It's a little bit the owner's personality, a little bit the list of clientele and how loyal they may or may not be, a little bit location, a little bit accessibility, a little bit image, and a whole lot of maybes.

The investment approach allows you to circumvent the good-will question to a large extent. You're looking at the bottom line, your return on invested capital. All the bickering—and bickering is inevitable—over the value of good will on the sale of a business could probably be swiftly resolved if both the buyer and the seller called in their accountants to determine the effect of the good-will valuation as it pertains to the individual's tax situation. What, for example, would be the tax implications of selling at a high price fixtures that have long ago depreciated to zero value, as compared with the possible tax gain that would obtain if the fixtures were conveyed for salvage value and the bulk of the sale were reflected as good will? From the buyer's standpoint, the same considerations have to be evaluated. You and the seller can argue all you like about how much the good will is really worth, but the tax counselors will be able to put the issue in better perspective, and you should listen to them.

• You and the seller of the business will enter into a written agreement, a contract, which your lawyer should have examined, that can have very profound effects on your chances for success. The contract should give you some protection if you later determine that the seller made material misrepresentations to you about any phase of the business. At the very least, you should be entitled to void the contract, and get monies refunded, if not outright damages as the result of any misrepresentation. The contract will also set forth the time and place of closing, and the method of payment. The seller will expect you to comply with all of the dates in the contract, and will, no doubt, seek protection in the event that you don't perform as promised.

If the seller's attorney has prepared the contract, you have to assume that it will have advantages for the seller built into it. You, as a layman, are not likely to recognize these disadvantages to you, which is precisely why you should have your own attorney review the contract before you sign it. At the very least, your own attorney will be able to offset any disadvantages written in by the seller's attorney, and quite possibly may be able to negotiate certain advantages for you.

*"Come on, Rosefsky, do I really have to go through all this rigmarole in buying a business? It seems like an awful lot of time involved, and by the time I get done checking everything out, I'll probably be so sick of it that I won't want to buy it anymore. You're taking all the fun out of it."*

*"No, of course you don't have to do all of this work. You can just blunder across the mine field like tens of thousands of other would-be entrepreneurs do all the time, and get yourself blown all to bits. Of course, you may be lucky, and that won't happen. A few do make it across unscathed. You may think I'm wrong in suggesting all of this preparatory work. That's your privilege. But what if I'm right?"*

## 5. Buying a "New" Business: The Franchise Route

We take a quantum jump from the previously discussed routes of getting free to this route and the ones that follow. While the foregoing modes offer some tangible, financial evidence of a success factor, the latter modes fall largely into the higher risk, or crapshoot, category.

The franchise route, if you've chosen it carefully, can minimize many of the risks because of the proven performance of other franchise operators within the same company. But the franchise route, if not carefully investigated, can be an instant and costly disaster.

The franchise route preys on our natural attraction to the line of least resistance. Developing your own business, it is soon learned, demands a great deal of hard work, patience, time, study, and plain old sweat. That's the hard way.

The easy way, we tend to rationalize, is to put up our money and buy someone else's hard work and expertise. Why should we waste time developing a formula, when we can buy a formula that already works? (That's the voice of the salesman you're hearing.) Step right into it, so to speak.

That's the gentle delusion upon which the franchise boom of the 1960s was built. Like weeds, our landscape was sprinkled with all manner of franchise operations, the bulk of them having been seeded by family life savings, often ranging to $50,000 and more. If you were successful, fine. But those who were quickly recognized that the reason for their success was hard work. For every nickel of profit, they had to fry a burger, clean a grill, sweep a floor. Sweat, plain and simple.

Others weren't as fortunate. Deceived by unregulated salespersons and their fancy brochures, thousands invested—and lost—their fortunes, chasing after the dreams described in grossly exaggerated sales pitches.

"But it all seemed so easy," is the hindsight moan.

I personally examined scores of franchise offerings when the boom was on. Clients would come to me with their tongues hanging out, seeking my advice on their proposed venture. Time after time, I was amazed at the brazen statements made in the literature. Projected operating figures were juggled, twisted, misrepresented. I particularly remember a hotdog-stand franchise offering that projected a very handsome annual profit based on a labor cost of only the manager/owner and two helpers. But one didn't have to be a CPA to determine from the projected figures that the manager and the two helpers would each have had to work a minimum of twenty-four hours a day, seven days a week, to come anywhere near the volume that the fancy brochure said was likely to be done.

Sometimes salespersons' promises were never written into either the sales brochure or the contract. Sometimes the verbal promises were directly contradicted in the written material. In one of my cases, a client had asked the salesman to define his exclusive territory, and the salesman told him verbally that it would be the entire city limits. In the contract, however, there was no mention of exclusive territory, and the embarrassed salesman told the prospect that he would see to it that the company wrote such a clause into the contract once he had signed it. Fortunately, before the prospect signed the contract, he learned that two other prospects had been told the exact same thing, and that all were expecting exclusive territories for the same city.

The recession of 1970–1971 put the crunch on the franchise boom. Tight money, bad publicity, fear of investing in single-purpose buildings, and some general sobering up made the "easy way" seem not quite so easy.

But what a breeze it might be if, with a much smaller investment, maybe only $2,000 to $10,000, you could set up right in your own home and find a way to riches! And, no, you won't even have to go knocking on doors, sweating and all that, to get rich! Just sell distributorships and take half of the proceeds for yourself!

That was the quivering delusion upon which the pyramid selling operations of the early 1970s were built. "But it all seemed so easy," is the same hindsight moan.

Cosmetics, household cleaning products, and motivational courses were the alleged "products" that were the subjects of these schemes, which the promoters called "multilevel distributorships."

The meetings at which prospects were lured into joining these programs were a cross between a carnival and a Holy Roller gathering. Shills, clutching huge wads of money, would proclaim how, just the year before, they were making only $100 a week doing menial labor and how this year they were on the way to $70,000 plus!

And, no, it wasn't just the unwitting, the uneducated, or the disadvantaged who dug up their savings to get involved. Many intelligent business and professional people were caught by the gleam of greed and the lure of fast money. Even after the debacle, few of them will talk about it. Some may say that they learned a lesson. Others may still have some of the glitter dust floating around in their heads, causing them to still suspect that they could have made it if the authorities had not cracked down on the promoters.

These schemes were designed so that participants would make their big money not by selling the product itself, but by selling subdistributorships within their community. Unfortunately, nobody thought to limit the number of subdistributorships, and sub-subdistributorships, and sub-sub-subdistributorships that could be sold. Consequently, once a participant had put down his cash and gone out into the field to find subparticipants, he found himself competing with other participants for very slim pickings.

The psychological arm-twisting that was applied to the participants/victims was, in many cases, nothing short of brutal. Launched into orbit by the quest for independence, money, rainbows, and other things, the takers were cleverly persuaded to believe that they could survive in the business world as well as anybody. It was an ego trip that, had it not had the profit motive attached, could have truly extracted many people from the doldrums that they exist in.

Once they were in orbit, and lightened by the removal of their wallets, they were persuaded that if they didn't make it, it was not the system's fault, but their own. They weren't working hard enough or didn't have the right measure of devotion or just didn't understand the system well enough. This was often a carefully placed wedge used to extract more dollars from the victims, to sell them an educational course that would enable them to better understand the system and increase their measure of devotion to it.

Then they'd be sent back into orbit, a few more hundred dollars lighter, to try again. Their zeal and the realities of the business world were so drastically far apart, that there was no hope of ever closing the gap. So it was for many thousands who thought they were going to make it the easy way.

By the mid-1970s, the franchise boom had faded, and the promoters of multilevel distributorships were derailed. But they'll be back. There's no question about it. In spite of a smattering of regulations and a supposedly greater public awareness of some of these schemes, there's a whole new generation of gullible victims emerging. When the time is right—that is, when the economy is booming and money is flowing freely—the promoters will be back.

Certainly, there are some legitimate franchise operations that can provide the franchisee with excellent training, sound management systems, and perhaps most important, a name that the public will be attracted to automatically. These are expensive, and they don't require any less work or dedication than do flaky franchises. But the chances for success are greater.

With respect to buying the sweat of others, or paying to learn how others sweat, consider the following precautions.

Before you sign anything, have a lawyer check the contract. It can have more loopholes than a gross of yo-yo strings. Of particular importance are the extent of your territorial exclusivity and the extent to which you are required to buy supplies from the franchisor. The latter item can play havoc with your business operation, for you might find it far more economical to buy certain supplies from local provisioners, yet your contract may prevent you from doing so.

On your own, find others who have invested in the same deal, and learn firsthand of their experiences. Don't rely on the names of people that the promoter himself will give you. He's not about to give you the name of anyone who will have anything bad to say. Seek out people on your own, and if you can't find any, keep in mind that it may be because there are none.

Have your banker and/or accountant check out the financial and business credentials of the promoters. Check with the Federal Trade Commission, the attorney general in both your own state and the promoter's state, local consumer-protection agencies, the Better Business Bureau, and local news media regarding the reputation of the firm and the individuals behind it.

With your accountant, go step by step, item by item, through each and every point of the promoter's financial projections. Are the projections based on the actual experience of other franchises, or are they simply pie-in-the-sky guesstimates?

## 6. Starting from Scratch with an Existing Product or Service

''Never has the demand been greater! Never have opportunities been greater! Yes, now you can become a disc jockey/truck driver/computer programmer/medical technician/electronic engineer/nuclear physicist/brain surgeon/TV pitchman! Don't delay one more minute! Call this number right now for a recorded message that may change your life!''

Yeah. And your bank account too. For the worse.

As common as the vocational-school pitch are the ads that appear in countless periodicals, offering easy ways to riches. Common among these are ''courses'' and ''kits'' that will teach you the secrets of success in such businesses as mail order and direct sales, and in other vaguely defined ways. Very often these pitches are nothing more than cleverly concealed means of selling some very inexpensive (and likely valueless) literature for enormously inflated prices.

I hope that the lessons will be cheap ones for those who fall for the ''get-rich-quick'' seductions in such advertising, and that these people won't be deterred from expressing their full potential in other endeavors. A wise investment in vocational training can return itself many times over. A mistake can not only mean lost money, but it can also set up a mental block that will hold people back from trying again through legitimate channels.

There are many fine correspondence schools offering a wide variety of vocational-training courses that can indeed be the key to new career opportunities. But the sad fact is that there are also many deceptive operations, and you may not know which one you've joined until it's too late. Getting involved in a flimflam is easy. Dropping out is easy. Not rising to the challenge is easy. These are some of the reasons why, during a five-year period (1966 to 1971) studied by the Veterans' Administration, fully three out of four vets receiving benefits for correspondence failed to complete their courses. Bear in mind that no course of training, whether by mail or in person, can guarantee you anything. You've got to work at getting the knowledge and putting it to the proper use. And that's not easy.

If you're considering embarking on a correspondence course or instruction to lead you into a new venture started from scratch, consider the following suggestions.

Check first with local colleges and junior colleges to see if similar training might be available in your home town. You might be able to obtain more adequate training at far less cost, but you won't know until you've checked around on your own.

Do a series of frank interviews with business people in your community who would be your competitors. Try to determine if the field is overcrowded or if there is, indeed, room for another. Ask them if they know anything about the course you're considering. Since they're in the business, they might be able to give you valid information about the program's reputation. Your banker can also be a source of information about your community's need for another entrepreneur in your chosen field.

Once you've signed a contract for a course, plan on being bound by it. Find out what your rights will be if you fail to complete the course, and what their refund policy is.

Beware of schools that offer "guaranteed jobs," "placement," "guaranteed income," or the like.

Check with others who have taken the same course to see how things went for them. Also with the Federal Trade Commission, the Better Business Bureau, the attorney general, and the local consumer-protection agencies as to whether there have been complaints against the school and how the complaints have been handled.

Above all, whether you're considering a school, a franchise, a distributorship, a mail-order course, or whatever, remember that the promoters are out to sell you something—although they might try to make it appear otherwise. You're being pitched to. Don't let yourself believe anything to the contrary. And if a moment of skepticism grabs you, ask yourself, "If what these guys are selling is supposed to be so good, why are they selling it? Why don't they just keep the secret to themselves and reap the fortunes that they say I could be making? They must be making more money pitching it to people like me than I'd be able to make actually doing it, or they'd be doing it themselves instead of selling it."

What about recourse if things go wrong with one of these outfits? Well, if worse should come to worst, and it might, did you ever think how far you might get in suing a company that didn't exist any longer?

If you don't feel the need for any kind of training or instruction or franchise assistance, and you're starting from scratch to sell an existing product or service, you'll have to pay special attention to each of the steps in the section on creating your plan and making it work. Except for the fact that you are dealing with a product or service for which there is already some level of proven public acceptance—be it preparing tax returns, driving a taxicab, or doing taxidermy—you're plunging headlong into unchartered waters, and you're going to need all the help you can get in order to make a success of it.

## 7. Starting from Scratch with a Totally New Product or Service

This is, without a doubt, the riskiest of all the routes to getting free. This is the ultimate ego trip, along a road strewn with every conceivable hazard to the would-be entrepreneur. For every hoola-hoop and frisbee and mood ring and pet rock, there are thousands of products that never saw the light of day. For every novel and painting and sculpture and handicraft, there are thousands that have never been seen except by their creator, the creator's spouse, and the creator's in-laws. The world of better mousetraps and great American novels and golden records exists far more in the Walter Mitty fantasies of its millions of aspirants than it does in reality. In addition to the risks of money and time, many who follow this course are unwittingly playing Russian roulette with their self-esteem, except that there's only one blank cartridge and five real ones, not the other way around.

Yet, despite the risks, probably no better attempt at realizing the American dream can be made than by taking this route at least once. If you do so impulsively, your chances of success are microscopic. But if you do so with the proper patience, the proper planning, and the proper skills or talent needed to make your venture go, there may be a chance for success in your future. Can a living be made this way? For a very small percentage of those who try, yes. In spite of the long odds, is it worth giving it a try? Yes, provided you have something to fall back upon.

Let me guide you, briefly, through and around some of the predominant hazards you'll find on this road to getting free.

The first, and most common, hazard is that as you embark, you will probably have your eyes and mind firmly fixed on that glittering vision of freedom and success in the distance. Yes, that's where the road leads to, ideally, but you become so dazzled by this image that you fail to keep an eye on where you're walking. Eyes to the road, friends, watch every step along the way.

Watch out for the doldrums of rejection—they can destroy you right at the outset, and send you back to the haven of security that you were so anxious to be rid of so recently. Fear of rejection, or the inability to cope with rejection, is probably the most frequent reason for failure in these endeavors.

Whether you are selling an invention or an artistic creation, you have to be accepted at three important stages. First, you must be accepted by the middle man—the manufacturer, the distributor, the producer, the publisher, the retailer—who will usually venture his own time, money, and/or space to display your product.

If you get past that first step, you must then be accepted by the public. The third step is perhaps the most difficult: you must be accepted by the public a second time. The consuming public is a curious breed. They'll try almost anything once, if it's brought to their attention in an appealing enough way, and packaged and priced in ways that whet their curiosity. But will they come back and try it again? On its first exposure to the public, it must satisfy a whim. On its second exposure, the crucial one, it must satisfy a very real need.

Rejection often convinces the rejectee that he or she is not any good. While this may, in fact, be the case, it needn't be so. You may simply be in the wrong place, or in the right place at the wrong time, or in the right place at the right time but with the wrong product.

Knowing your marketplace and knowing your competition are essential if you want to minimize rejection. In industry, large staffs of research and development people are maintained to create new products for the marketplace. You're competing with them, and with their enormous resources of capital and marketing skills. And yet, even with the giants within the consumer-product industry, the eventual failure rate of new products runs close to nine out of ten.

If your creation is artistic or literary, you're competing with established artists, authors, and artisans who have a direct relationship with the publishers/producers/manufacturers as a result of their past successes with them.

Two case histories will illustrate these pitfalls.

The first involves a couple who visited me to consult about a new product that they had developed, and a pitch that they had received from a product-marketing firm. They had developed what could be best described as a new type of bandage, with the gauze pad containing some form of soothing lotion that had never before been used in a bandage. They were reluctant to divulge the specifics to me, but I was able to gather that before their invention, if you received a mosquito bite, you would put calamine lotion on the bite and then put a plain bandage over the lotion. Their product already contained the calamine lotion, or whatever else it may have been, and thus you wouldn't have to bother with that intermediate step of applying the lotion. It would be contained in the bandage.

It didn't sound like anything earthshaking, and apparently all of the pharmaceutical firms to whom they had submitted their idea didn't think so either. They had received a file full of rejection letters from these firms, and were now becoming desperate to have their product manufactured and marketed. They were attracted to an advertisement offering market analysis for new inventions—many firms promote this service, and a high percentage of them have been uncovered by state and federal authorities to be nothing more than a new twist on the vanity publishing schemes: they take your money, massage your ego, and disappear into the night.

The couple had communicated with such a firm, and were now debating whether or not they should spend the necessary $1,500 to acquire the "marketing study" and "feasibility research program" that the firm was offering. The pitch was ludicrous, to say the least. The couple had had to disclose the general nature of the product to the firm, and the firm had written them a glowing letter telling them that they indeed were standing at the brink of untold wealth, if only the firm's services were utilized to bring the product to its full fruition. The marketing-research program would consist of exposing the product to "at least 12 million prospective customers on a worldwide basis," and held out the promise that the rate of acceptance would be so high as to assure immediate success. The couple had taken the bait and had been ready to withdraw the money from their savings account when they spotted my newspaper column, which warned of a similar scheme that preyed on would-be songwriters. With the last vestige of their common sense, they decided to seek my advice.

I determined that the full extent of their own market research had been to produce a few dozen of these bandages for use on their immediate family, close friends, and neighbors. Everyone who had used the bandages had been ecstatic. I alerted them to the possibility that very often good friends and close relatives are reluctant to tell the truth about such matters, and that even if they had been truly ecstatic, that market testing was far from sufficient to prove the worth of the product. I strongly urged them not to send any money to the invention firm, but rather to proceed to use the money in the following, much more sensible fashion.

With the money available, they could produce many hundreds of boxes of the product, a large enough supply to give them a decent market test within their own community. I suggested that they make up the products, hire a designer to create an attractive package, and proceed to local pharmacies and similar outlets to convince the proprietors to put a few boxes on their shelves. Even if they had to offer the retailer a larger than standard profit, and have nothing left for themselves, it would at least be a way to see if retailers would accept the item, which is the necessary step before seeing if the public will accept it for the first time and for the second time.

After manufacturing the limited run, there would be enough money left over for some window posters, point-of-sale displays, and a modest amount of advertising in local media, including the "penny-saver" type of shopping guides. If they could get the retailers to display the product, then there was at least a chance that the public would have the opportunity to buy it. If, in fact, the public bought it, then there'd be an opportunity to see if the public was pleased by it and would come back and buy it again.

If they reached that level of acceptance, they should, on the basis of actual orders from the field, be able to start a more extensive production run. They'd have to expend a great deal of energy (sweat) to do the manufacturing on their own, to do the delivering, the invoicing, the selling, and the praying. If sales continued to increase, eventually they could hire a manufacturing firm to produce the product for them, and they could retain sales representatives to carry the line on a commissioned basis. If, eventually they made substantial penetration into the regional retail market, that would be the time to go to a national distributor, perhaps sell the rights, and reap the royalties therefrom.

They had never thought of doing any of this. And it didn't sound appealing to them. It meant hard work, and a chance of finding out all too soon that their product would not be successful. They had bought the ego message, and would have gone along with it until their bank account had been bled dry, and would still have never known whether or not the product had any chance of being accepted by the public. Had the product been more conducive to mail-order sales, I would have recommended this kind of market trial—placing limited ads in local publications, varying the ads until they found a level of acceptable returns, then increasing the advertising accordingly in broader-based publications.

Was there a happy ending? I'm not sure. I never saw them again, nor did I see their calamine-lotion-soaked bandages. Perhaps they learned soon enough that the product was not acceptable to the public and they abandoned their efforts. Perhaps it was a cheap lesson, and they were thankful that they didn't waste untold hours and thousands of dollars pursuing an impossible dream.

The other case history is my own. I hope that some of my random experiences in the marketing of the printed word can indicate to others in artistic fields some of the tribulations that have to be faced.

**THE MAGAZINE EPISODE.** There are bad rejection slips, and there are good rejection slips. Very early in my career, I would regularly submit a flurry of article ideas to various major magazines. At first, it seemed as if I was doing nothing more than subsidizing the post office with the round-trip postage that went into each idea submission. Fortunately, my previous years as a businessman had given me a rather thick skin with respect to rejections. I also realized that if Jonas Salk had become discouraged at the rejection slips he received from nature, polio might still be a great danger to us today. Thus, I remained hopeful, even in the face of an unending barrage of rejections.

Then, one day, I received a good rejection slip. It was indeed a flat-out rejection, but it was personally typed, and it was from one of the major women's magazines. (It should be noted that most major magazines receive between 200 and 400 idea submissions for every article or story that they run.) I took the personal note as a sign that I had not just my little toe, but my entire foot, in the door of this prestigious publication. I immediately fired off another idea to them, for the writer of the note had said, "Please think of us in the future should you have any more ideas." A few days later, I was elated by my success: another personally written rejection letter. At this point, I knew that the writer of the rejections, an "editorial assistant," and I were destined to do big business together. It was just a matter of time and the right idea.

A third idea was submitted, and my elation turned into total despair when the mailman arrived with the third rejection letter—this one a printed form. The article idea had been a spoof on the astrology craze, and I had felt certain that this would be my major breakthrough in a long, hard battle. But, alas, first they build you up, then they let you down with a bang.

But I was undaunted. Some weeks later, I was in New York City, and realized that I was in the same office building as this magazine. Gathering my courage, I marched in and told the receptionist that I wanted to see Miss So-and-so, an editorial assistant. Who was I? A writer. The look of astonishment on the receptionist's face told me that writers have no business coming to the office of the publication. That just isn't heard of. All of the rejection slips are handled through the mail. But I inisted that I see the young lady, commenting that I had flown all the way from Phoenix, Arizona, for the sole purpose of resolving a problem.

A few minutes later, a very frail and frightened young lady, probably recently out of college, came into the waiting room to confront me. In spite of the two endearing personal notes she had sent me, she hadn't the foggiest notion of who I was. I refreshed her memory by referring to the various ideas that she had received from me, and then hit her with the overpowering question: "I thought that after those two first personal notes we really were going to have something going. Then all of a sudden, a standard-form rejection. What happened? Where did I go wrong?"

"Oh," she explained. "Those first two personal notes I sent because I didn't have much to do that afternoon, and I wanted to practice up on my typing. As for the printed rejection, we have a firm rule here that we never do anything on astrology, even a spoof. So I just automatically sent out the rejection."

My lesson was simple and easy to swallow: hereafter, I would review at least the past year's editions of the particular magazine before submitting any ideas; review the content and the style of writing of all of its material; determine wherever possible, often by telephone to the editor, whether they had any particular taboos or already had articles in progress similar to the one that I was planning. In short, I was formulating the early phases of Rosefsky's Rule Number 738B: You don't ask, you don't get.

**THE TELEPLAY EPISODE.** Around the same time as the magazine episode, I was casting my ideas westward, in hopes of finding some writing assignments in the television industry. An old friend and successful television scriptwriter had offered to set up a meeting for me with his agent. Elated, I flew to Hollywood for an early-morning meeting with this agent, who had a desk slightly smaller than a handball court, with nothing on it but a telephone that kept ringing with calls from Desi and Lucy, George and Gracie, and the like. At the end of the meeting, which took approximately seven minutes, the agent told me that, out of deference to his old friend and successful client, he would read my material if I cared to send it to him. That alone set my juices flowing, and I could already see myself with a writing career consisting largely of endorsing checks for teleplays and residuals.

I returned home and concentrated on writing a sixty-minute teleplay for a now long defunct series. Less than a month had elapsed when I sent my first submission to this very important agent. For reasons that I really don't recall, except perhaps that the agent was so prestigious, I sent the manuscript via registered mail. Naturally, I had my own copy of it, but I think I may have felt that this original manuscript could be of such great value in Hollywood's archives in years to come that I wanted to protect its value against an accident at the post office.

It was returned two days later, unopened. Shocked, I called the agent to find out why. "You wise young punk lawyers who want to be writers!" he yelled. "Don't ever send me anything by registered mail. I'll return it just the same way I did this one. If I had opened it, read it, and sent it back to you, and then ten years from now you saw some other show with some plot lines that looked vaguely like yours, you'd sue me and the producer and everyone else in sight, wouldn't you?"

I was speechless. Such thoughts were beyond my comprehension. I had only wanted to protect my valuable manuscript from post-office vandals. "If you want me to read any of your stuff," he went on in a more moderate tone, "you'll have to sign release forms."

"Why didn't you tell me that before?"

"I forgot."

The release forms came in the mail a few days later, and I signed one reluctantly, fearing that I had given away all but my future, unborn children. The release accompanied the manuscript to Hollywood, and back again, two days later.

"Now what's the matter?" I asked him in a frantic telephone call.

"I don't like it."

"I don't care if you don't like it. I want to see if the producer of the show likes it or not. Why don't you just send it over to him and let him decide?"

"Because," the agent shot back, "I put my own reputation on the line every time I send something to a producer. He looks to me to screen the good stuff from the junk. If I send him one piece of junk, he might not even look at the next five good things I send him. I'm not going to jeopardize my own reputation or that of my other clients if I don't like a piece of property. But maybe you can find another agent who will handle it for you."

The real world was beginning to dawn. Instead of endorsing royalty checks, I was signing a lot of my own checks to pay for telephone calls and airplane flights. I contacted three other agents whose names had been referred to me by friends. None of them liked the teleplay, and none of them would agree to submit it to the producer, for the same reasons the first agent had given me.

I finally asked one of them why I couldn't submit it to the producer myself. "He won't look at it," was the reply. "Producers only look at stuff that comes in from agents they know. They'd be doing nothing but wading through crap all day long, looking at lousy scripts. That's what they use us for, to screen out the bad stuff. If you send it to him, you probably won't even have it returned, even if you enclose a stamped return envelope."

Now, I asked myself, what's the worst thing that could happen if I sent the script directly to the producer? Would he come and bomb my house? Would he kidnap my children? Would he put up a sign in the post office, saying, "No manuscripts by Rosefsky should be accepted here"? No. The worst that could happen would be that he wouldn't return my script and I'd be out a few extra dollars on copying costs. I mailed it directly to the producer, and was elated about ten days later when it was returned along with a very friendly and encouraging letter from the producer himself. He didn't buy my manuscript because, as he said, it wasn't suitable for him. But he did comment that I had a suitable writing style, and he encouraged me to continue with my efforts.

And the lessons: the need for perseverance; the need to try things when others say, "That isn't done"; the willingness to embarrass yourself.

**THE BOOK EPISODE.** A few months after my newspaper column had begun national syndication, I wrote a piece warning my readers about some of the problems they might face on moving day. It was a brief column, only 500 words, and it touched only lightly on some of the problems that the family on the move faces. But the column caught the attention of a gentleman in the New York area who suggested that I expand the subject into a full-length book, since some 10 to 15 million people moved each year and the market seemed right for a "how to" book on this often frustrating experience.

The man presented himself as a "free-lance publisher," one who would seek out properties, see them to completion, and then try to sell the package to a publishing firm. He seemed to be sort of an unnecessary, extra middle man, but he was willing to give me a contract and a $500 advance to tackle the project. Recognizing that he was as much a free-lancer as I was, the lawyer in me told me to include in my contract a clause that would have all rights revert to me if he failed to find a legitimate publisher within six months after he received the manuscript. He agreed, and I proceeded to write the manuscript.

As if fate were trying to tell me something, he failed to find a publisher, even though he had gone to his own expense to create an attractive dust jacket for the book. I waited the requisite time and the rights reverted to me. And there I sat with a manuscript all typed up and nowhere to go.

It was now early summer, and I was well aware of the eight- to ten-month period that it takes to produce a book once the manuscript has been completed. I was also aware of the unwritten rule in the publishing industry that "thou shalt not submit a manuscript to more than one publisher at a time." I never questioned the whys or wherefores of this rule. I just accepted it, as apparently do all of my colleagues. I determined to make one major effort to get the book published for the following spring season (being a book on the subject of moving, it's imperative that it come out in the spring, the time when most families are in the planning stages of their summer moves).

A friend in the publishing field suggested a major firm that might be interested in such a book. I contacted them by telephone and found that they were interested. I sent off the manuscript and waited for a contract. After weeks had gone by, I made a telephone inquiry and was answered with, "The editorial board is all on vacation this month, so it'll be a few more weeks until we can make a decision. But we really are interested. Just be patient."

After two more months of diddling around like this, they finally rejected the manuscript. It was now August, and if there was to be any chance at all of having the book published by the following spring, I had to have the work in progress within just a few weeks. I vowed that if I wasn't successful, I'd just stash it away in my closet as my first great, unpublished manuscript.

Then I remembered the lesson I had learned with the television producer: if I send the manuscript off to one publisher at a time, following the time-honored rule, it could take thirty to forty years before one agreed to publish it. What, then, is the worst that can happen if I send the manuscript, or at least an inquiry letter and the dust jacket, off to a whole passel of publishers at once?

Accordingly, I prepared and mailed out inquiry letters to fifty-five different publishers, all of whom I had determined, from my research, were likely prospects for such a book. In the letter, I explained how the rights to my manuscript had reverted to me, and I enclosed a photostat of the dust jacket to indicate some of the promotional possibilities of the book.

Out of the fifty-five letters, I received forty-four rejections and eleven requests to see the manuscript. I thought that was a rather good performance, for a 20 percent positive response is quite high for a novice. However, of the eleven requests to see the manuscript, eight of them were typewritten form letters. And it would cost me many hundreds of dollars to send out all of those manuscripts. Thus, I abandoned the eight printed requests and concentrated on sending copies of the manuscript to the three publishers that had written to me personally.

Two weeks later, one of them called and offered to buy the manuscript from me for $3,500. I didn't even wait to hear from the other publishers, for then and there I had an opportunity rare for authors: I was able to write to two publishers and explain to them that the property was no longer available. I had sent out my first rejection slips.

And the lessons: there's no tradition that isn't worth trying to crack; marketing a literary or artistic property is no different from marketing a mousetrap, a deodorant, a can of chicken soup—it has to be exposed to the potential marketplace as strongly as possible, has to be followed through vigorously, has to be presented not as a creature of your ego, but as a property through which the publisher/producer can reap a profit.

Your invention or creation may be truth, beauty, and the divine light to you, your spouse, and your children. But to the middle man who has to manufacture and/or distribute and/or market that product, it's one thing and one thing only: a way to make a profit. And if you can convince him of how it can become profitable, you may be taking a major step toward your own success.

The way to profit most by working for yourself, whether you're hiring yourself out as an independent contractor or inventing the perpetual-motion machine, is to follow the hard and fixed disciplines of the businessman. Not the promoter. Not the dreamer. The businessman. He's the one who has survived the rigors of getting started, who has shaped and honed a plan that suits both his product and his personality, who has been willing to forego certain other desires for the sake of seeing his machinery work smoothly and efficiently, who has learned how to cope with the predictable and unpredictable ups and downs that accompany any work venture, and who has developed his own definition of success and achieved it.

Let us look now at the specific tools that he has used to accomplish those ends.

# Creating Your Plan and Making It Work

Your profit potential depends directly on how carefully you've planned, how closely you stick to your plan when it's right, how quickly you can spot what's right and what's wrong in your plan, and how easily you amend your plan when it's wrong.

The basic elements that must be considered in your plan are listed below. They are referred to in general fashion, as they might apply to any venture. The Appendix will provide you with more detailed sources of information regarding specific ventures and variations on them.

1. Getting help: Your F.A.I.L.-Safe team and how to use it.
2. What form will your business take? Individual, partnership, corporation, other?
3. Financial and capital needs: analysis and projection.
4. Establishing a location.
5. Insurance.
6. Tax considerations, and how the new pension law can aid you.
7. Marketing.
8. Managing a small business: the saga of Paul Pill.

First a word about some of the important side effects of breaking loose from your existing job or career. You may be giving up certain valuable benefits when you leave your current work, some of which might not be replaceable, and some of which might cost considerably more to replace than you're now paying (directly or indirectly) for them.

For example, you may now be covered by a group health-insurance plan, which includes basic medical expenses as well as major expenses. The group costs for this kind of insurance are considerably lower than what the same coverage might cost you as an individual or as a member of a much smaller group. The same can be true of group life-insurance programs.

Perhaps even more important, if not critical to many careers, could be the fact that you would not be able to obtain the desired health insurance or life insurance individually, because of your own health conditions that have developed over the years. The same might be true of members of your family—they are likely to be covered under your group plan, but because of their own physical conditions, they might be excluded from private coverage that you'd seek to obtain when you leave your current work.

The possible risk of loss of either of these kinds of insurance can pose a severe obstacle that should not be taken lightly. It's essential that you determine the insurability and the cost of insurance for all the members of your family, including yourself, that you wish to be insured once you have left your current work. This must be done before you terminate your present position, for once that act has occurred, it might be too late to get back into the fold. You should also check with your current employer to determine if the existing policies, whether health or life, can be assumed by you, upon your payment of the premium, should you terminate your work there. This may be the easiest way to continue your present plans, but don't overlook other, outside sources.

What pension or profit-sharing benefits might you be forgoing by terminating your current work? Either of these benefits could amount to a considerable number of dollars. The Pension Reform Law of 1974 (Employee Retirement Income Security Act, or ERISA) spells out very specific rights that you, as an employee, have under any existing pension or profit-sharing plans. You should determine what those rights are, and determine also how much you might lose by leaving, or how much you might gain by staying an additional period of time until certain rights become vested and irrevocably yours. Under certain circumstances, it may be possible for you to "roll over" your existing pension benefits with your current employer into a new plan that you could maintain on your own or that you could transfer into another employer's plan. Find out what your rights are in this respect. We'll discuss this "roll over" situation in more detail in the section on taxation and pension plans.

What rights might you be forgoing with respect to stock options or other agreements that could give you a piece of the business you're now involved in? If any such sums are substantial, you must ask yourself most seriously whether your desire to get free is really worth losing the benefits that you have accrued. As with pension and profit-sharing plans, will you be able to obtain these benefits if you remain in your present job a bit longer, and if so, will it be worth it to you to remain in order to latch on to those benefits?

Miscellaneous benefits that you might be leaving can include the use of an automobile, membership in clubs, dues and subscriptions to various organizations and publications, certain tools of the trade, clothing allowances. These may seem insignificant, but if they're all added up, they could present you with a considerable question mark before you make your ultimate decision.

I don't mean to suggest that any or all of these termination matters should discourage you from making your decision. I merely suggest, nay, urge, that you have a total grasp of the impact of all these items before you make an irrevocable decision. You'll want to replace many of these items out of your own earnings at some time in the near future, and the cost of replacing them can have considerable effect on your overall cash flow in your new career. Know what you're getting into before it's too late to change your mind.

## 1. Getting Help: Your F.A.I.L.-Safe Team and How to Use It

Your F.A.I.L.-Safe team is that group of professional advisors without whom you cannot function properly as a prudent business person. The time to begin counseling with the members of the team is in the formative stages of your endeavor, long before you have reached any definite conclusions as to how you'll proceed. These are the people who will help you shape your conclusions in a sensible and viable manner. Some of them will cost you money. Others will not. There is no way to determine the total cost of these services until you've had at least initial consultations with all of them. But be prepared to spend the money where needed, for it's essential to your ultimate well-being.

And don't give me any backtalk like, "What do I need it for?" You do need it. Unless you, yourself, have the professional skills to function objectively in any of the areas you'll need information about, you need the assistance of a trained expert who can anticipate the problems that you're not yet aware of, and can thus help resolve them before they occur. Ask any lawyer, and he'll tell you that the bane of his existence is having to say to so many of his clients, "Why didn't you come see me *before* you signed all of these papers? Now that you've signed them, the cost of getting you out of the mess will be ten times what it would have been had you consulted with me at the outset."

Or ask any doctor how often he says to a patient, "Why didn't you come see me when the pain first started, not now when it's eating up half of your insides?"

And so on. Human nature being what it is, most of us fail to seek assistance until we reach a crisis point. By that time it's often too late for help, or the help will be extremely expensive compared to what it could have been. Choose the members of your F.A.I.L.-Safe team now, and get to work with them, diligently and with full cooperation. The more work you do with them at the outset, the less you'll probably need them later on. The cheapest professional help is that which allows you to avoid problems. Call it what you will—an ounce of prevention, an apple a day—there's no better advice I can give you than to tell you to make use of these experts, if you are to realize the maximum profits and maximum satisfaction in your venture.

These are the members of your F.A.I.L.-Safe team, as they apply particularly to a new business venture:

*F*inancial, which includes your banker, management consultant, certain suppliers, and Small Business Administration staffers.
*A*ccounting.
*I*nsurance.
*L*egal.

Your primary financial teammate is your banker. Not just any banker will do. It behooves you to check the banks in your community for a loan officer who has had some experience in the kind of business you're embarking upon. Every bit of experience that he's had he can pass along to you and you can evaluate it and probably benefit from it. If he is aware of some of the pitfalls you might be facing, he's in a knowledgeable position to point them out to you and to help you avoid them. For general consultation purposes, the banker's services cost nothing. You can't beat that price. In return for this service, the banker, of course, hopes that you will become a customer of the bank, keeping your checking accounts there, and borrowing from the bank as it suits your needs and the bank's abilities to lend.

A word of caution about bankers: in the course of your dealings, you can establish a very strong and worthwhile relationship with an individual, only to find that he is suddenly transferred to another branch or another city, or has left the institution altogether. Often, there can be a problem in reconstituting your relationship with his replacement. Much of the banking relationship is based on personality and on mutual trust. The right chemistry between banker and customer is an invaluable asset, but it may be impossible to reestablish it with a replacement behind the loan desk. Therefore, try to make certain that another banker, in addition to the one with whom you're working directly, becomes familiar with your overall situation, and try to establish a kind of second line of communications with this other officer. Then, if your main banker is replaced, you might find it much more convenient and comfortable to shift your activities over to this second person, rather than take your chances with your own officer's replacement.

The Small Business Administration (SBA) is a federal agency that can be of considerable help to you both at the outset and during the progress of a new business venture. There are close to a hundred SBA offices throughout the country (see Appendix for listing). In addition to assisting you with direct financing for your business, the SBA conducts special programs and conferences that can assist you in the management of your activities. And the SBA publishes extensive literature on a variety of business ventures, a listing of which is included in the Appendix.

Suppliers can also be a source of financial assistance. Many may extend short-term credit, which can be invaluable in helping you get started. Many also may be in a position to assist you with layouts, traffic-flow diagrams, and other technical assistance that you'll need in laying out your physical plant. In choosing among various suppliers for a specific product that you'll be using or selling, you may find yourself being influenced by the collateral services that one supplier is able to offer you as compared with those of others. Dig as deeply as you can when interviewing would-be suppliers, to determine the full range of services—financial and other—that they could make available to you.

The more grandiose your plans, the more sense it makes for you to hire a management consultant at the outset. A consultant can guide you in many of the important phases of setting up a new business and getting it running, including the specifics of buying your inventory, pricing it, handling security problems, obtaining advertising, and investing. The larger the city you're in, the better the chance you'll have of finding a management consultant who's had experience in the area of your particular endeavor. Look also to the SBA for their assistance in this regard. Within the SBA framework, there is a subgroup called SCORE (Service Corps of Retired Executives). These are volunteers who offer their counseling services to small businesses, often charging only their out-of-pocket expenses. If there are no management consultants in your community, it may be worth the expense of visiting a larger city to seek one out and determine what services he can provide for you, and at what price.

Next in your F.A.I.L.-Safe team is your accountant. This isn't someone whom you visit only at income-tax time. A good accountant is a constant ally in your new business venture, and one whose services can't be taken too lightly, particularly if you're not familiar with the complexities of keeping books. Confer with him early to seek his aid in helping you set up your bookkeeping systems, your cash-control systems, and your necessary forms and equipment, such as cash registers. At the outset, his primary job will be to help you set up a bookkeeping program that will be as easy as possible for you to follow and maintain on a day-to-day basis. With this as your foundation, his work at tax time will be that much easier for both you and him. He should also assist you in setting up an audit program, an internal double-check system to make sure all the money is going where it's supposed to be going, to ensure that employees' handling of money is done properly, and to provide you with signals that will show up if anything is going wrong with your internal cash-flow arrangements.

Try to obtain an accountant who has had experience in your line of business. If he is willing to divulge the name of other clients who are in similar endeavors, you'd do well to interview them to determine their level of satisfaction with the accountant's services. Usually, an accountant's fees are based on hourly rates. Determine the fees in advance, and how they are computed, including telephone consultation, visits in his office, and visits at your own place of business. If you don't know any accountants personally, the other members of your F.A.I.L.-Safe team might be able to put you in touch with some.

Next comes insurance. As an employee, your business insurance problems are minimal, if not totally nonexistent. Your employer probably provided you with health and life insurance, and he also maintained the necessary workmen's-compensation insurance and other programs to protect you, his property, his customers, and his good name. Now this will all be on your shoulders, and it's no small matter to cope with. The proper management of a sound business insurance portfolio requires an expert right from the beginning. We'll discuss the specific insurance requirements later, in the section on insurance, but for the moment, it's time for you to consider interviewing agents and/or brokers who will be willing to work with a new entrepreneur in setting up all of the risk-protection devices that you'll need.

It's essential that you be aware of the distinct difference between an insurance policy and the agent who sells that policy. The policy is a legal contract. All the rights and obligations of the parties are spelled out in detail, and there's very little room for interpretation, except in extremely rare instances. In other words, once you become the insured, you're bound by what that policy says.

The individual who sells you the policy is in a position to evaluate your needs, show you the best coverage to meet those needs, and connect you with the policies that meet your particular needs. An agent who is untrained, overzealous, or who simply does not pay attention to detail could easily do an improper evaluation of your needs, and could create an insurance portfolio for you that might be either too costly (because of duplicity of coverage) or inadequate (because of lack of coverage). The insurance field is vast and complex, and finding the right agent can be a stroke of excellent fortune for you. Interview many agents, get personal references, and make your choice wisely. Part of an agent's job is to provide proper counseling, but you must understand that the agent doesn't eat unless he sells policies. Therefore, there has to be a limit to the amount of time he can spend counseling you. You'll have to make your own estimate, based on your interviews, of the amount of time and energy he'd be willing to expend on your behalf. The more you examine the field, the more knowledgeable you'll become, and the more probing questions you'll be able to ask. This will assist you in choosing the agent who will best suit your needs.

Last, but far from least, in your F.A.I.L.-Safe team, is your lawyer. When you go into business on your own, you will, needless to say, have to do it in accordance with the law. Even the most modest venture will require the services of a lawyer.

You may be able to take many of the steps on your own, such as obtaining a city sales-tax license, or obtaining the necessary state licensing for any occupation that requires such licensing. But beyond such minor matters, an attorney's assistance is a virtual necessity in many ongoing aspects of establishing and running a business. At the outset, the legal form of your business must be determined—sole proprietorship, partnership, corporation. In conjunction with your accountant, you must establish your program to comply with all of your tax obligations, including federal and state income taxes, employment taxes, unemployment taxes, excise taxes, and any applicable sales and use taxes.

You'll need an attorney to assist you with any contracts regarding the purchase of an existing business and the leasing or purchasing of your business premises, contracts with partners, backers, employees, unions.

As government regulations increase geometrically, you are likely to need an attorney to assist you in complying with zoning ordinances, building codes, local health regulations, special-use permits, pollution control, consumer protection, fair hiring practices, waste disposal, wage and hour requirements, safety and health regulations, pension and profit-sharing requirements, and on and on and on and on.

Naturally, one-person shops will be exposed to these situations far less than bigger businesses will be. Nonetheless, there is always the possibility that you'll have to comply with certain regulations, fill out certain forms, be audited, be harassed, be provoked. It's all part of being in business for yourself in modern American society.

## 2. What Form Will Your Business Take?

You can't build a building without blueprints, and you can't establish a new business without knowing the underlying legal form in which you will operate. The three most common forms of business entity, ranging from the simplest and cheapest to the most complicated and expensive to establish, are the sole proprietorship, the partnership, and the corporation.

To some extent, your overall objectives may determine what form your business will take, if not now, then in the future as your plans begin to take more definite shape. For example, if you are not able to provide all of the skills that the endeavor will require, you may think in terms of establishing a partnership with an individual who can contribute those skills. Depending on the specifics of your operation, this choice may or may not be more feasible than hiring a person as an employee who can provide those skills.

If your capital needs are more than you can meet out of your own resources or borrowing capabilities, you may think again in terms of a partnership, whereby the partner would contribute capital and/or skills and/or management experience of his own. If the scope of the business is large enough, you may consider forming a corporation in order to sell stock to the public, or a limited partnership that would, if successful, result in an infusion of capital from a limited number of co-venturers.

**SOLE PROPRIETORSHIPS.** The desire for sole proprietorship can fulfill your wish for complete control over the destiny of the business, but may leave you vulnerable if you become disabled and are unable to manage the affairs of the business. This may indicate a need for partnership, again depending on the nature of the business. The cost of maintaining each of these business forms can vary, as will the respective costs of taxation and other advantages or disadvantages.

Even though the sole proprietorship is the simplest entity to establish, you should still choose this form only after counseling with the appropriate members of your F.A.I.L.-Safe team. Regulations regarding business entities vary from state to state, and in some cases from community to community, depending on local customs. As a sole proprietor, you'll no doubt be required to file a "doing business as" certificate with your county clerk or other appropriate official, so that the public has effective notice of whom they're dealing with, particularly if you use a business name. As a sole proprietor, you are totally on the hook for all of the obligations and responsibilities of the business. It's all your ball game. There are a minimum of governmental forms and regulations to worry about, and all income and expenses flow through your own individual tax form (via schedule C of Form 1040).

For most one-person enterprises, the sole proprietorship will probably make the most sense, at least in the beginning. After a few months, or a year or two, of progress, you can examine the characteristics of the other forms to see if they offer any advantages. It may not be wise to spend the money at the outset to set up one of the more complicated forms, at least not until you've had some inkling as to the potential for success. If the business endeavor is predominantly dependent on your own energies and expertise, the corporate form will not increase those skills, and indeed you might find yourself bogged down with the paper work that running a corporation entails.

**PARTNERSHIPS.** There are two basic types of partnerships—general and limited. A general partnership is an agreement between two or more individuals to carry on a business endeavor. Commonly, the general partners will share and share alike in their contribution to the partnership (labor, capital, etc.) and in their distribution of the profits and losses. A limited partnership usually consists of at least one general partner and a number of limited partners, who have contributed capital to the enterprise, but who may not be contributing any labor, and who will be limited as to their liabilities regarding the venture. A limited partnership thus allows the moving force, the general partner, to solicit capital from a limited number of investors, offering them a share of the proceeds but limiting their risk, all without the expense of forming a corporation to sell stock to the public.

Either kind of partnership should have a written agreement setting forth all of the rights and obligations of the partners. Technically, a general partnership may be established without a written agreement, but it would be foolhardy to do so. There are simply too many ifs, buts, and maybes to contend with in the course of running a business to leave it all to chance and your supposed willingness to consent to the others' actions. Nothing can come between even the best of friends as swiftly as a dispute over money. If all of the rights and obligations are spelled out in a legally binding agreement, the most disruptive element of a business venture—dispute—can be largely eliminated. Remember, this is a business deal, not a hand-holding, buddy-loving friendship situation. Business is business, and it should be designed, planned, and executed as such.

One of the most important aspects of a partnership agreement is the termination phase. In the event of the death, disability, or retirement of one of the partners, what are the rights of each of the parties? In the event that one party wishes to buy out the other, this possibility should also be spelled out in the initial agreement. A buy-out agreement can be based either on a flat sum of money, or on a percentage of profits over an agreed-upon period of time. If a buy-out agreement isn't established between the parties, some chaos is sure to result if and when that event occurs. You can always draw up a new agreement on any of these matters as time passes, and as conditions change. But a set of agreements should also be made at the outset, so that there's never any question in anybody's mind as to who gets what, if, and when.

Partnerships, particularly limited partnerships, will likely be governed by the Uniform Limited Partnership Act in each state. Your attorney should see to it that your papers comply with the provisions of that act, which are likely to include filing a registration form in the county in which you're doing business.

A partnership as such is not a taxable entity. But a partnership must file an extensive tax return each year (on Form 1065) and each individual partner takes his specific share of the income or loss from the partnership return and applies it to his own individual 1040 Form.

Partnership activity may go under different guises, such as a syndicate, a group, a pool, a joint venture, or any other title given to an unincorporated organization that is carrying on a business venture. Generally, for tax purposes, all of these endeavors are considered partnerships.

What about two individuals joining forces as a sole proprietorship—is this a partnership? For tax purposes, it probably is. If you and your joint venturer are sharing profits and losses, and if each of you contributes cash or property or labor or skills to the business, the Internal Revenue Service is likely to consider your business to be a partnership, thus requiring the filing of Form 1065. Beyond IRS concerns, you are, for all intents and purposes, engaged in a partnership whether you've signed a formal agreement or not. And since that's the case, you might as well sign a formal agreement, if for no other purpose than to protect each partner in the event that one wants to withdraw. With a formal agreement, there'll be no question about the distribution of assets and liabilities at the point of withdrawal.

**CORPORATIONS.** People tend to think of corporations in the context of General Motors, IBM, and AT&T—"big business." What many people do not know is that a sole individual can incorporate, and many thousands do every year. A corporation is a legal entity in its own right. It's like a person, a body. The name is derived from the Latin *corpus,* or body. The corporation is a legal device that offers the individual a shelter from claims of the public. When you deal with a legitimate corporation, your dealings are with that entity, and you have no claims against the individuals who have established the corporation, except possibly for their own initial investment in the corporation. The letters "I-n-c." after a corporation's name are intended to notify the public that they are dealing with a corporation, an entity in its own right, and not with an individual, even if it is a one-person shop.

So forming a corporation sounds appealing—you pay the money, file the papers, go into business, and your creditors can't touch you if things go bad. Right? Wrong. In all likelihood, the beginning business owner will have to sign individually to guarantee all of the corporate obligations. In effect, then, the insulation from liability that a corporation offers is really of little benefit to the beginner. It may take many years of strong, profitable performance before a corporation is regarded by lenders and suppliers as creditworthy in its own right.

Putting aside the question of credit, what if you incorporate and agree to supply 10,000 widgets to an important client within ninety days, and then fail to do so? Can the client sue only the corporation for lack of performance, and not yourself? Prudent businessmen dealing with newly incorporated firms are likely to require the individual principals to guarantee the corporation's performance, thus keeping you on the hook for everything that your corporation promises it will do.

So, if a newly formed corporation can seldom take advantage of the shielding that the legal structure offers the big wheels, what good would a corporate form be for a new business venture? As a way to raise capital, through the sale of stock? This may be possible, but not feasible. The legal and brokerage fees involved in such activity can be extensive, and there is no guarantee that the capital will be raised. Prudent investors will look to the principals for the extent of their own capital involvement in the venture, and unless you have enough money or skill or exclusive ideas, their confidence is not likely to be won easily. The limited partnership would probably be a better way to proceed if you do need to obtain capital from outside sources (other than by borrowing it). Or the hybrid subchapter S corporation would probably be more desirable. This is an entity that is allowed to have up to ten shareholders, but that does not pay its own taxes. It's akin to a limited partnership in that it files only an informational return, and then each of the venturers is attributed his own share of profit or loss for his or her particular individual return.

Prior to the passage of the Employee Retirement Income Security Act (ERISA) in September 1974, the corporate form was looked upon with great favor by many small individual business owners and professional people (doctors, lawyers, dentists, etc.). The attractive features were not the insulation from liability or the ability to raise capital through the sale of stock, but certain advantages with respect to establishing pensions funds, profit-sharing funds, and otherwise stashing away current income for future use, free of current taxation. Prior to the passage of ERISA, a self-employed individual could have established a Keogh plan, which would have permitted him to contribute up to 15 percent of his annual income into a do-it-yourself form of pension program. The contribution was limited, though, to an annual maximum of $2,500. Thus, if a self-employed businessman earned $30,000 in a given year, he could contribute only $2,500, not $4,500, which would have been 15 percent of his income.

Under a corporate structure, the individual could have contributed a much higher amount to his pension plan, and realized substantial tax savings in the process. Further, many other kinds of expenses, such as certain life-insurance premiums, medical reimbursements, and the like could have come out of the corporate till as deductible expenses, rather than out of the individual's pocket where they are not deductible, or where the deduction is severely limited.

But ERISA changed much of that. As an adjunct to ERISA, the annual limitation on the Keogh plan was raised to $7,500, thus strictly limiting the appeal of the corporate form to a vast number of small business owners who couldn't contribute that much anyway. Further, ERISA imposed a mind-boggling array of regulations from both the Internal Revenue Service and the U.S. Department of Labor on the maintenance of pension and profit-sharing plans. The book work and legal expenses involved in maintaining such plans had, by late 1975, caused thousands of such plans to be terminated because the small businesses couldn't put up with the added burden that ERISA had imposed on them.

Another recent development that has cast doubts over the value of the corporate form for many small businesses is the Social Security Tax, or self-employment tax, as the case may be. The very rapid rise in these taxes in the past few years has created a wide discrepancy between the two. And the result has been that the sole proprietorship has become the favorite over the corporation, particularly if you're operating strictly on your own.

As a sole proprietor, you pay a self-employment tax, which constitutes your contribution to your Social Security program. For 1976, your contribution will have been 7.9 percent of the first $15,300 of your earnings, or a maximum of $1,208. If you incorporated, and were the sole employee, both your corporation, as the employer, and yourself, as the employee, would have to contribute 5.85 percent of the first $15,300, or a total of 11.7 percent, for an ultimate obligation of $1,790. That's a difference of $582 right off the bat, not an insignificant sum, particularly for the individual just starting out on his own.

Further, if you are the sole employee of your own corporation, you'll have to pay the federal and/or state unemployment tax, which can amount to another $134 each year. Also, you'll be obliged as an employer to provide workmen's-compensation insurance for your employee (yourself) at a sum that varies, depending on the kind of work you're involved in. Although this workmen's compensation does provide a measure of insurance in the event of disability caused by a work-related accident, it may do nothing more than duplicate the coverage you already have in your private health policy.

When you add these taxation costs to the ongoing legal and accounting costs that you're likely to have with the corporate structure, you'll find that there's a very heavy load to carry if you want to operate under the corporate umbrella. The benefits, which you'll have to pin down precisely with the aid of your F.A.I.L.-Safe advisors, will have to at least offset those added cost burdens. Otherwise, it probably won't be worth it to incorporate.

Another area that requires investigation and that could have a bearing upon the form of business that you should adopt is the licensing requirement in your state or community for the type of business you'll be involved in. These requirements will vary from place to place, and the lack of proper licensing can be a costly mistake. Occupations that may require various degrees of licensing include accountants, architects, auto-repair shops, barbers, cemetery brokers and salespersons, chiropractors, collection agencies, contractors, cosmetologists, dentists and dental hygienists, dry cleaners, electronics repair dealers (TV, radio, etc.), employment agencies, engineers, funeral facilities, furniture and bedding manufacturers, geologists, insurance adjusters, insurance salespersons, landscape architects, lawyers, manicurists, marriage and family counselors, nurses, opticians, osteopaths, pharmaceutical manufacturers and wholesalers, physical therapists, physicians and surgeons, podiatrists, private patrol operators, psychiatric technicians, psychologists, real-estate agents and brokers, repossessors, shorthand reporters, social workers, stockbrokers, structural pest-control operators, and veterinarians.

## 3. Financial and Capital Needs: Analysis and Projection

The prime cause of failure of any new business endeavor—be it buying into an existing situation, franchising, or starting from scratch—is the lack of proper financial planning and capitalization. Compounding the problem is the question of timing: an entrepreneur may estimate the right amount of money to get his operation under way, but fail to account for the length of time it will take before the venture starts returning a profit.

It takes, on average, from two to three years before a new business venture breaks into the black. Until that time, the venture can be a drain on your assets and your borrowing capacity. If you don't prepare yourself to survive that initial ordeal, you may have to pack it in prematurely, which can be a bitter disappointment. If you can hit a point of profitability before two years have elapsed, more power to you. If you haven't hit the profit mark by the end of three years, it may be time to get back to the drawing boards.

Whether you're setting up to do free-lance accounting or typing in your home or you're opening a retail outlet in a shopping center, you have to pay attention to the necessary start-up costs, the capital you need to get you to a break-even point, and the projections that will indicate to you how much income you can expect for yourself once the project is in operation.

Prior to doing those projections, it's necessary to take a close look at your own personal life style, and how much flexibility you have in it to allow you to follow your dreams, should it become necessary for you to make sacrifices. I've drawn up a series of questions that will help you to focus on that very important point. They're based on the assumption that you'll do no borrowing, for loans will have to be repaid sooner or later. It's a hard-nosed look at how much sacrifice you may be willing to make, should the need arise—and you should expect the need to arise. If you're fortunate enough to continue at your income level without missing a beat, as many of the individuals in the case histories were, that's fine. But if you're not prepared for the contingency of lost income, your whole psychological framework and motivation can be affected negatively, and this may cause the project to fail prematurely. Please answer the questions as honestly and as realistically as you can. This may require some estimating, but keep it in a sensible range. The answers to the questions won't predict the probability of success or failure, but rather your ability to cope with temporary cutbacks in your overall financial situation.

1. What is the economic value of your current work, including your salary, your fringe benefits (health insurance, life insurance, other benefits), and the amount that is being set aside for you for pension or profit-sharing?
2. What is the current personal cost to you of the work that you're now doing? This would include travel expenses, clothing, equipment, food and other personal consumption, dues, subscriptions, etc.
3. Assuming you want to maintain your current life style for at least the next year or two, how much will you have to take in to replace your current salary and the value of all the fringe benefits, subtracting the costs of your current work (question 2) that you won't have to incur in your new venture? For example, if you'll be working out of your home, you can eliminate substantial travel and clothing costs from your current situation.
4. What would you be willing to eliminate or modify in your current life style if your income (as determined in question 3) were cut by 10 percent per year as a result of your new venture? If it were cut by 20 percent? 30 percent? How far could you trim back your life style if your income were reduced by an even greater percentage?
5. How much capital do you now have available to you out of your own individual resources? These resources include your existing savings accounts, life-insurance reserves, pension and profit-sharing benefits that you would be able to take with you on leaving your current work, stocks, bonds, other investments, equity in your home.
6. How much of this capital would you be willing to risk in your venture, if you knew it might take five years to replace it? if it took ten years to replace it? fifteen years? twenty years? if there were a chance it might never be replaced?

7. If your new venture did, in fact, cause a drop in income, to what extent might you dip into your available capital to maintain your life style, and/or to what extent would you modify your life style in order to leave your capital intact for other purposes?

8. If, in fact, you did dip into capital to maintain your life style during your new business venture, how long do you realistically think the capital would last?

9. If you didn't dip into your capital in the event of a drop in income, and instead modified your life style to suit the new income, how long do you think you could be satisfied with these imposed limits on your life style?

10. Are there any windfalls—gifts, inheritances, etc.—in your foreseeable future? How certain are you of receiving any such fortune? Would you apply that money directly to your new business venture, or hold it in reserve for later personal use? If you would do both, what would the proportions be?

Discuss these questions, and your answers to them, with anyone close to you who might be directly or indirectly involved in your venture, such as spouse or partner. This mini-self-analysis will be important in evaluating your actual financial projections, because if your projections don't indicate enough cash flow, or if actual experience doesn't generate enough cash flow, you'll have to tackle the issue of where the extra money will come from. You can borrow it, and have to repay it later out of personal or business sources. Or you can seek outside investors who may be willing to take a risk on your plans. But if the borrowing isn't feasible and the investors can't be found, you'll have to look to yourself, and only yourself, to make up any deficits that do occur. How much of your funds you'll be willing to contribute, and for how long, will largely be a product of your own energies and motivations. Be prepared for any eventuality.

Let's examine the specific financial projections that you'll have to make as part of your work in setting up on your own. Warning: this discussion is by no means a substitute for the actual pencil-and-paper work that you must do with your accountant and/or banker. It is, rather, intended to provide you with guidelines that will help you to shape your own specific projections to suit your own needs and goals.

**START-UP COSTS.** These are the costs you'll incur before Day One, opening day. They represent the sum total of all that you will have invested, or borrowed, prior to the earning of your first nickel. They will, of course, vary from business to business, but the main categories are common to most endeavors.

**Research expenses.** This category includes all of the out-of-pocket expenses that you will have incurred in teaching yourself all that you have to know about the business. They include such items as books, magazines, consulting fees, travel expenses related to research, educational programs.

**Fixtures and equipment.** This item includes everything you'll need to open the door. Don't overlook any costs involved in installing such equipment. In shopping for your fixtures and equipment, make certain that you understand the exact cost of any installation, including any special electrical wiring or plumbing that has to be done, and any structural changes necessary to fit the equipment in its proper place. If your quoted prices for fixtures and equipment from the suppliers do not include installation, you may be in for a very rude surprise.

**Starting inventory.** Not too much, not too little, but just the right amount of whatever it is. Remember to plan to have your starting inventory available as of opening day, but not much before that. Timing is as important as the amount of inventory and the price you pay for it.

**Office supplies.** This category includes such things as typewriters, adding machines, stationery, invoices, and all other forms and equipment that you'll need for the proper operation of the office and bookkeeping of your business.

**Decorating and remodeling.** Be careful on this one. These expenses can easily fool you. Depending on the existing decor and quality of the premises you'll be occupying, the renovation costs can vary tremendously. Prior to committing yourself to a lease or purchase of a building, conduct a thorough survey of the premises to determine that all of the basic equipment is in satisfactory operating order, and that the structure itself is sound. Decor is particularly important in any business that deals with the public. The right decor can win customers, the wrong decor can chase them away. Consider obtaining the services of a professional commercial decorator. Firms that supply commercial interior furnishings often have a decorator on their staff whose services are included in the price of what you buy from the firm. Obviously, you're not getting these services free, but they may be well worth the higher price for the equipment if the office is decorated right. In using a decorator, it's essential that you examine other commercial interiors that he or she has designed, and discuss the success of the design with the proprietors of the premises. You may feel more comfortable hiring a decorator on a flat-fee basis. This would free you to buy whatever you need from whichever source offers you the best price. In the long run, this might represent a substantial savings. Discuss the matter with various firms in your area, and shop for the best deal.

**Deposit for utilities.** You'll probably have to place a deposit with the telephone company and the utility companies in advance of receiving service. This is customary in most communities, and while it doesn't amount to an awful lot of money, it's an item that must be figured into your start-up budget.

**Deposit or down payment.** It's customary for landlords to require a deposit of two months' rent in advance. One month's rent will apply to the actual first month of occupancy, the other will apply to the final month, and/or to any repairs that the landlord may incur to put the premises back into suitable condition should you damage or abuse it. Negotiate with the landlord to have the last month's rent deposit put into an interest-bearing account, payable to you. The interest may not seem like a lot of money at the beginning, but at the end of a number of years, it can amount to a tidy sum. If you're purchasing a building, include the amount of the down payment in your start-up budget. The mortgage payments that you make subsequently will be considered as a form of operating expense, but in the meantime, you have a substantial amount of money tied up in the premises.

**Legal and professional fees.** This item includes all of the F.A.I.L.-Safe expenses relative to your new venture: legal fees for drawing all appropriate papers, including leases, partnership agreements, corporate documents, mortgages, contracts with suppliers, employees, etc. Accounting expenses include all costs incurred relative to the initiation of the business.

**Licenses and permits.** Be sure you obtain all licenses or permits that your business might require and add their fees to your start-up budget.

**Preopening advertising and public relations.** These include expenses of announcements, media advertising, public relations and other publicity.

**Operating cash.** During the period immediately prior to opening, and for a short period thereafter, you're likely to need cash on hand to pay salaries of employees who are helping to set up the operation: janitors, sign painters, movers, printers, and any other related workers. This is a sort of catch-all, but it can catch quite a lot.

**Owner's draw during pre-start-up time.** If you'll be drawing out any income prior to opening day, that amount should be figured in your start-up cost. Whether or not you do so depends on your cash needs and on the amount of cushion you have to work with. Obviously, the less you draw out in advance, the more there will be to help see you through the actual operation.

Some of these start-up costs you may pay for in cash, out-of-pocket, either with your own money or with money from outside investors. Other expenses may be paid over a period of time, such as your equipment or fixtures. You may have borrowed from the bank to buy these items, or the supplier may have extended credit to you for their purchase. To the extent that you'll be paying in the future for any of these items, these amounts must be transposed to your actual operating budget and the accounts maintained regularly.

**THE PROJECTED OPERATING STATEMENT.** This may be the most important key to your overall plan to go into business for yourself. The accuracy with which you project your income and expenses, and the flexibility you allow yourself should your projections be off target, can make or break your venture. If you overestimate sales, or underestimate expenses, you can be doomed before you start. You can't do enough homework on this subject. And even after all the homework, your success will still be largely up to the hands of the fickle public. Professional help from a banker and an accountant who are familiar with your type of business can be invaluable. Here are some additional sources that offer guidelines for establishing projections.

*Annual Statement Studies.* The Robert Morris Associates, Philadelphia National Bank Building, Philadelphia, Pennsylvania 19107. $10. It may also be available at your public library. This book contains samplings of operating statistics for a wide variety of businesses. But they should be construed only as broad guidelines, for in the final analysis, no two businesses are really alike. Two identical shops in identical locations with different owners can produce broadly different statistics, if for no other reason than that the personalities and energies of the owners differ. The Robert Morris Associates makes this necessary disclaimer with respect to the statistics contained in the book:

"Robert Morris Associates can not emphasize too strongly that their composite figures for each industry may *not* be representative of that industry (except by coincidence), for the following reasons:

"1. The only companies with a chance of being included in their study in the first place are those for whom their submitting banks have recent figures.

"2. Even from this restricted group of potentially includable companies, those which are chosen and the total number chosen are not determined in any random or otherwise statistically reliable manner.

"3. Many companies in their study have *varied* product lines; they are 'mini-conglomerates,' if you will. All they can do in these cases is categorize them by their *primary* product line, and be willing to tolerate any 'impurity' thereby introduced.

"In a word, don't automatically consider their figures as representative norms, and don't attach any more or less significance to them than is indicated by the unique aspects of the data collection."

With a disclaimer like that, you might conclude that there's little value in researching these studies. Not so. They can give you some bases for judgments that you'll make on your own, and this is certainly far better than proceeding blind. Study them, evaluate them, and try to shape your own projections accordingly.

*Barometer of Small Business.* Accounting Corporation of America, 1929 First Avenue, San Diego, California 92101. Published semiannually. Yearbook for previous year available each March. $10. Mid-year published each September. $6. Both can be obtained as annual subscription for $12.

*Key Business Ratios.* Dun & Bradstreet, 99 Church Street, New York, New York 10007. This publication is usually available in local Dun & Bradstreet offices.

In addition, explore the Appendix of this book for the resource materials appropriate to your own venture. The Small Business Administration series, *Small Business Bibliographies,* contains an abundance of reference material for the most common types of small businesses. These reference materials include books, trade-association publications, governmental statistics and publications, magazine articles and much more. They are available at no charge from your nearest SBA office. (Please note that all prices for the above books are subject to change without notice.)

In preparing your operating projections, you should look at least three years into the future, and you should project high, medium, and low ranges for all items on the list. Strenuously avoid the temptation to fudge your projections to show an early break-even point. If your projections indicate a break-even point between the twenty-fourth and the thirty-sixth months, you'll be fairly close to the norm for most businesses. That doesn't mean that you shouldn't strive to break even as quickly as possible. But if you've set too optimistic a break-even date, and you find yourself not meeting it, you're liable to become discouraged unnecessarily.

How do you account for inflation in establishing a projection of operating expenses? With some difficulty. Many businesses will be able to automatically adjust for inflation by increasing the prices for their goods or services as the prices for their own operations increase. But not all businesses can do this effectively. Unfortunately, inflation is largely an unknown element that you'll have to contend with as it occurs. For the sake of the initial projections, you might want to assume that you can slide your prices up and down in line with your own costs. If you do so for the sake of making the projections easier to handle, don't forget for a moment that this is an ideal situation, and that the real situation may differ appreciably.

A simple profit and loss projection will contain the following items:

1. Gross sales. This is the total revenue received by you as a result of marketing your product or your service.
2. Cost of sales. This pertains to the goods that you have had to purchase in order to realize the sales: the inventory, the parts, etc.
3. Gross profit. This is the difference between your gross sales and cost of sales.
4. Salary of owner/manager. This is what you pay yourself.
5. All other salaries and wages.
6. Rent, or your interest, real-estate taxes, and property taxes if you own the building. The principal portion of your mortgage payment is considered a repayment of debt, which, theoretically, should come back to you when you sell the building, and is, therefore, technically not an operating expense of the business.
7. Advertising.
8. Delivery expenses and other transportation requirements. This includes your own car to the extent that it is needed for business purposes.
9. Supplies.
10. Telephone and postage.
11. Utilities. This includes electricity, heating fuel, water, and any special assessments for sewage, street cleaning, etc.
12. Insurance. The whole bundle. See the section on insurance for a more detailed view of this item.
13. Taxes. This includes Social Security taxes, unemployment taxes, and any other taxes related to the operation of your business. This does not include income tax.
14. Interest on any business loans that you may be repaying.
15. Maintenance. This includes the building, the parking lot (if any), the sidewalk, and the equipment. It also includes janitorial expenses.
16. Legal and other professional fees.
17. Depreciation or reserve for replacements. This is one of the most overlooked and dangerous areas in your financial projections. As any business owner knows, and as any novice will soon find out, the tax laws allow you to write off, or depreciate, certain equipment that by nature becomes obsolete. This can include fixtures, equipment, and even the building itself.

    The tax write-off that's allowed for depreciation is very attractive to the business owner, but he often fails to recognize the other side of the coin: that these items do, in fact, depreciate in value and eventually have to be replaced or renovated or repaired. If he has failed to set aside the necessary reserves to pay for the replacements, he can find himself in a financial bind when replacement time rolls around.

It's as true with household budgets as it is with business budgets: you know for certain that some day your television set and your washing machine and your hot water heater are going to expire. But as long as they're working properly, you tend to take them for granted. Then, when their end comes, and you're suddenly looking at a budget busting many hundreds of dollars to replace them, you curse the item for expiring prematurely. If you haven't set aside a reserve for replacements, you'll likely have to borrow to replace the item, and that can add 10% to 20% to the cost of the item. And, if your household is anything like mine, when one thing goes, at least three things go. It's almost as if fate had decreed the common expiration date of all these costly appliances.

In your business endeavor, you should attempt to project realistically the expected life of all replaceable items, and project whatever fund you think you can afford to accomplish their replacement. You may not want to set aside the entire amount for replacement, preferring to borrow a part of it. That's all right, as long as you have planned in advance for the contingency, and programmed your borrowing needs so that the replacement of an appliance or a fixture won't interfere with other, perhaps more important, borrowing needs that may occur at that time.

18. Bad debts and returns. No business is without them. Don't think that you can escape this headache. The extent of your bad debts—that is, those that you can not collect—will depend largely on the care you give to the granting of credit, and the follow-up procedures you use in collecting obligations owed you. The cost that you absorb on returned merchandise will vary depending on whether the manufacturer is willing to accept returns, or whether you'll have to accept them yourself. This should be understood when you make arrangements with suppliers.
19. Factoring costs. This represents the expenses you'll incur should you sell your accounts receivable in order to obtain cash on the barrelhead. One common way that retailers and service firms do this is through the ubiquitous bank credit card. These cards are a wonderful way to get your cash immediately, but the advantage comes at some cost. The cost will vary depending on the banks in your area, and on the volume of business that you do with them. You can determine these expenses at the time you sign up with the banks for your credit-card arrangements. If you're granting credit to customers, you may wish to sell your receivables directly to a bank, or to a factoring firm. A factoring firm is one that specializes in the purchase of accounts receivable and then takes its own chances on collecting the amounts due. The cost of factoring in this way will also depend on your volume and on the quality of the accounts. The cost can be considerable, particularly if the quality of the accounts is poor. To keep this cost at a minimum, or to eliminate it altogether, it's essential for you to exercise all of the proper precautions in the granting of credit.

These include the proper credit search on the customer, available at your local credit bureau and through Dun and Bradstreet. Your banker can assist you in determining the proper precautions to take before you grant any credit to customers or clients.

20. Miscellaneous. The whole grab bag. If you haven't included fringe benefits for yourself and your employees, include them here. Other items are travel and entertainment expenses related to the operation of the business, temporary help expenses; appropriate costs of maintaining and operating your automobile; necessary cleaning and laundry expenses, business gifts that you make to valued clientele; subscriptions and dues for professional publications and organizations; subscriptions to technical journals; books and professional equipment necessary for the business; public relations expenses related to promoting the good will of the business, regulatory fees and license fees paid to local, state, or federal government; charitable contributions made by the business; dues to civic organizations such as the Chamber of Commerce; expenses that are necessary for your education or for that of your employees; and amounts that you pay to secure or protect franchises, trademarks, or trade names.

Proceed through this checklist again and again, with your accountant at your side and with the research materials referred to earlier. Anticipate absolutely every possible expense, and project them at high, medium, and low ranges. Also project your income and cost of goods at high, medium, and low ranges. Then start the juggling of figures to try to arrive at reasonable and rational projections for the first year, the second year, and the third year. Start with a projection of low income/high expenses and proceed to the reverse, high income/low expenses. Don't forget to figure in the ongoing expenses from your start-up costs that you'll have to be repaying.

Settle, if you can, on a feasible projection that you think can be obtained, but play it conservatively. It's always better to be surprised with a windfall than it is to be disappointed by an unexpected loss. The bottom line of your projection—the gross profit less all expenses, will illustrate your range of net profit.

From the net profit, you deduct any income taxes payable by the business, and any repayment of debt or distribution of profits to investors, such as dividends. The final amount that is left is the true profit picture, which represents the return on your invested capital. If it's in the black, and experience proves your projection to be correct, you're doing pretty well. If it's in the red, you're going to have to determine where additional funds will come from to support the business for the subsequent years, or where you can reduce expenses to put the bottom line into the black.

The overall operating projections will help you to determine adjustments that have to be made in your start-up expenses, and vice versa. The two interact. They can't be looked at separately.

**TIPS ON BORROWING.** If it appears that you will have to borrow to get your projections in line, meet with your banker at the earliest possible time to determine what your borrowing capacity is. Borrowing *needs* and borrowing *capacity* are two vastly different things. If you don't have the capacity to borrow what you need, you're going to be in trouble. After getting an overview of your total financial situation, and after reviewing your realistic projections, your banker can help you determine what your borrowing capacity should be currently, and in the future, assuming the projections are met.

If he feels that your borrowing capacity isn't adequate to suit your needs, he may recommend that you seek a co-signer, or that you obtain collateral to secure the needed loans. If you can provide either of these two kinds of protection for the lender, he may be willing to take more than the usual risk related to your questionable ability to repay. Banks and bankers are all different, and even though most have operation manuals, the rules can be bent depending on how you present yourself and your business activity. If you are realistic and have the right amount of controlled enthusiasm, the lender may be impressed favorably. If your figures are pie-in-the-sky, and your enthusiasm bears no relation to reality, he will spot it and act accordingly.

The proper relationship with your banker can assist you greatly in acquiring the funds you need and can reasonably repay. Consider these tips before approaching your banker with a specific loan request:

Do all of your homework beforehand. Know as precisely as possible exactly what you need, and how you plan to repay it. If, for example, you're borrowing to buy equipment, shop for the equipment first and have written offers from the suppliers to show your banker. The loan officer can serve you best when your specific needs are clearly stated. A loan application with question marks still on it simply cannot be processed as readily as a completed one. If the loan officer has to say, "We'd like to help you, but come back when you have all the details," you've wasted your own time as well as his.

Make sure that all of your credit accounts are up to date before you apply. If need be, check with each creditor and with your local credit bureau to make sure that your history is clear and accurate. A credit report showing late accounts may not kill your chances of getting a loan, but it could cause delays and aggravation. A loan officer would rather see you with dirty workclothes and a clean credit file than the other way around. Under the Federal Fair Credit Reporting Act, you can determine from your local credit bureau just what is in your file. A nominal fee may be involved, but it's well worth it. Very often, without our knowing it, erroneous matters slip into our credit history. If a loan officer examines your credit history in conjunction with a loan application, and he sees derogatory material that you didn't know existed, it could have a damaging effect. The Fair Credit Reporting

Law stipulates how you can have erroneous material removed from your credit file. Examine your credit file periodically—perhaps every year or two—to make sure that it is correct and up-to-date.

Shop in advance to determine what kind of rates are being charged by various lenders. But remember that interest rates aren't the only thing you're shopping for when you seek a loan. Service and convenience also have to be taken into account.

When you visit your banker, bring with you a complete and up-to-date record of your financial situation. He's going to want all that information, and if you have it prepared in advance, it will save both of you time. Make sure you divulge all pertinent credit information, even if it's not good. He'll find out about it anyway, most likely, and if you haven't told him, he'll be liable to wonder why.

Inquire in advance about whether there are any specific requirements or taboos with the lender. Taboos may include age, length of employment, how long you've been living in the community, minimum down payments. Many lenders have set basic policies along these lines, and if you can't meet them, you may as well know where you stand early in the game.

Bring your spouse, if you are married, to complete the application and sign all the necessary papers. Under recent federal laws, discrimination because of sex is ruled out in all lending procedures. Technically, that means that your spouse may not have to sign the papers. But since your debt is a family situation, both partners should have a full and complete understanding of their involvements.

Go easy on hassling over interest rates. If you tell the loan officer that you can do better elsewhere, he'll probably tell you to go ahead and do so. If you've shopped in advance for rates, you should have a good idea before you go in as to what you'll be charged. Often, rates are flexible at institutions, and an inquiry might be in order. But petty bickering is likely to gain you nothing, and may well lose you a potential friend.

Don't act as though you're doing the lender a favor by coming to him. By the same token, don't make it appear as though the lender is doing you a favor by making you a loan. It's a business deal and should be treated as such by both sides.

Don't be disturbed if the loan officer asks you to give your other business to his institution, such as your savings account and/or checking account. This is part of his job, and he's expected to ask you these questions.

Don't wait until the last minute to apply for a loan. Anticipate your needs far enough in advance to take care of all the details. Very often other matters will hinge on whether or not you get the loan. If this is the case, keep the parties concerned informed as to your progress. Careful and thoughtful planning in this regard can avoid a great deal of last-minute nailbiting.

Don't demand an answer to your application within a certain time. You do have a right to have your papers processed promptly, assuming that everything is in order, and the lender will make every effort to do so. But delays can happen, such as receiving an incomplete or confusing report from the credit bureau. Often, too, an application may have to be considered by the loan committee, and this can take extra time. The loan officer isn't "passing the buck" when he refers an application to the loan committee. Your request may be for more than he has authority to approve, or he may want to get other opinions on a puzzling point in the application. The committee can be very helpful, simply by giving the borrower the benefit of all its best thinking. When you make your application, the officer should be able to give you a fairly good idea as to how long it will take to process. Perhaps he can speed it up a bit for you. But if you give him a deadline, an "or else," you're liable to antagonize him.

Don't balk if the officer asks you for a co-maker or collateral. He's trying to help you get your loan, and lending policies may require him to obtain more security. You may disagree with him, but instead of arguing about it, which won't help matters, ask him for an explanation. There's often room for compromise, but you might shut that door by being obstinate. A request for a co-maker or collateral doesn't necessarily mean that your credit isn't good. There might just not be enough of it. And remember, the loan officer doesn't have to ask you for extra security. He can turn you down flat, but in this case he doesn't want to.

Above all, remember that the loan officer is a human being. He has bosses to answer to and policies to adhere to. He wants to make good loans, and he wants to create good customers who will come back again. A loan interview can be easy, smooth, cordial, and efficient. The loan officer can become a friend, a helping hand, and a most valued advisor.

Or you and he can be quarrelsome, difficult, and tense during the interview—often because the borrower hasn't followed these simple suggestions. In such a case, the loan officer isn't liable to go very far out of his way to help you.

A loan officer is doing his job. Like yourself, he can be made happy or unhappy. He is there to help and advise you, but he has to stick to certain patterns. Know the patterns. Be prepared. Make a good friend and build your credit on a firm foundation.

## 4. Establishing a Location

Particularly if you're dealing with the public on a walk-in or drive-in basis, your location can be an instant make or break factor in your venture.

Attempts at overcoming the disadvantages of a bad location can take a tremendous amount of energy and money, and may never be successful. On the other hand, even a haphazard operator in a good location can succeed in spite of himself. If the public doesn't come to your door, the problem of location isn't as critical, but it's not to be sloughed off lightly. You still have to be accessible to suppliers, delivery people, and facilities that you'll be making use of, such as post offices and shipping locations.

Earlier we discussed some of the hidden factors that have to be examined in choosing a location. To recap briefly: Are there any plans afoot that would create excessive competition, such as the construction of a major shopping center in the immediate neighborhood? Are there any impending changes in the highway and traffic patterns that could divert traffic away from your place of business, to your disadvantage? Are there any imminent zoning changes that might permit uses of land or buildings near your premises that would be incompatible with your type of business or that would discourage customers from doing business with you?

Can you observe any subtle shifts in traffic patterns that may have a bad effect on your business, particularly if you're in a retail endeavor? A perfect example of some of these factors exists on the street on which my office is located. The changes have no effect on me because I'm not dealing with the public, but to the many dozens of retailers along the street, the change in the past few years has been near disastrous. The street is Fifth Avenue, in Scottsdale, Arizona. Until the early 1970s, it was regarded as one of the most prestigious retail shopping areas in any resort area of the country. Winter visitors by the tens of thousands descended on the area each year, their pockets laden with money to be spent on souvenirs and exotic merchandise not generally available elsewhere. In addition, thousands of residents of the greater Phoenix area, particularly the more affluent ones, came to Fifth Avenue for many of their luxury purchases. Until that time, the street was barely four blocks long, with a luxurious Trader Vic's restaurant in the middle of the strip. Some of the finest art galleries, jewelry stores, clothing boutiques, and other specialty shops in the West were among the tenants. And rentals for stores on Fifth Avenue were substantially higher than comparatively sized shops anywhere else in the greater metropolitan area. But for those merchants willing to spend the rental dollars, it was generally well worth it. It was a retailer's paradise, literally too good to be true.

At the western end of Fifth Avenue, there were four blocks of mostly vacant land, whose value had skyrocketed due to their proximity to the shopping activity. The lure of the heavy and wealthy traffic was so great that developers picked up the vacant lots, even at exorbitant prices, and proceeded to extend the Fifth Avenue shopping area by the additional four blocks, thus doubling its size. Further, more development sprouted along the side streets that intersected Fifth Avenue. This was the beginning of the end. The volume of traffic and the volume of square footage had struck a nice balance when Fifth Avenue was only four blocks long. Now, with its length doubled, the traffic was diluted and the result was a severe cut in the business of many of the retailers.

Then, in 1974, a major new shopping center was completed less than a half-mile from the Fifth Avenue strip. Two major department stores and a number of fancy specialty shops opened up in the shopping center and began to drain the Fifth Avenue traffic even more seriously. In 1975, three blocks to the south, a major motel and pedestrian mall opened, with dozens more shops around its perimeter. "For Rent" signs started sprouting along Fifth Avenue like mushrooms after a spring rain. In desperation, many of the Fifth Avenue merchants started to vary their product lines to appeal to a broader base of clientele. Their shops began to be filled with lower-grade merchandise, gimmicks, and junk. The typical stroller along Fifth Avenue now jingles his coins, whereas the former shopper used to riffle his bills.

Physically, Fifth Avenue is still extremely attractive, particularly at night when the western-decor storefronts are illuminated by strings of soft and appealing lights, which cast shadows on the majestic palms that line the sidewalks. But the heyday is over. Rental values are dropping, empty stores are going begging, and the fortunes that once were realizable have now evaporated. It's still by no means a disaster area, but people who signed long-term leases even three or four years ago are ruing that day. It all seemed so right at the time, but in the space of just a few short years, the whole picture has changed drastically.

Similar situations have occurred in well-established shopping centers. In 1975, the W. T. Grant Company went out of business. In many hundreds of medium to lower-priced shopping centers throughout the country the Grant stores had been the main shopping magnet. Without that major pulling power, many merchants in those centers found their traffic suddenly diminished, if not gone altogether. And there's barely a major city in the nation that hasn't had an interstate highway bypass its former through-traffic route, throwing into chaos countless motels, gas stations, fast-food restaurants, and all the businesses that cater to and supply those tourist-related activities.

Thus, extremely careful analysis of neighborhoods is in order. When you do find one that you're confident will remain relatively stable for at least enough years to allow you to build your reputation, you have to concentrate on picking precisely the right spot within that neighborhood. Of primary consideration is whether or not the product or service you're offering is in demand by the people who live within your marketing area. You don't open a fancy jewelry store in a lower-income neighborhood. And a low-end clothing store, or any other discount endeavor, might not succeed in or near a higher-income area. Your audience and your product have to be complementary, and you can help to assure success in that regard by paying attention to the demographics of your chosen community. Demographics refers to the relative affluence and age and the occupations of the inhabitants of the immediate area.

Depending on the type of business you're in, the following factors might be critical to your succss.

—The number of persons and families in the trading area, and how this has changed over a period of time.
—Where most of the inhabitants work.
—The number of young and old persons, and the numbers of children and teenagers.
—The number of families with small children and teenagers.
—The number of one-person households, and the number of small and large families.
—The incomes of the families and individuals.
—Whether the area is an older, established one or one in which most residents are newcomers.
—The number of families that own their homes. The number that rent.
—The value of the homes. The approximate monthly rental.
—The age and quality of the homes.
—Whether the homes have air conditioning, and other appliances.
—The number of families that own an automobile. The number that own two or more.

It doesn't take much imagination to see that the answers to these questions can be an important determinant of success or failure for a wide variety of businesses, particularly retail ones. By dovetailing these demographics with the projected audience for your product or service, you can see whether or not you're on the right track.

The demographic information can be obtained easily through the census data available for every community in the United States. The U.S. Census Bureau breaks down its analysis of cities into census tracts, with an average tract having a population of between 4,000 and 5,000 residents. The statistical information on the residents of each tract is considerable, including breakdowns as to race, sex, country or origin, years of school completed, occupation, income, housing value, rental value, structural equipment, appliance equipment, automobiles, and overall condition of housing. These publications are available for reference purposes at most major libraries. They may also be used or purchased at any of the offices of the U.S. Department of Commerce, which are located in forty-three major cities. In addition, some 700 "cooperative" offices run by local Chambers of Commerce offer Bureau of Census leaflets and other informative printed matter. As a general guide to this valuable asset in choosing a location, ask your nearest Small Business Administration for their publication number 154, *Using Census Data to Select a Store Site*. It's free, and well worth reading. It contains a listing of where you can find additional information on this subject.

Whether you're buying or renting, retail or industrial, large or small, it's imperative that you examine the premises thoroughly before you sign any commitments to take occupancy. Even if the landlord is responsible for all repairs and maintenance, it's nothing but a headache to move into premises and have to be hassling the landlord to fix the roof, patch up the walls, or do whatever else he's responsible for doing. Even if he does this work swiftly and properly, it still can cause you some inconvenience in your day-to-day operations. In the event that the landlord is slow to respond, your aggravation will grow rapidly.

For a relatively small investment, you can hire a contractor and/or the appropriate tradesmen to give the premises a complete inspection, including the structural elements, the plumbing, the wiring, the heating, the cooling, the insulation, the roof, the parking lot, the hardware and locks, the alarm system, if any, the hot-water heater, if any, and any other mechnical appurtenances on the premises.

Turn the faucets on and off. Turn the lights on and off. Flush the toilets. Try all of the locks. Does everything work properly? Are there any strange noises or vibrations that occur as a result of using the plumbing or any machinery on the premises? Do the windows and doors open and close properly, and can they be locked to the satisfaction of the insurance company covering you for burglary? Does the premises have adequate electrical power and drainlines to satisfy any special needs that you'll have?

As important as these inspections are for a tenant, they're ten times more important if you're to become the owner of the building. A building, like a human body, decays over the years. It shows its age, and not always gracefully. If you don't know what infirmities you're taking over, you're going to have to patch them up when they become visible. And that could cost a bundle.

What kind of occupancy should you consider as a new entrepreneur? Leasing? Buying an existing building? Owning your own building? Proceeding with the most conservative course, it makes the most sense to rent, with an option to buy. A straight lease without any option to purchase might be less costly at the outset—the owner of the building is likely to charge you a premium for the privilege of buying the building from him at a set price at some time in the future. But the protection that you obtain by having the option to purchase may make paying the premium well worth it, particularly if it turns out that the location is just right for you. Actually, even more ideal than a lease with an option to purchase is a lease with an option to renew the lease and then with an option to purchase. Generally, any leasing arrangement should be for as short a term as possible, say, one to three years, with renewal options attached. This gives you the flexibility of getting out if things don't work out, or of extending your lease if you are happy with the premises. If your business is successful enough, and you have the option to purchase, you can tackle that alternative when the option comes due.

If the owner of the building is reluctant to negotiate an option to purchase, consider offering him this deal: a lease with a right of first refusal to purchase. A right of first refusal is somewhat different from an option to purchase. With an option to purchase, the owner has given you the contractual right to buy the building, at an agreed-upon price, no later than an agreed-upon date. In other words, suppose you lease the premises for a three-year term, with an option to renew for an additional three years, and with an option to purchase before the end of the sixth year, for $100,000. This means that any time until the end of the six years, you can exercise your right to purchase the building for $100,000. Presumably, the amount of down payment and other terms will have been included in the original option.

The option to purchase, in effect, takes the building off the market for the owner. He can't sell it to anyone else because he has obliged himself to sell it to you. This is why he is likely to charge a premium, that is, a higher rental—because he is taking the building off the market.

If you have a lease with a right of first refusal on a purchase, your agreement is, in effect, the following: if, during the term of your lease, or any renewals thereof, the owner comes up with a bona fide purchaser who is ready, willing, and able to pay a certain sum to buy the building, the owner must come to you and give you the right of first refusal. In other words, if you can meet or beat the prospective buyer's price within an agreed-upon time (usually not more than thirty days), you can then buy the building. If you don't exercise this right of first refusal, and the owner sells the building to the other purchaser, your lease should stipulate that the new purchaser obtains the building subject to your lease rights.

By giving you the right of first refusal, the owner is not taking his building off the market. He's still free to offer it for sale to anybody, at any time. You have a measure of protection in that you can choose to meet any actual price that's offered to the owner. That price might be higher or lower than what you might have agreed on in an option to purchase arrangement. That's the chance you'll have to take. But since the owner is not taking the building off the market, you have a strong negotiating point to keep the terms of the lease as low as possible. The landlord is giving up nothing, and he can thus afford to be more moderate with you on the lease terms.

A lease, whether it has options or not, is a legally binding contract, and you shouldn't sign it without legal counsel. The purpose of a lease, other than to assure you a continued right to occupy your desired premises, is to offer you some stability with regard to this major aspect of your overhead. In other words, you want your costs to be as controlled as possible, and the proper arrangements in the lease can assist you with this. In the language of the realtor, there are gross leases and net leases. The gross lease is the one in which the tenant pays a flat sum for the term of his lease, and the landlord pays for all of the necessary expenses, including utilities, taxes, repairs, and maintenance. The net lease is one in which the tenant pays everything. Obviously, at the outset, the cost to the tenant of the gross lease will be higher. But the ultimate, total cost of everything may be lower on a gross lease. The reason is that the extra costs for utilities, maintenance, and taxes will keep going up, and if the net lease tenant is responsible for all of those, he eventually may pay more than he might have on the gross lease. A smart landlord will figure out the year-to-year increases in the various areas, and will probably build them into the lease.

To defend yourself and allow for the most favorable lease terms, consider calling in a local realtor who specializes in commercial leasing and getting his opinion as to the long-term differences between a gross lease and a net lease.

Landlords generally prefer net leases, because that relieves them of a lot of the headaches of paying the extra bills and worrying about the increases. One common compromise between the gross lease and the net lease is a lease that contains "stops." A tax stop, for example, will stipulate that the landlord pay a certain amount of the real-estate taxes, often up to the amount paid for the previous taxable year. If taxes increase beyond that point, the tenant bears the cost of the increase. Similar "stop" provisions can be included with respect to utilities and special assessments. It would be to the tenant's benefit to put a stop on top of the initial stop—that is, a provision that would limit the tenant's liability after a certain point.

For example, if the basic tax-stop clause requires that the landlord pay the first $1,500 in real-estate taxes, and that the tenant pay anything over and above that amount, the tenant should request a provision that would limit his liability to the next, say, $500. In such a case, the landlord would pay the first $1,500, the tenant would pay the next $500, and the landlord would then assume liabilities for anything over the $2,000 level.

What about buying your own building or having one built to order for you? Is this only for the "big wheels"? Not necessarily, though perhaps it should be. I've seen too many small enterprises go under prematurely because they tied up too much capital and too much brain power in their own small building—perhaps as small as 1,000 to 2,000 square feet, and often designed with such singularity of purpose that it becomes unsuitable for other uses unless there is extensive renovation.

Conquer the impulse to get involved in your own building. Cut your teeth on the other person's capital. If you have a successful venture in the palm of your hand, leasing for the first two or three years isn't going to hinder your ultimate success. But ownership of a building can put serious crimps in your capital availability, and can turn a business destined for success into a muddle.

On the other hand, if your venture is destined for failure, you compound the problem if you own a building in addition to the business. Yes, there's always the possibility that you can sell the building and break even or make a profit on it. But that's a big maybe. If you're embarking on a new business venture with the hope of turning your profit on the ultimate sale of the building in the event that the business itself doesn't work out, I think you're a bit misdirected in your planning. If a business fails at a given location, very often a stigma will attach to that location, even though the business itself, and not the location, may have been the total cause of the failure. Thus, the failure of the business can have a negative influence on the ultimate sale of the building.

Assuming that you have limited capital to work with, isn't it likely that your capital can return a better yield for you if you put it to work within the business itself, instead of tying it up in real estate? If your capital, as invested in the business, can't be as productive as capital invested in real estate, then why not build a building and rent it out to some other tenant, to get the best possible return on your money?

Granted, there will be some types of businesses that require a specific location. Fast-food franchises are a typical example. If you are embarking on such an endeavor, and you can't find a rental situation that closely approximates what your ownership situation might be like, you may have to tackle the prospect of buying, or building, your own building. In such an event, extended deliberations with all the members of your F.A.I.L-Safe team are essential before you arrive at any conclusions. It is true that ownership of a building offers you attractive tax advantages via the depreciation of the building. But those advantages might not be of any value to you if you're not earning money in your venture. If you exhaust your capital in establishing the building, you'll probably have to borrow heavily for the capital needed within the business itself. And that extra 10 to 20 percent interest cost can more than wipe out whatever profit margin you're projecting. Plan extremely carefully in this regard, and become involved only if an appropriate rental situation, with an option to purchase, can't be found.

## 5. Insurance: Why Take Chances?

Embarking on any new business venture involves many risks. A number of them are unknown to you. Will the public respond to your offering? Will they pay the price you're asking? Can you produce your goods or services and make a reasonable living from the prices the public is willing to pay you? Will your success in one month, or one quarter, or one year repeat itself the following year? These are the risks you're willing to take in order to shoot for the goals that you've set for yourself. Very likely, you're going to need all of the energy and expertise you can muster to get on the better side of these risks and reach your payoff. To operate with maximum efficiency, you need a clear head, as free of worries, doubts, and concerns as possible.

Doesn't it make sense, then, to protect yourself against all of the possible known risks that you might be confronting? Why take additional chances when many of these can be eliminated by the proper insurance program? The trade-off is simple and attractive: for a small, known, fixed bet—your premiums—you're protecting yourself against possibly large and unknown losses should they occur. A sound insurance program, coupled with a prudent loss-prevention program, will allow you to maintain the most constant financial stability possible in your profit and loss statement. Following are the primary areas of insurance that you must examine in establishing your overall business plan. Discuss each of these types of coverage in specific detail with your insurance advisor.

**Basic fire and extended coverage.** Your basic fire-insurance policy protects your premises, your fixtures and equipment, and your inventory against loss due to fire and lightning. In addition to the basic fire protection, you'll probably want to obtain an extended-coverage endorsement, which extends the protection to such risks as windstorm, hail, smoke, explosion, vandalism and malicious mischief. In addition, if you'll be holding property that belongs to others, such as in a laundry, dry-cleaning plant, or repair shop, you'll want to be certain that this coverage extends to the customers' property. Also, you may want a special endorsement to cover specific loss of currency, securities, and other valuable papers.

Although fire insurance will compensate you for damaged goods and property, it won't protect you against the costs that you'll incur due to the interruption of your business. These costs will include the rental or mortgage payments that would continue in spite of your damaged premises, and also the profit that you'd have realized otherwise. Obtaining business-interruption insurance is the proper way to protect against this contingency. An extensive business-interruption policy can add greatly to your security. In addition to the above costs, a full-fledged business-interruption policy can also provide for payment of salaries to key employees, taxes, interest, and utility costs, as well as expenses incurred in the cleaning up and reopening of your business. It may not even be necessary that you close up shop completely: if you are seriously disrupted by the insured peril, you can still realize some recovery. Depending on the type of business you're involved in, you may also want your business-interruption insurance to cover losses that occur as a result of fire or other peril closing down a principal supplier or customer of yours; coverage can also be obtained if your operations are suspended because of a failure or interruption of the supply of power, light, heat, gas, or water furnished by a public-utility company.

Your basic premium for fire, extended coverage, and business-interruption insurance can be altered by two important factors: the loss-prevention precautions that you take and your willingness to carry a coinsurance clause. The insurance company can tell you the steps you can take to prevent losses, and thereby keep your premiums at a minimum. As for coinsurance, if you participate in this clause, which requires you to carry insurance usually equal to 80 or 90 percent of the actual value of the insured property, your premiums can be reduced, and you can collect the full amount of any loss. Commonly, if you don't have the coinsurance clause, you may not be able to collect the full amount of smaller losses. If you carry less than the prescribed coinsurance amount, the amount you can collect on a given loss will depend on the percentage of the full value of the property that you have insured it for.

**Liability insurance.** If someone is injured on your premises, or if the property of others is damaged as a result of your negligence, you can be sued for the amount of damages claimed. In the case of personal injuries, this can run into enormous sums. Liability insurance is an absolute necessity, particularly if you're dealing with the public on your premises. Under a proper liability policy, not only will the company pay any damages, but it will also defend you against any claims for damages. In addition to your premises, you should also have all vehicles and their drivers covered, as well as any employees who use their own cars for company business.

**Automobile insurance.** If you are using your own vehicle for business purposes, or others are using vehicles that you own, or others are using their own vehicles in pursuit of your business, you should have comprehensive protection against damages caused to or by any such vehicles. Coverage should include medical payments for anyone injured in an automobile accident, collision insurance, and comprehensive protection for fire, theft, and other hazards. If you will be carrying the property of others in your automobiles, see to it that that property is also protected.

**Crime insurance.** Burglary insurance protects you from losses where there are visible marks of a burglar's forced entry onto your premises. In recent years, with crime rates rising in many major American cities, insurance companies have been extremely careful about the manner in which they write these policies. Be certain that you understand all of the exclusions that exist in a given policy, and be sure that you fulfill all of the needed precautions so as not to void the policy. These precautions might include the installation of certain types of locks on your premises, and similar security measures.

Robbery insurance protects you from the loss of property, money, and securities by force, trickery, or the threat of violence. The insurance can be arranged to protect you both on and off your premises.

Most companies will offer a comprehensive crime policy for small business persons covering both burglary and robbery, as well as losses due to embezzlement by employees, mysterious disappearance, and like situations.

**Glass and boiler insurance.** Many business owners, particularly retailers, will want to look into glass insurance, which can cover them for damages to plate glass, glass signs and doors, show cases, counter tops, and similar glass installations. The policy will cover not only the glass, but its lettering and ornamentation as well, provided that such coverage is spelled out in the policy. The insurance can also cover the cost of temporary boarding up when necessary.

Boiler insurance, for the building owner or tenant responsible for the boiler, can cover losses due to explosions in the boiler. Discuss the details with your agent.

**Life insurance.** The proper life-insurance program for the small business owner can assure stability and continuity of the business in the event of the death of one or more of the key individuals. This is usually referred to as "key man" insurance. If you're operating solo, the proceeds of a life insurance plan can be available to the heirs to assist them in the continuing operation of the business, or they can offset the possible diminution in value on the sale of the business due to the loss of the principal. Further, a key-man policy for a sole proprietor can be a form of forced savings to provide a retirement program for the owner when the time arrives. In a partnership or corporate structure, key-man insurance can provide funds to buy out one of the principals in the event of his death. For example, if Joe and Tom are equal partners, and each of them has a key-man life-insurance policy on his life for $50,000, and Tom dies, the proceeds of the policy go to Tom's heirs as the buy-out price, and Joe thus owns the entire business at no out-of-pocket expense to him. This type of arrangement is, of course, subject to the initial agreement between the partners. In some situations, the payment of premiums on key-man life insurance may be deductible for a corporate structure. Discuss it with your agent.

**Disability insurance.** Where will you be if illness or accident renders you unable to work, either partially or totally? Disability insurance provides a regular monthly income for an agreed-upon period in the event of disability. This can help offset fixed overhead expenses, as well as provide a modest source of income for you during your disabled period. In some situations, you might be entitled to certain disability payments through Social Security or workmen's compensation, and you should determine what those payments might consist of, and under what circumstances they become payable. You are likely to find that those payments are not adequate, and you'll want to obtain a private policy on your own. If you have key employees, whose absence from work would be costly to you, you also might want to obtain such coverage for them, either at your own expense or on a shared expense basis with the employee.

**Workmen's-Compensation Insurance.** If you have employees, the basic common law requires you to provide them with a safe place to work, competent fellow employees, safe tools, and adequate warnings of any dangers. In addition, the Federal Occupational Safety and Health Act can impose stringent requirements along these same lines. In most states, you're required to provide workmen's-compensation insurance to cover employees who are injured on the job. In states that don't require the insurance, you can still be liable for injuries suffered by employees as a result of their work. Further, failure to provide adequate safety precautions under the federal law can result in the imposition of penalties on you. The cost of workmen's compensation is generally determined by the nature of the actual employment, and the benefits are defined under the policies and law applicable. If you are operating under a corporate structure, and you are the sole employee, you'll have to conform with state laws with respect to any required workmen's-compensation insurance on yourself, even though you're the only employee. Some employees may not have to be covered by workmen's-compensation laws. You should determine the specific regulations within your own state with respect to who must be covered and who need not be covered. But you should protect yourself in any case for injuries that may arise on the job, because it may be possible for an employee to bring a claim against you, even if you weren't required to cover him under the law.

**Employee-benefit coverages—fringe benefits.** The most common of these are group life and group health insurance. It's not mandatory that you provide these coverages for any of your employees, and, indeed, you may find the cost more than you care to bear. But if for no other reason than that you can provide protection for yourself at far lower than individual rates via group plans, they're well worth looking into. Commonly, employees may not be eligible for such protection until they have served in your employ for a specific amount of time. The cost and benefits of these programs should be weighed carefully. In theory, generous employee benefits should tend to reduce labor turnover. But there's no assurance of that. Much depends on your overall relationship with your employees, their continuing high morale or lack of it, working conditions, etc.

**Bonding.** Bonding is a form of insurance designed to prevent you from losing money due to various financial activities within your business. A fidelity bond, for example, can be placed upon an employee, particularly anyone having access to books or funds, to protect you in the event of an embezzlement or theft by the employee. When application is made for fidelity-bond coverage on employees, the insurance company usually does some investigating into the background of the individuals involved. Such investigation could disclose that the individual has been involved in questionable activities in the past, and you might, therefore, want to consider not hiring that particular employee.

A surety bond may be called for where certain work is to be performed, either by you or for you, and there's a question as to whether or not it will be performed fully and properly. For example, if your chosen new business is plastering, and you win a contract to do the plastering in a building under construction, you might be asked to provide a surety bond to guarantee that the work will be done properly. If you fail to do the work, or if the work is improperly done, the person who hired you will be compensated for any differences by your surety bond. On the other hand, if you hire someone to do plastering for you, you might require that person to have a surety bond to assure you of compensation in the event that he fails to perform properly.

## 6. Tax Considerations, and How the New Pension Law Can Aid You

The federal tax laws offer two unique ways in which you, as the independent business person, can shelter considerable earnings from taxes while at the same time setting up an attractive pension program for yourself.

When you chose to get free, you made a decision, conscious or otherwise, that nobody can take care of you better than you can yourself. You did this in spite of the fact that your employer had a pension or profit-sharing program to which he was contributing for your benefit, which would theoretically provide you with the means to live on once you had retired from your job. Now that you're forgoing his largesse, you have to take those positive steps to take the better care of yourself than he was doing.

Having money stashed away for the future can be painless when someone else does it for you. You never saw the money in the first place, since it was deducted from your paycheck. But it can be quite different when you have to consciously extract the money out of your available funds and exercise the willpower to put it away for the future instead of spending it now.

The concept of profiting most by working for yourself requires that you establish a program to take care of your future needs. The issue, more simply stated, is this: when it's time for you to retire, resign, or take in your shingle, if you find that you don't have enough money to live in the style you'd like to, *you don't get a do-over*. You can't go back to age 25, or 35, or 45 and enjoy a decade or two of stashing away money for the future. You have to do it while the doing is good, or it's too late. If I must, I will impose one criterion of success on anyone purporting to venture off on his own: success means that you've provided for your nonworking days as adequately as you did for your working days. Your work today, in effect, buys you freedom for the future.

The two attractive tax laws that allow you to create your own pension program have enough features built into them to help motivate you to take these important steps. If there were no tax incentives to stash money away for the future, many of us would neglect to do so. Indeed, that's the case with millions of people already. But these incentives do exist, and you should take advantage of them.

The two tax shelters are known as the Keogh plan and the IRA plan. Keogh is the name of the originator of the law, back in the late 1950s. IRA stands for Individual Retirement Account, which became law as part of the Pension Reform Law of 1974 (ERISA).

**THE KEOGH PLAN.** The Keogh plan was originally designed to induce self-employed individuals to establish retirement plans for themselves and for selected employees. Prior to the existence of the Keogh plan, self-employed individuals had no particular tax incentives with respect to retirement plans. The law sought to change that. As the Keogh plan now stands, a self-employed individual can contribute up to 15 percent, but not more than $7,500, of his annual earnings to the plan, and the amount contributed is tax-deductible for him. Under the Keogh plan, a self-employed individual must also make contributions for certain full-time employees, generally those who have been with him for three years or longer. Though the contributions for employees are tax-deductible for the employer, they are an out-of-pocket expense, the benefits of which must be weighed in accordance with their cost.

**INDIVIDUAL RETIREMENT ACCOUNT.** The other program, IRA, is essentially designed for individuals who are not covered by a qualified pension plan at their place of work. For the most part, this is the way IRA has been promoted across the country. But as regulations stand as of this writing, self-employed individuals are also eligible for IRA plans, provided they are not covered by any other kind of IRS-qualified pension programs.

There are two essential differences between IRA and Keogh. The amount that can be contributed to an IRA plan in any given year is 15 percent of earned income, but with an annual maximum of $1,500. Unlike Keogh, though, an IRA-plan participant need not make contributions for his employees, if he has any. In other words, if you don't wish to contribute for the benefit of your employees, you can choose an IRA, but you'll be limited to the $1,500 annual maximum level of contributions. If you wish to contribute more than the IRA-limited $1,500 per year, then you can choose the Keogh plan and contribute up to $7,500 a year (or 15 percent of your income, whichever is less), but you'll have to make contributions to employees who qualify under the law. Your accountant can assist you in determining which of the two programs is more suitable to your current and future needs. It is possible that the annual ceiling on IRA will be increased in years to come. You should pay attention to the current regulations on IRA and Keogh if and when you have to make a choice.

Beyond those two basic differences, the IRA and the Keogh programs are generally similar. For example, in addition to your contribution being tax-deductible to you with both IRA and Keogh, the earnings that each plan generates are also tax-free. What does this mean to you in dollars and cents?

Let's assume that your taxable income is between $14,000 and $16,000 per year, and you're filing a joint return. Your income puts you in the 28 percent tax bracket. If you had contributed $1,000 to an IRA plan, you'd be entitled to take that as a deduction from your income. You can do this even though you don't itemize your other deductions, such as charitable contributions, interest expenses, and the like. In other words, you are paying taxes on $1,000 less of taxable income. Being in the 28 percent bracket immediately means that you pay $280 less in taxes than you would have if you had not made the IRA contribution. That's $280 cash in your hands instead of Uncle Sam's hands. It can't be made any simpler.

What happens to the $1,000 that you contributed to your IRA account? It earns tax-free interest for you. Let's say you put it in a savings account where it earns 6 percent per year. In a non-IRA account, you'd earn $60 during the year, and it would be fully taxable to you. After paying the taxes (assuming the same tax bracket as above), you'd have a net of $43 in earned-interest income. That goes back to work for you the following year to be compounded, to earn, and to be taxed. But the IRA account earns $60, and it all stays in your account. It's not taxed. The $60 goes back to work for you in the account, to be compounded, to earn, but not to be taxed.

Over the years the double tax advantages of IRA and Keogh can make an enormous difference in your total nest egg. But you have to let the money ride for a long pull to realize the ultimate benefits. The money can't be withdrawn from an IRA or Keogh plan until you reach age 59½, without having to pay penalties. (Withdrawals can be made without penalty in the event of death and certain disabilities.) When you do withdraw the funds from either IRA or Keogh, the funds are taxable at that time. But, theoretically, you'll be retired at that time, thus in a much lower income bracket, and thus pay a much smaller tax on the fund than you would have had you been paying taxes while you were earning the money. Once you've reached age 59½, the money can be withdrawn in one lump sum, or the withdrawal can be spread over a period of years. The penalty on early withdrawals is currently set at 10 percent of the amount withdrawn. This would be in addition to the taxes you'd have to pay on the money at the time of withdrawal. This may seem harsh, but the amount of the penalty is actually not much greater than the interest you'd have to pay if you had to borrow the same amount of money from a bank on a straight loan basis. Thus, the penalty factor should not deter you from salting your money away in one of these plans.

IRA and Keogh plans can take many shapes, including approved forms of savings programs, insurance, annuities, mutual funds, and certain retirement bonds issued by the U.S. government. It would make no sense at all to speculate with either IRA or Keogh money—the most conservative course would be the soundest, for you're then assured that the money will be there when you need it. If you need any reassurance on this point, seek out the many professional people, particularly doctors, who invested large numbers of Keogh dollars in mutual funds in the go-go years of the mid and late 1960s. By the early 1970s, after two market debacles, they had watched large portions of their retirement fund go down the drain. Don't let this happen to you. Avoid the appealing pitches that would have you believe your money will grow in value under certain management programs. There are no wizards on Wall Street. You'll have to shop around carefully for a sensible IRA or Keogh receptacle that will suit your long-term investment needs. Remember: an *investment* is a program whereby you are assured of how many dollars you will have X, Y, or Z years in the future. A *speculation* is a program whereby you have *no* assurance of how many dollars you'll have X, Y, or Z years in the future. You may have more, you may have far less. You can't afford to play games with your retirement fund. It has to be there, and you have to take positive steps to assure that it will be.

**Rolling over with IRA.** One of the most innovative aspects of the Pension Reform Law was a provision allowing people to transport their pension rights from one company to another when they changed jobs or when they left one job to go off on their own. Prior to the law, it was difficult, if not impossible, for an individual moving from one employer to another to take his accumulated pension benefits with him. If one was leaving a job to become self-employed, the pension benefits could be withdrawn, but substantial taxes had to be paid on them.

The Pension Reform Law allows an individual to use an IRA plan as a pension transporter—to collect his pension benefits accruing from one employer, and to roll them over into another pension plan of a new employer (both employers willing), or to establish a new retirement fund using the initial pension pay-out as a basis. Here's how an IRA roll-over would work for someone who's leaving a job to become self-employed: Upon leaving your current employer, you obtain whatever lump-sum distribution of pension benefits you're entitled to. Previously, you might have had to pay income taxes on the total amount you received. Under ERISA, any portion of the lump-sum distribution that you yourself had contributed would still be taxable now upon withdrawal, but the portion that the employer had contributed can be temporarily saved from income taxes by depositing the total sum into an IRA account within sixty days. You can then leave the money in the IRA account for the duration, or if you obtain new employment, where a qualified pension plan is available to you, you can, new employer willing, deposit your IRA funds into the new plan. This allows you to defer payment of income taxes on a substantial sum of money from a high-income bracket time of your life until retirement, when the taxes will take a much smaller bite.

The roll-over is especially attractive to those who are leaving their job and will not need the use of the accumulated pension money for many years. If you do need the money now, such as to help yourself get started in your new venture, you probably would not want to consider using the IRA, since it ties up the money for a long period of time. But if you have no need for the funds until you reach retirement, you'd be foolish not to explore the benefits of the IRA program.

Please bear in mind that the regulations of the Pension Reform Law are subject to continuing revision, and that the specific elements of the law pertaining to the IRA accounts and Keogh plans may be changed from time to time. It's important, therefore, that you subject whatever plan you choose to a periodic review by your financial advisors.

## 7. Marketing

Successful marketing is perhaps best described as an indeterminate combination of art, science, genius, and luck. It's a group of activities designed to find the audience that will be interested in buying your product or service, induce them to examine the product or service in surroundings that will put them in a buying mood, motivate them to buy it at a price that can throw off a reasonable profit to you, and leave them in a frame of mind that will lead them to return to consume your product or service again, and, you hope, again. Whatever your product or service, you have to market it. Whether you're creating song lyrics, repairing transmissions, teaching the tuba, purveying edibles, crafting jewelry, teaching yoga, or doing anything else that suits your fancy, you must package your product attractively, display it convincingly, and sell it profitably.

There is no such thing as thc perfect marketing formula for any product or service. The ideal item may go begging because of the personality of the proprietor, and a piece of junk may sell at a handsome price because of the selling expertise of the creator. The finest goods in the best location can bankrupt the owner because he had not purchased wisely, and a concept may miss its market altogether because of improper advertising. The right marketing plan for you will be the plan that ultimately works. That means a protracted period of trial and error, revamping, reshuffling, rewording, revising until you come up with the right combination that generates the right amount of dollars.

But as haphazard as the marketing approach may seem at first glance, there are some basic guidelines and pitfalls that should be borne in mind by the prudent entrepreneur. Failure to pay heed to certain marketing basics can cause chaos; proper attention to certain marketing techniques can minimize the margin of error. Some of the guidelines that you should bear in mind in developing your market plan follow.

**CUSTOMER ANALYSIS.** In the language of the trade, this might also be known as targeting and/or positioning. In essence, who are your most likely customers? Who is most likely to pay your price for what you're selling? Define your best potential customer list and concentrate on it.

Particularly in retail endeavors, you should attempt to get a reasonable estimate of the total market available to you. This will necessitate an evaluation of the competition and how much of a share of the market they currently control. How much penetration can you make into the existing market? What might you have to do to improve your penetration—lower prices, increase quality, present a broader selection of goods, offer more convenient hours?

Make use of industry sources in order to help you anticipate what your customers will be wanting and needing. Frequently, customer demand is based on what the industry offers them. Trade associations, publications, shows, and conventions are invaluable in teaching you what goods will be pushed in the coming season. The more knowledgeable you are about forthcoming trends, the better you'll be able to satisfy your customers' wants and cope with the competition.

Specific customer trends can be localized to your market area: Do people shop mostly in evenings, on weekends, or weekdays? Are your target customers cash or credit buyers? Try to determine if there are any trends in your market area that can affect your business, either short-term or long-term: Is the income base of the population fluctuating? Are there any physical changes in the market area that can add to or detract from your business potential? Are there changes in the make-up of your competition?

Once your business is ongoing, probably the best source of marketing information is the customer himself. Questionnaires or a suggestion box can be invaluable aids in determining whether the customers are satisfied with the product or service they're receiving, whether the price is acceptable, whether the location is accessible, whether the service is being rendered satisfactorily—and can they recommend any constructive changes that would enable you to serve them better?

**BUYING.** This is particularly pertinent for retail operations. The best salesperson in the world can't turn a profit if the goods haven't been bought right. Buying is a talent unto itself, and it takes many retailers years before they catch on to the best tricks of the trade.

As a retailer, you are the ultimate point of sale, and there are dozens of suppliers for every product you can offer vying for your few square feet of space. Getting to know your suppliers and what they can offer you is the first order of business in establishing a sound buying plan. This extends not just to the product itself, but to the service that the suppliers may have available with respect to display and counseling, the credit terms that they can make available to you, and the punctuality of delivery. In some retail businesses, return privileges may be important to your bottom line, and you should determine what those privileges might be, depending on the volume of your purchases.

Since many suppliers offer highly similar and competing merchandise, it may be worth your while to try to consolidate your suppliers into a small handful, rather than to attempt to deal with dozens of them. The more suppliers, the more paper work you'll have, the more invoices to pay, the more inventories to attend to, the more salespersons to deal with. All of these take time, and your time is money. Establish early on a form of evaluation for your suppliers: How do they hold their prices? How do they perform? etc. Much of this evaluation will be subjective because you're dealing with personalities. Don't be fooled by the hail-fellow-well-met who is fun to go out with on the town, but whose prices are out of line, or whose deliveries are unreliable.

An important element of smart buying is to keep in touch with new items that will be forthcoming, and to be totally flexible with respect to seasonal changes. The retail mix is constantly changing, and so are the public's tastes. If you're in tune with the changes and have anticipated them far enough in advance, you can ride with the happy trends and avoid the bad ones. This requires an investment of your time for researching new products (as noted above, the trade shows, publications, and associations are an invaluable source of information in this respect). It may also require more of an investment of your time in chatting with salespersons than you care to make. Pick your salespersons wisely, and they'll deliver the information you're seeking with a minimum of travail.

**KNOWING THE COMPETITION.** Espionage isn't necessarily recommended, but the more you can learn about your competition, the better you'll be able to market your own products and services. Visit their places of business. Examine their advertising. Analyze their packaging. Shop their aisles. Drink their booze. Eat their food. Utilize their services. And wherever possible, talk with their customers.

Can you spot their weaknesses? their strengths? their flexibility? their quickness or slowness to act? Some people are more competitive than others. You might, if you're keenly competitive, grab onto every weakness in your competitor's portfolio and try to capitalize on it. You might try to undermine your competitor's strong points, either in pricing, display, manner of service, or any other aspect. If you're not of the competitive ilk, perhaps you should beware of churning waters where competitive skill is necessary for survival. But there are some endeavors in which competition is not the key to success. If you're doing whatever you do as well as you can, you might satisfy your needs in the marketplace. But the other guy may not look at you that way. He may be fiercely competitive, out to do you in, and you may not be aware of it until it's too late. So, competitive or not, you have to be aware of the jungle that you're in, and deal with it accordingly.

**PRICING.** Once you've analyzed your customers, established a sound buying program, and gotten a bead on your competition, you have to establish a pricing program that will provide you with the profits you're seeking. Based on your analysis of the other elements, should you price below, at, or above the current market? Will you hold your quoted prices firm, or will you allow yourself to bargain with clientele? Will you offer discounts for quantity purchases, or to special groups? If you have products that aren't moving, do you have a set plan as to when you'll mark them down and how much? Goods that aren't moving take up valuable space that could be used for more successful merchandise. How long will you try to ride a dead horse?

Which of your products or services will attract customers when special pricing is offered, and what is the maximum pricing you can get away with in your market area on various products? What products or services can be used successfully as loss leaders?

Much of your pricing is subject to forces beyond your control—such as the prices you have to pay to the suppliers, which may fluctuate widely from time to time, and the prices that the competitors charge. Are you aware of these forces? Can you anticipate them? Can you cope with them adequately in the face of what your competition is doing?

An important aspect of your pricing program will be the extent that you offer credit facilities to your clientele. In recent years, the bank credit-card programs—Master Charge and Bankamericard, along with a growing number of local bank cards—have become far and away the most popular type of credit facility for the small business. Depending on the volume of business you do with a credit-card company, the cost of these services to you will vary. But in most cases, it will probably be considerably less than it would cost you to establish your own in-house credit program.

With your own in-house credit program, not only do you have the headache of examining all credit clientele and making judgments accordingly, but you're saddled with the bookkeeping and collection procedures that go along with it. Not offering credit facilities when your competition does can be a critical problem. Even offering lower prices than the competition may not offset his easy availability of credit, and the simplicity for the customer of giving you a card in order to consummate a deal. Interview your local banks to determine the terms on which they can offer their credit-card services to you, and discuss the matter with your accountant and attorney to be certain that you're in compliance with the Truth in Lending Law and the Federal Fair Credit Reporting Act, in addition to any specific state regulations governing the offering of credit.

Will your pricing policies give you a reputation that you might not desire? Will you become known as a "schlock shop," even though you don't think you are one? On the other hand, will you become known as too inflexible in your pricing when your competitors have a more liberal pricing stance? Will you allow your pricing policies to affect the basic service you give your clientele? On the other hand, if you charge what the traffic will bear, do you provide a similarly high quality of service to go with the high prices?

I'm sorry that there are no specific answers to all of these questions. The questions are really posed to stimulate your thinking in order to create boundaries within which you can operate profitably. In order to maintain some constancy of cash flow and profitability, there must be certain boundaries within which you function. You can always draw customers in by putting everything on sale, but you can also lose money in the process. By the same token, competition and the prices you yourself pay for raw materials will often necessitate changes in your own price structure. But the changes can't be haphazard. You have to establish some rules for yourself and hew to them. Establishing rules and following them are one way to avoid insanity in the sanity-testing endeavor of owning and running your own business.

**PROMOTION.** Promotion of your product or service may range from personal contact to the use of mass media. Promotion is how you tell the public about what it is you're offering them. Some products may be advertised successfully in certain media, and disastrously in others.

If your product or service is promotable through advertising, you must get to know all of the media available to you, and the firms that provide this service. The media include radio, television, newspapers, telephone directories, handbills, outdoor billboards, the so-called "penny-saver" or neighborhood shopping tabloids, direct mail, telephone solicitation, point-of-purchase displays, shopping bags, display cards in mass transit (buses, subways), magazines (don't overlook national magazines, which can offer regional or localized buys for specific firms or products at a very attractive price), and even skywriting.

In addition to the common advertising media, you may be able to promote your product or service through public relations. This generally entails hiring a firm that specializes in that activity, to obtain exposure for you in the mass media. It may include interviews of you, or stories about you and your product, on television, on radio, and in the local newspapers.

Meet with representatives of all of your local media, and learn their price structures and services. Many small businesses may not do enough advertising or public relations to satisfy the needs of an advertising agency. This doesn't mean that you can't get professional help with your promotional program, for many media, including radio, television, and newspapers, will offer considerable assistance in getting a decent program under way for your venture. You can also tie in with your suppliers, who frequently offer cooperative advertising dollars, scripts, and other aids for the various media.

Pay close attention to the advertising not just of your competitors, but also to other successful businesses that are dealing in lines similar to yours. Why do you think their advertising is successful? Naturally, advertising alone can't carry the ball—the businesses have to deliver the product or service to back up their claims. But advertising, which is what brings the bodies in, can make a tremendous difference.

While it's necessary for you to learn the various prices and services available from the media, it can be very confusing. Advertising people often talk in terms of cost per thousand—that is, how much it will cost you per thousand impressions. There are some media that are right for some products and wrong for others, regardless of the cost per thousand. An outdoor billboard may claim the lowest cost per thousand, and direct mail may be an exceedingly high cost per thousand. But some products deserve the higher-priced exposure, while others can get by with the lower-priced exposure. Much depends not just on the *number* of exposures, but on the *quality* of each exposure you're getting. An outdoor billboard may be seen by 100,000 people in the course of a given day, but the sighting of the billboard may be so repetitious that after the first one or two times, the effectiveness of the message is lost. The billboard becomes a part of the scenery. This doesn't mean that billboard advertising can't be effective. For the right product, and for the right purpose, it can be very effective. It can introduce the public to a new activity in a given area, or to a new product, or to a new pricing of an existing product. It can reinforce advertising in other media.

This same kind of interplay works with all of the media. You've heard television announcers suggest that you "see the ad in your local newspaper." And you've seen advertisements in newspapers urging you to watch a specific television show, which is sponsored by the same firm that placed the newspaper ad. But it's the advertising on the television show that will sell the product, and the newspaper is being used to get you to watch the actual sales pitch.

Advertising is a complex and confusing field, one that many business people say they can do well without, but one that almost everybody eventually tries. You can't ignore it completely, nor can you allow yourself to be awed by it. Experiment. Try a little here, a little there. Establish a sensible advertising budget for yourself and use this money wisely.

**DISPLAY AND DECOR.** You can't please everybody all the time, but you certainly have to give it a try. Display of your product and the decor of your premises can be a valuable asset to your business or a turn-off for your clientele. My thoughts turn to the ultra-posh doctor's office, replete with waterfalls and bubbling fountains, presumably to put the waiting patients into a restful, pastoral frame of mind. All I could think of was the money that went into this nightmarish decor, and how it would add to my bill. As I said, you can't please them all, but there are certain basic guidelines of good taste that you can seek out. I know many professional men who allowed their wives to be the decorator of their business premises. I'm not knocking their wives. In many cases they had nothing else to do and were glad of the opportunity to show off whatever talents they thought they possessed. But effective interior decor is a skill unto itself, not picked up at mah-jongg games or in the course of visiting department-store decorator boutiques. I'm certain that many wives turn out elegant quarters for their husbands, and I applaud them for it. But perhaps as often, they can be overindulgent, and lacking the necessary skills, create an environment that is not conducive to sound business activity as much as it is to wow their friends.

If you're seeking a professional decor that can accomplish the right psychological effects on your clientele, do it professionally. Interview designers, see the work they've done, and hire accordingly.

The same goes for display in the retail business. You've all seen hodgepodge shops that leave you scratching your head. And there are shops in which the merchandise all but jumps out and says, "Buy me."

Make the most effective use of items that have the most unusual eye appeal. Set a sensible schedule for changing your various displays, for even the best display, when maintained for too long, ceases to be effective. Display your best attention-getting items where they'll call attention to other products as well, particularly those that will sell auxiliary items. Put your impulse items in the heaviest traffic areas, and do as the supermarkets do in putting your highest-profit-margin items at eye level, not up or down.

Window dressing can be intriguing to look at, but it doesn't do you any good unless it draws people into the store. This, too, is an art, and it takes talent to do well. You're paying for window exposure to the street, and you might as well put the space to the best possible use by hiring professional talent to assist you with your window dressing. Determine from your suppliers whether or not they can assist you in this regard, for it may save you considerable money to use their displays and/or ideas.

**PERSONNEL.** So far you've established the sharpest marketing plan that anybody in the business has ever seen. You've got your customers pegged down to their last spendable nickel. You've done your buying like a wizard. You've established a pricing program second to none. You've cased the competition so that you know what time they go to the bathroom. You've enlisted the finest talent to create your advertising and public relations. Your display is a prizewinner, and your decor is dazzling. You take great pride and satisfaction in all that you've done, and you're confident that the expense of time and money will prove to have been worth it.

Now you want to screw up the whole works? Put in the wrong personnel. You think it's tough to shop for merchandise and professional services? Try shopping for human beings who will do the job just as you want them to. Handling of personnel is probably one of the most challenging aspects of marketing, and it's certainly one that deserves a considerable amount of your attention, patience, compassion, sensibility, sensitivity, intelligence, discipline, humor, and saintliness. You have to find personnel who will be compatible not only with the public but with yourself as well. You're brand new at this whole thing yourself, yet you have to train your people to deal as you want them to deal. If you're not careful, they'll train you to deal as they want you to. You have to be flexible to adjust to your employees' ever-changing moods and attitudes, and they have to be equally flexible to put up with you. Both of you have to be capable of putting up with those ever-changing tides in the public.

This is your business venture. To them it's just a job. They can go somewhere else if they're not happy, but it's not quite as easy for you to change your whole scheme if you're not happy with them. Remember that each and every employee is a potential reader of this book—a person doing a job who some day may wish to get free. If that person is of value to you and you wish to retain him, perhaps it would be a good idea for you to reread the early chapters of this book to be certain you know what caused you to want to break loose, and treat your personnel accordingly.

There are no statistics on the subject, but I would venture to say that the most discouraging aspect of being in business for oneself is that of dealing with personnel. Consider: if you were so easy to get along with, you'd have been happy at your previous job and wouldn't have thought of getting free. What makes you think that now that you're on your own you're any easier to get along with? It's a two-way street, and you have to take the initiative in establishing smooth and efficient personnel relations. If you've ever done business with a firm that has good personnel relations, you know it in a flash, and I'll bet you do business there repeatedly. If you deal with a firm that has sour personnel relations, you know that in a flash too, and you'll probably stay away. The public will react the same way when it deals with you. Be prepared. It's not easy, but no one ever said it would be.

**FLEXIBILITY.** Nothing is as constant as change. The seasons change. The neighborhood changes. The customers change. You change. Your stock in trade changes. Buying habits change. Advertising techniques change.

Your personnel changes. Your competition changes. Your needs change. Your desires change. Your family changes. And if any of these things stop changing, you get bored silly.

Maintaining an attitude of flexibility in your business endeavor is essential. You have to always be ready to introduce new products when you sense the public's need for them. You have to be capable of coping with the ups and downs of business trends, locally, regionally, and nationally. You have to be capable of changing with your own personal whims, needs, health, finances, and motivations.

Your whole marketing plan, and each element in it, must be ready to change on short notice. This means that you cannot neglect any of these items for any length of time. In some cases, constant review may be necessary. In other cases, review can be done every few months, or even every year or two. But you must pay attention and be willing to change when change is called for.

Set out a formal plan as to when you will review all the aspects of your marketing plan, and follow through with the plan. So many of us strive always to maintain the status quo. Yet in the business world, maintaining the status quo can be the kiss of death. You have to assume that others are always moving ahead, and can leave you eating their dust. Even major national firms with proven products are continually revamping their marketing plan to cope with changing tastes and with new thrusts by the competition.

Consider, for example, Coca Cola. The product itself hasn't changed in generations, as far as we know. And yet the company's packaging, advertising, displays, and pricing are undergoing continual change. These aspects all change at different rates. The advertising jingles may change a few times a year. The corporate logo may change once a decade. Even the formula itself may change, although the public probably isn't aware of it. And why should a product with such a proven track record have the need for constant change? Perhaps it's because it does change so regularly that it has been able to maintain its unparalleled success.

Your marketing skills will be the ultimate test of your success. Give them fair time in which to develop. But always question them. And above all, don't let pride stand in your way. Don't ever hesitate to admit to yourself that you may have done something wrong. The farther you go down the wrong road, the more lost you'll get. As soon as you sense that things aren't working right, go back to the drawing board and try again a different way. Some of your marketing techniques, if they've gone awry, can be corrected with a slight adjustment of the fine-tuning knob. This may involve little or no cost. Try whatever you can that doesn't cost you anything, and proceed with caution on any new investments for your marketing plan. But don't be afraid of those investments. The right one can pay off in bonanza form.

# 8. Managing a Small Business: The Saga of Paul Pill

Management is the umbrella—the overall activity of handling your affairs. After you've acquired your professional advisors, decided on a form of business, established your financial program, found your location, set up your insurance program and your bookkeeping system, and developed your marketing plan, you boil down to the ultimate: managing your affairs, including your time, your employees, and your emotions. Management is concerned with the ongoing day-to-day elements of running your business.

The Saga of Paul Pill, which follows, illustrates twenty important Don'ts and Dos of running your own business. The object of illustrating the twenty Don'ts and Dos is to help you create an atmosphere of consistency in your business operation. With everything functioning smoothly, the successful manager is able to devote the maximum time to creating and implementing plans that will result in profitability and contentment. His time is not wasted in petty problem-solving, but is directly utilized in programming sound, achievable progress. Unless you're achieving a degree of recognizable progress, it's not going to be long before you start saying to yourself, "I wish I were back at the old job again where I could call my soul my own." The numbers in parentheses refer to these specific Don'ts and Dos, which will be explained in more detail at the end of the story.

As Paul's saga unfolds, I ask you to keep in mind one fact of life, one principle, one law, and one redundancy. These axioms are essential guidelines for anyone who thinks he has the necessary components to become a successful operator of his own business. The components are bookkeeper, personnel wrangler, buyer, salesperson, building inspector, judge, jury, benevolent despot, form filler-outer, public servant, optimist, pessimist, and stoic. The axioms are:

Fact of Life: With rare exception, it takes two to three years for any new business to get into the black.

The Peter Principle: "In a hierarchy, an individual tends to rise to his own level of incompetence." Needless to say, a business enterprise is a form of hierarchy, and no one is excluded from the operation of this principle.

Murphy's Law: "Nothing is as easy as it looks; everything takes longer than you think; if anything can go wrong, it will."

Rosefsky's Redundancy: "If I've said it once, I've said it ten thousand times. Seek out, find, and make use of the proper professional assistance in running your business!"

These axioms weave their way in and out of the Saga of Paul Pill. The certainty of their existence, particularly in human business activity, is unquestionable.

**THE SAGA OF PAUL PILL.** Fresh out of pharmacy school, Paul Pill was pleased to get a job as assistant night pharmacist at Doc Drudge's Drugstore. The store was in a small shopping plaza in what had been a tranquil suburban town. But as the population began to overflow from the nearby city into the suburbs, the store—the only drugstore in the area—began to do a booming business. Where Doc and one night pharmacist had handled all of the prescription business in the past, now it took two men on each shift to handle the load. Young and eager, Paul took to his task and did a commendable job not only professionally, but also personally, with the store's customers.

A few years later, when Paul was about to take a Mrs. Pill, Doc promoted him to the position of Chief Night Pharmacist, since the erstwhile Chief had departed for another community. Paul continued to work energetically as ever, and whenever he had a spare moment, he would try to learn about other aspects of the store. Little by little, Doc would call upon him to do some buying, to handle some of the paperwork, to interview prospective sales clerks.

More time passed, and Paul began to acquire a crop of little Pills. With an ever-growing family to support, Paul asked for and was given a day position with increased responsibilities. Paul succeeded the retiring Chief Day Pharmacist and became responsible for running the store in Doc's increasing absences.

Paul's eye was sharp and his ambition was boundless. As he watched the operation progress over the years and watched the town grow, he began to spot ways that the business could be improved. He suggested, and Doc agreed, that the unproductive and often messy soda fountain be removed and racks of panty hose and prepacked cameras and toys be installed in its place. He recommended, and Doc agreed, that trading stamps be offered to the customers as an incentive to have them increase the size of their purchases.

Doc didn't heed some of Paul's suggestions because of the cost involved—such as installing air conditioning, erecting a new sign, and revamping the lighting from the old incandescent fixtures to new fluorescent ones. But Paul was not dismayed, for he had a plan.

As Paul's little Pills began to grow into, then out of, adolescence, Doc generously recognized that a growing family needs ever more income to thrive on. Doc put Paul on a profit-sharing plan, and Paul rose to the occasion by working extra hours to help boost the store's volume.

Meanwhile, Paul formulated his plan. Doc was nearing retirement, and had often mentioned that he'd like to sell the store and move to a warmer climate. Paul had been salting away a nest egg against the day he might approach Doc with a deal to buy him out. Paul knew that if all of Doc's old-fashioned ways were thrown out and his own modern thinking put in their place, the store could double, if not triple, its income within a year or two.

Paul carefully calculated some of the changes that he would make, and the results of his figuring did project substantial increases in the store's volume.

Doc, Paul thought, was foolishly liberal with his credit policies. Many old customers had run up charge accounts of hundreds of dollars. They paid irregularly, and Doc never dunned them for payments. Many were the times that these customers would move or die, and no effort was made to collect on the debts. By tightening up these procedures, cash flow could improve and there would be an abundant source of capital—many thousands of dollars worth—that could be collected.

Another of Doc's idiosyncrasies was to be a little too kind to customers. When a customer brought in a prescription for a brand-name product, Doc would often suggest that he buy the generic brand instead, and save perhaps 50 percent of more. By eliminating this practice, Paul reasoned, the prescription department revenue would soar.

There were still many areas in the store that weren't making full productive use of the space. The truss-fitting rooms would be converted to a high-volume greeting-card section. The seldom-used waiting area next to the prescription counter would be replaced by a display of fast-moving and high-profit men's cosmetics. Even the bicycle rack in front of the store would be replaced by a row of newspaper vending machines, from which the store could reap a rental fee.

The old image would go. Paul would renovate from top to bottom, including installing his long-desired fluorescent lights, air conditioning, and a new sign.

In short, Paul began to calculate how his income would increase, how his work hours would decrease, and how he could begin taking long-awaited vacations with his family. He had heard rumblings about a new chain discount drugstore opening a few miles away, but he knew that his steady clientele wouldn't abandon him to drive the extra distance to save a few pennies. (1)

The day finally arrived. Doc called Paul into his office and told him of his desire to sell out. It didn't take them long to come to terms. Doc wanted $60,000 for the business, and Paul was ready, willing, and able to pay it. Doc had long since written all of the store fixtures down to zero, so he put no value on them in the transaction. Twenty thousand dollars of the $60,000 represented the complete inventory, at cost, and Doc promised to make arrangements to have major suppliers finance the total sum. That way, Doc would have his cash and Paul would have a good working-credit arrangement with his suppliers to carry the inventory.

The other $40,000 represented Doc's "going business value," and Paul thought it was certainly fair enough. Paul would raise the $40,000 as follows: he had $10,000 in his savings account, which he would "borrow," though he knew that he didn't really have to repay it, since it was his own money; $20,000 had been offered to him through a "loan" from his parents, and he felt confident that in a few years they would forgive the debt to him in the form of a gift; and the remaining $10,000 he would borrow from his local bank. This, to Paul's thinking, was the true extent of his invested capital. He would take an additional loan of $15,000 to accomplish the desired renovations.

His projected cash flow indicated that after his annual loan obligations were met, there would be a net profit of $1,000. This would be 10 percent of his allegedly invested capital of $10,000. This, Paul felt, was certainly a fair return on his investment, particularly considering that within eighteen to twenty-four months after completion of the renovations, the volume would start going up; and later, when he refinanced the various loans, his net profit would start reaching closer to $5,000. Paul signed the appropriate papers, and he was now the proud owner of one drugstore. (2)

Paul wasted no time in proceeding with his plans. He had worked so diligently for so long in sketching out his desired renovations that he decided to assume all of the duties in accomplishing the work, including negotiating the contracts with the suppliers and tradespeople, supervising the construction, and so on. He knew that this would keep him so busy that he would have to relinquish his other duties.

Thus, he promoted Percy Pestle from Assistant Day Pharmacist to Chief Day Pharmacist and General Store Manager. Percy, with a charming smile and a winning way, had always been very popular with the customers. He was a natural to take over Paul's duties, but an important part of Percy's duties had been to spend time as the cosmetics buyer, and Paul knew that Percy wouldn't have time for that while he assumed the larger tasks.

So, Paul chose Lola Lipstick, his best salesperson, to assume Percy's role as the cosmetics buyer. Sherman Shelf, Paul's nephew and star stockboy, was promoted to cosmetics clerk, working for Lola. (3)

The ensuing months were anything but smooth. Paul lacked the skill of a general contractor to properly schedule the work of the various subcontractors and, consequently, they were stepping all over each other trying to get their work done. Paul's pharmaceutical skills did not extend to dealing with construction laborers, and tempers were almost always at their very shortest. The construction job lagged on for weeks beyond the anticipated deadline, further fouling up Paul's "grand opening" plans.

As old Doc Drudge had done when he had run infrequent special sales, Paul announced his grand-opening by sending a mimeographed letter to his extensive list of customers. Paul sat back and waited for the surge of traffic to come flowing in. But he waited in vain. The old clientele, it seemed, had not been impressed with the chaos in the store during the past months. Paul's initial perplexity turned to dismay, when, in the weeks that followed, it became apparent that there was to be no surge of new customers. The old customers still showed up now and then, along with some new ones, but that old, steady, reliable flow wasn't there the way it used to be. (4)

The opening of a chain drugstore a few miles away finally did happen, but Paul didn't worry about it. Deep down inside, he knew that some day the chain store could be a formidable competitor, but for now he was more concerned with working out his own internal problems, and wondering where his projections had gone astray.

Paul found more and more of his time being occupied by salesmen. Salesmen from the local radio and television stations and newspapers would visit him regularly to urge him to spend money on their media to bring in the public and counteract the competition. Salesmen from paper companies tried to sell him new supplies of paper bags for wrapping his customers' purchases. They even offered to create new logos for him, hinting rather strongly that the old logo that had been used since the beginning of Doc Drudge's days didn't really have the "zing" that would catch the public's eye today. Merchandise salesmen were constantly haranguing Paul to install racks and display kits to push their various products. Paul remembered that he used to be critical of Doc Drudge for not paying more attention to these promotional ideas, but he had to admit to himself that now that he was in the driver's seat, he couldn't bring himself to break away from the old, established patterns. (5)

The worst was yet to come. Even after all these months, it appeared that Percy Pestle was not cut out to be a store manager. Percy's forte, it seemed, was with customers, not other employees. The other employees resented Percy's pedantic ways, and morale began to suffer.

Lola Lipstick also proved a flop. She had been such a good saleswoman that she neglected to realize that everyone wasn't as good. Thinking that Sherman Shelf could push the goods as well as she had, she tended to overbuy. Not only did this throw Paul's payables way out of whack, but it created a warehousing problem in the storage room. Without Sherman acting as a competent stockboy, boxes of goods piled high, creating confusion and inefficiency.

Sherman's promotion to cosmetics clerk was also a disaster. Never having dealt with the public, he had found himself at a complete loss. The net effect of all this was that customers started staying away in droves.

Percy, Lola, and Sherman all complained to Paul, trying to point out to him that morale was suffering and business would suffer accordingly. But Paul, so preoccupied with wondering where his profits were going, failed to heed them in time. (6)

The problem compounded itself. Sherman, diligent nephew that he was, would leave the cosmetics counter to go into the stockroom and assist the regular stockboy every chance he could. But it always seemed that when Sherman left, a number of cosmetics customers would come in. Lola was unable to take care of all the customers, and Percy, spotting customers standing around not being helped, would start bickering across the aisles at Lola. This would unnerve prescription customers who were waiting for Percy to fill their orders. And down, down, down went the volume. (7)

Through it all, Paul still continued to have unbounded faith in his fellow workers. After all, he had worked with Percy for many years; he and Lola still continued to enjoy occasional forbidden moments in the back of the stockroom after the store was closed for the night; and Sherman Shelf was his wife's brother's only son. Paul was a pharmacist, yes; a psychologist, no. Though his key employees continued to complain, he continued to assure them that time would get all the bugs out, and that everything would be okay. (8)

By now, well into the first year of his new venture, Paul realized that his original projections had no chance of coming true. His own personal net income had begun to slip from the level it had been at when he was still Doc Drudge's employee, and the bank was getting a bit impatient when Paul slipped one month, then two months, behind in his payments.

Things were looking bleak for Paul, when suddenly, out of the blue, some miracles happened. As Paul approached the store to open up one gray winter morning, feeling in the depths of despair, he noticed two envelopes under the front door. With great curiosity, he opened them, and as he read them, he uttered a series of sounds that were a combination of relief, despair, joy, and anger. The contents of the first letter disclosed that Lola Lipstick had run off with a contraceptive salesman and was quitting her post; the second letter revealed that Percy Pestle had run off with Sherman Shelf, and they were moving to the West Coast to open up a leather boutique.

Employee-less, Paul frantically combed the want ads and called the employment agencies. Within two days, he had replaced his three errant employees with well-qualified people. To his amazement, within a week, Paul found the entire operation running much more smoothly and happily than it had been when his original triumvirate was in charge.

Then, a few days later, even better news struck: it was announced that a major, and very dynamic, supermarket was going to build a large store adjacent to Paul's north wall. Construction was to begin within six weeks, with completion scheduled within twelve months. The additional traffic that would be generated by such a store made Paul's head fairly spin.

The months ahead were bright for Paul and his pharmacy. His new employees were functioning smoothly, and he joyously watched the construction of the adjoining supermarket.

"Everything has a way of working out," he remembered telling his wife one evening during the spring of that year.

But Paul's perils weren't over yet. The supermarket opened on schedule, and the crowds came in droves. Paul was among the first to survey the new premises and was the first person who had to be carried out of the store in a state of shock: one large aisle in the supermarket contained what seemed like miles of shelves laden with the same products—cosmetics, soaps, sundries, lotions, potions, and notions—that Paul carried in his store next door; and the supermarket was selling them all at lower prices.

His first reaction was to check his lease, which immediately disclosed to him that any stores that were built in the shopping plaza could carry any merchandise they wanted without restriction. The original landlord, it seems, had anticipated the possibility of a supermarket some day in the future, and he didn't want to risk losing a good supermarket tenant by putting any restrictive clauses in the leases of other tenants.

How could Paul compete? He had been buying the same merchandise from the same suppliers all these years and his prices were pretty well established. He couldn't sell for less than he was now selling without seriously cutting into his profit margin. When he told some of the salespersons who called on him that he might have to look toward other, cheaper brands of certain products, they all leaned heavily on him with their well-rehearsed and justifiable pleas that they had done him a lot of favors over the years; they had carried his financing when he was in a bind; they had provided him with a lot of free extras that he used for his own purposes. (9)

If Paul thought he had troubles, the little gourmet shop that adjoined him on the other side had even worse troubles. The supermarket carried a complete line of gourmet foods, priced far lower than the specialty shop could afford to carry them, and the gourmet shop promptly went out of business altogether. And the light went on in Paul's head. He remembered his early days with Doc Drudge, and how that messy, noisy, smelly soda fountain in the corner used to annoy him. But now he thought of all the traffic coming into the plaza, and all of the employees of the supermarket, and all of his own customers, and all of the other employees in the plaza—and there was not a luncheonette within five blocks. What a drawing card! What a moneymaker it could be!

Paul made immediate plans to take over the lease of the defunct gourmet shop, make an opening through the adjoining wall, and set up a modern, clean, attractive luncheonette. Naturally, in his enthusiasm, he would handle all of the renovation himself and his now trusty Chief Pharmacist, Morris Mortar, would take over the managerial duties of the drugstore in the interim. His other key employees, Corrinne Compact in the cosmetics department and Calvin Carton in the stockroom, would be given added responsibilities to take up the slack.

So the second vicious circle of Paul Pill started to spin. As soon as the luncheonette was opened, Paul received a notice from his fire-insurance company that his rates were going up. The ventilation fans didn't work right and couldn't be fixed for over six weeks. Smoke and the odor of burning grease filled the store constantly, and when it began to seep into the adjoining supermarket, Paul received an angry letter from the market's attorney threatening a lawsuit. (10)

Things deteriorated rapidly. The exhaust fan was fixed, but it was impossible to get the odor of burning grease out of the store. Instead of a drawing card, the luncheonette had proved to be a repellent. Financing for the luncheonette equipment and renovations had stretched Paul's available credit sources to the limit, and now, with no income from the luncheonette, but the rent still falling due regularly, along with the financing payments, Paul was ready to give it all up and go find a job as a pharmacist in a nice, quiet suburban store.

Then the ever-mysterious hand of fate rested on Paul's head once again. The supermarket needed Paul's space for their own expansion. They offered to assume all of Paul's existing debts, including the luncheonette equipment and leases, and in addition offered him an extra $5,000 in cash if he could vacate within thirty days. Battered, beaten, but still confident that he could make it on his own, Paul saw the $5,000 as his stake toward getting started in another store of his own.

He had been through the mill. He was older. He was wiser. He saw his mistakes. Now he was going to make it.

Paul reflected at length on his experiences. He had, he felt, been through all of the rigors that an independent businessman could be expected to go through in the venture of his choice. He reflected on how he, as a *magna cum laude* graduate of the school of hard knocks, could make use of the tribulations he had been through. As an interim move, he took a day job as a pharmacist in a large local store and enrolled in a number of courses at the night-school session of the local community college. He studied accounting, business law, and personnel management. He realized that academic training was no substitute for actual battle conditions, but he found the text studies and lectures valuable. The study of actual case histories pointed out to him where he had gone so far wrong in the past, and how he could avoid such traps in the future. (11)

Now, slowly, carefully, he began to plot his next move. He scouted neighborhood shopping centers within a ten-mile range of his home, looking either for a likely drugstore prospect that he could purchase, or a spot that seemed right for construction of a new drugstore. He came across a proposed shopping-center development adjoining a large tract of land that was to become a residential subdivision.

A few days of scouting around at local real-estate offices disclosed to him the expected residential growth pattern for the area. Some research among suppliers and store managers disclosed the type and quality of products that would be carried by the merchants in the shopping center. There was a supermarket under construction in the center, and, with the help of his attorney, Paul was able to negotiate mutual lease clauses whereby certain types of higher-priced products that he would carry would not be carried by the supermarket. Similar written agreements were made with other merchants in the center. Paul had picked his objectives carefully. His would be a specialty pharmacy, including a select line of goods not generally available in that area of the city. The residential developments were to be of the upper-income variety, and he would concentrate on meeting the needs of those people. He would compete with the lower-priced discount stores within a few miles of him by concentrating on personalized service and offering a line of goods not available at these discount stores. (12)

With his accountant's aid, he worked out a realistic three-year projection of his income and expenses. He conferred with his banker about the financing needed to accomplish his goal. Suppliers of the merchandise and equipment, aware of his past difficulties, were nevertheless anxious to please him since he had always ultimately lived up to his credit promises. Taking the advice of his insurance agent, he obtained a substantial life-insurance policy on himself and assigned it to the bank as part of the collateral for obtaining the needed financing. Obviously, the life-insurance policy was only good as long as it remained in force (as long as somebody pays the premiums), but it made a good psychological icing on the cake to seal the financing deal. (13)

With what he learned in his accounting course and the direct assistance of his own accountant, Paul prepared a series of recordkeeping programs that would enable him to keep total control on all of his business matters with a minimum of effort. Matters that had stymied him in the past—such as payroll and tax records—now fell into place so simply that he couldn't believe that he had had so much trouble with this detail work in his previous go-around. (14)

Major fixture suppliers offered to provide Paul with a detailed layout of the store, along with their bids to supply the fixtures. Paul chose carefully and was then able to negotiate with the supplier's contractor to have all of the necessary work done on the premises, so that he could open up without complications at the appointed time. Paul kept an eye on the construction during its progress, but was content in the knowledge that the supplier had provided a foreman who was willing and eager to please. Paul knew that if he became dissatisfied with the progress of construction, the supplier would be at least morally obliged to correct the matter.

During construction, Paul took time to interview key employees, checking them out carefully as to references, past records, and credit history. He made it clear to his employees that while he hoped they would function as a happy family, he was the boss, not an old pal, not a potential paramour, not a relative, but the boss. They could come to him with their problems, and he would try to help them. He would exact good work from them for the good wages he was going to pay them. And he let it be known that good service to the customers was the prime criterion of continued employment. (15)

The store opened on time. Paul did a moderate amount of well-placed advertising and was happy to see many lookers and shoppers in the first days of his new venture. Customers were delighted with the service they received. (16) Paul kept alert to a daily inventory count so as to always have a needed supply of various products on hand to satisfy demand. (17) He studied his trade magazines religiously and went to trade shows whenever he could, in order to be the first store in the area to carry new products. (18) His direct personal supervision of all matters in the store kept things functioning smoothly. At the expense of one extra employee, he was able to see to it that every customer was served with a minimum of delay and with a maximum of courtesy. (19)

Now Paul was prospering—not necessarily getting rich, but he was comfortable. Moreover, he had a great sense of satisfaction in performing good work, keeping his employees happy, and receiving the gratitude of his customers for the service they were getting.

The nervous tension and mental aggravation that he had been so accustomed to in his previous venture seemed to have disappeared altogether. He wasn't lazy, he wasn't complacent, he wasn't resting on his laurels. He knew that continued updating of his products, continued training of his staff, and continued innovation in his marketing were essential to keeping a pleasant profit curve on the rise.

Moreover, he knew that as his performance improved steadily over the years, he would have that much more attractive a package to offer a prospective purchaser.

None of Paul's own children chose the pharmaceutical profession as they went through college. But that didn't dismay Paul. He knew that he had a tight, handsome, profitable little package that he should have no trouble selling to a worthy successor. Then one day, a young man named Claude

Capsule, fresh out of pharmaceutical school, came in to apply for a job as the night pharmacist . . . (20)

The twenty Don'ts and Dos for managing your own business follow. Paul's story may not be completely typical, but his ups and downs were all brought about by his observance, or lack thereof, of the basic rules of management that apply to any type of individual business enterprise.

1. DON'T wear rose-colored glasses. Paul's dream of glory may not have been unreal. It may not have been unattainable. But he let wishful thinking get the best of him, and heady optimism far outweighed common sense.

2. DON'T play games with money. Paul borrowed a lot of his capital, and because he didn't think he'd have to pay it back, he never really considered it as capital. He was kidding himself, and dangerously. Had his projections been properly analyzed, his $1,000 return on a factual $40,000 capital investment would have been so inadequate as to discourage him from proceeding. If you're borrowing money to get involved in a new business venture, you have to make plans to repay it. If you withdraw from your own savings, that's capital—money that should be earning more money for you—and if it doesn't, you're only weakening yourself financially. If, down the road, your debts are forgiven, count that as a windfall, but don't plan on it. The dangers are evident.

3. DON'T misuse your time. If you have talents in one direction, devote your time to the full exercise of those talents. Don't venture into someone else's area of expertise. Not only is your own time being put to poor use, but you could foul up whatever else it is you're getting into. Do that which you know best, and hire others to do that which they can do better than you.

4. DON'T depend too much on past history. The public is fickle. They may not react tomorrow the way they reacted yesterday, and you may never know why. We can learn from the past, but to rely on things always being the way they were can be a mistake. It's better to plan on how you'll cope with an unpredictable future than to have reveries as to how things will be tomorrow because that's the way they were yesterday.

5. DON'T ignore marketing. Whatever your endeavor, you're selling something. It may be yourself or a product or a service. That commodity has to be packaged, and the public has to be informed about it. The public has to be made to want it, and the public has to come to you to get it, either in person or via the mails. And they've got to want the commodity that *you,* as opposed to your competitors, are offering. In order to entice them away from the competitor and toward you, you have to know what the competition is doing at all times. This is all in the sphere of marketing, and you can't forget this aspect for a minute.

6. DON'T ignore your employees. You don't have to be a slave to them,

but neither should they be slaves to you. Listen to them. Be aware of their morale. Be aware of their work habits—whether they're overworking or not working enough.

7. DON'T allow confusion. One of the first things a customer will sense about a business enterprise is that there is an atmosphere of confusion. Confusion can result from many things—improperly trained employees, inefficient traffic-flow patterns in the public areas, inefficient procedures for delivering the product to the customer, poor recordkeeping.

8. DON'T procrastinate. When you get the slightest glimmer that something might be going wrong, jump right on it. The longer a problem is left to smolder, the more difficult it becomes to put out the fire. Procrastination doesn't work—if you stick your head in the sand like an ostrich, the problem isn't going to go away.

9. DON'T get lax about your buying policies. Smart buying is every bit as important as smart selling—perhaps more so. If you buy smart enough, you'll have many options as to how you can sell. But if you haven't bought smart, you might be locked into the price you sell for. Sales persons that come to call on you may become pesty, it's true, but you never know what they have in their satchels, and until you do, you won't know if you can make money on it. Keep in touch with a broad range of suppliers. Be on the alert for special deals that may be advertised or brought to you by word of mouth. Be on the alert against getting into too cozy a situation with a given supplier, lest you be in a position of owing him favors. Flexibility is more important.

10. DON'T overexpand. Proper, sound expansion is one thing. But the ruination of so many business enterprises is that when things seem to be going well, there is a pell-mell rush to expand, on the assumption that if big is good, bigger will be even better. It doesn't always work that way. Paul's case was particularly pathetic, but many successful businesses are equally pathetic in their greed and/or desire to enlarge more quickly than they're capable of doing. Plans for an expansion should be scrutinized as carefully as the plans for the original enterprise were.

11. DO acquire expertise. If anyone should have known about running a drugstore, it would seem that Paul Pill should have. Yet, as happens all too often, the tidbits of knowledge that one may acquire by observation aren't enough to help you cope with the day-in and day-out operations of a business. In addition to whatever on-the-job training you can get, read, study, and take whatever courses might assist you in meeting your goals. A man who's been successful in business for decades will still tell you that he's got a lot to learn. He knows whereof he speaks.

12. DO plan ahead. You can't foresee the complete future, but you can do enough valid research to eliminate a lot of unknown factors and zero-in

on the known. Paul had learned his lesson well, and it paid off for him.

13. DO make use of your professional advisors. Yes, this involves some cost. Yes, this may entail some delay in achieving what you want to achieve. But use them. If you know a better method, please let me know.

14. DO keep proper records. Aside from the mind-bending records that the government requires you to keep, you should, on your own, maintain exact and up-to-the-minute records of inventory controls, cash flows, debts, receivables, deliveries, shipments, and anything else pertaining to the movement of goods, people, money, and securities in your business affairs.

15. DO maintain your proper role. This applies not just to your employees, but to everyone else with whom you come in contact—your suppliers, your customers, your lenders, your debtors, your advisors. Never for a moment relinquish friendships, but keep your friendships and your business relations separate. Business is business, and business matters must be handled objectively, forthrightly, and, above all, with the utmost integrity.

16. DO keep your customers happy. No further amplification needed.

17. DO keep on top of all information that can affect the welfare of your business. *Keeping* all the records in the world (see item 14) isn't enough if you don't *scrutinize* the records regularly and thoroughly. In addition to statistical records, you should keep on top of an up-to-date list of your clientele, your suppliers, your debtors, and your creditors.

18. DO be alert to new trends and new products and new services that can affect the welfare of your business. Read trade journals. Visit trade shows. Such endeavors are what keep you a step ahead of the competition and in the favor of your customers.

19. DO be on the alert for bottlenecks. They can be distracting, discouraging, and destructive. They can happen on the premises. They can happen during the course of negotiating a deal. They can happen outside of the business proper by way of personal problems, personal legal entanglements, illness, disability, and death. Both overplanning and underplanning for avoidance of potential bottlenecks can be foolish and expensive. You've got to find a happy medium that's just right for your own situation.

20. DO plan for management succession. Part of your goal is to provide yourself with a means of income, as well as a means of personal satisfaction. But a great part of your endeavor also has to be devoted to providing future security for yourself and your family. If you or your children aren't planning on your endeavor becoming their endeavor, you have to plan for an orderly transfer that will yield you the ultimate fruits of your labors. With every step you take, you should be asking yourself, at least subconsciously, what will the new owners think of this one?

# But What If . . . ? A Closing Thought

I fervently hope that this book has stimulated you to think in terms of expanding your life. We only get a one-way ticket, and we have to make the most of it. We all have varying levels of potential, and we all want to strive to realize that potential to the fullest. I've tried to give you some of the guidelines to enable you to take the steps needed to do this.

It's necessary, however, to inject a note of caution. My close observation of, and participation in, the business world for many years has shown me countless times that failure—whether financial, personal, or a combination—is due to our almost blind neglect of the need to ask ourselves at each step of the way, "But what if . . . ?" It's fine to have enthusiasm and commitment, and to dive headlong into the fray when we believe in something. But if we do so without having a safety net under us, such a venture could be our ruination.

Thus, we have to ask, "But what if this step or that step doesn't work out the way we expect it to?" We can never ask this question enough. I'm not suggesting that you not take the step because the answer to the "But what if . . . ?" question is frightening. I'm suggesting only that you develop contingency plans to cope with whatever may come should the step not be the right one.

This is particularly important when one is contemplating a major career redirection, such as leaving an established position to get free and go into business on one's own. You may, as did many of the individuals in the case histories, have unbounded confidence in yourself. To that, you'll owe a measure of your success. Remember, though, that those case histories were chosen intentionally to illustrate successes. A random sampling of case histories of failures would be far more extensive. Yes, many of these successes never seemed to ask themselves "But what if . . . ?" At least, they didn't admit to me that they did. But deep down in their heart of hearts, I have to believe that each success story was founded on a knowledge that if things didn't work out, there was something solid to fall back on, for the sake of sanity, for the sake of soul, and for the sake of immediate family.

You who are about to break loose and get free are bucking long odds.

You will greatly increase your chances of making it by following the precautions set forth in these pages, and by acquiring the skills and professional guidance needed to see you through.

For your daring and for your courage, I say congratulations and Godspeed. Proceed with confidence, with discipline, with dedication. But before you go, sit by yourself in a quiet place and write out simply and briefly on a sheet of paper the answer to one simple question, "But what if . . . ?" I hope you'll never have to refer to it, but keep it handy in case you do.

# Appendix: Source Materials

The source material listed here is available through the Small Business Administration, a federal agency, and through Bank of America. Much of the SBA material is free, and is available at your nearest SBA office. Addresses of all SBA offices are on pages 252–255.

There is a charge for some of the SBA materials. These materials may be ordered by sending your check or money order to Superintendent of Documents, U.S. Government Printing Office, Washington, D.C. 20402. Prices are subject to change without notice, but your local SBA office can inform you of current prices.

## *SBA Small Marketers Aids*

These leaflets are available free and provide suggestions and management guidelines for small retail, wholesale, and service firms.

*Publication No. and Title*

25. Are You Kidding Yourself About Your Profits?
71. Checklist for Going Into Business
95. Are Your Salespeople Missing Opportunities?
96. Checklist for Successful Retail Advertising
104. Preventing Accidents in Small Stores
105. A Pricing Checklist for Managers
106. Finding and Hiring the Right Employees
107. Building Strong Relations with Your Bank
108. Building Repeat Retail Business
109. Stimulating Impulse Buying for Increased Sales
110. Controlling Cash in Small Retail and Service Firms
111. Interior Display: A Way to Increase Sales
113. Quality and Taste as Sales Appeals
114. Pleasing Your Boss, the Customer
115. Are You Ready for Franchising?
116. How to Select a Resident Buying Office
118. Legal Services for Small Retail and Service Firms
119. Preventing Retail Theft
121. Measuring the Results of Advertising
122. Controlling Inventory in Small Wholesale Firms
123. Stock Control for Small Stores
124. Knowing Your Image
125. Pointers on Display Lighting
126. Accounting Services for Small Service Firms
127. Six Methods for Success in a Small Store
128. Building Customer Confidence in Your Service Shop
129. Reducing Shoplifting Losses
130. Analyze Your Records to Reduce Costs
132. The Federal Wage-Hour Law in Small Firms

133. Can You Afford Delivery Service?
134. Preventing Burglary and Robbery Loss
135. Arbitration: Peace-Maker in Small Business
136. Hiring the Right Man
137. Outwitting Bad Check Passers
138. Sweeping Profit out the Back Door
139. Understanding Truth-in-Lending
140. Profit by Your Wholesalers' Services
141. Danger Signals in a Small Store
142. Steps in Meeting Your Tax Obligations
143. Factors in Considering a Shopping Center Location
144. Getting the Facts for Income Tax Reporting
145. Personal Qualities Needed to Manage a Store
146. Budgeting in a Small Service Firm
147. Sound Cash Management and Borrowing
148. Insurance Checklist for Small Business
149. Computers for Small Business—Service Bureau or Time Sharing?
150. Business Plan for Retailers
151. Preventing Embezzlement
152. Using a Traffic Study to Select a Retail Site
153. Business Plan for Small Service Firms
154. Using Census Data to Select a Store Site
155. Keeping Records in Small Business
156. Marketing Checklist for Small Retailers

## *SBA Small Business Bibliographies*

These leaflets are available free and furnish reference sources for individual types of businesses:

*Publication No. and Title*

*1. Handicrafts*
*2. Home Businesses*
*3. Selling by Mail Order*
*9. Marketing Research Procedures*
*10. Retailing*
*12. Statistics and Maps for National Market Analysis*
*13. National Directories for Use in Marketing*
*14. The Nursery Business*
*15. Recordkeeping Systems–Small Store and Service Trade*
*17. Restaurants and Catering*
*18. Basic Library Reference Sources*
*20. Advertising–Retail Store*
*21. Variety Stores*
*24. Food Stores*
*29. National Mailing-List Houses*
*31. Retail Credit and Collections*
*33. Drugstores*

*41. Mobile Homes and Parks*
*42. Bookstores*
*45. Men's and Boys' Wear Stores*
*46. Woodworking Shops*
*47. Soft-Frozen Dessert Stands*
*50. Apparel and Accessories for Women, Misses, & Children*
*51. Trucking and Cartage*
*53. Hobby Shops*
*55. Wholesaling*
*56. Training Commercial Salesmen*
*58. Automation for Small Offices*
*60. Painting and Wall Decorating*
*64. Photographic Dealers and Studios*
*66. Motels*
*67. Manufacturers' Sales Representative*
*72. Personnel Management*
*75. Inventory Management*

## *SBA Management Aids*

These leaflets are available free and deal with functional problems in small manufacturing plants and concentrate on subjects of interest to administrative executives.

*Publication No. and Title*

32. How Trade Associations Help Small Business
46. How to Analyze Your Own Business
49. Know Your Patenting Procedures
80. Choosing the Legal Structure for Your Firm
82. Reducing the Risks in Product Development
85. Analyzing Your Cost of Marketing
92. Wishing Won't Get Profitable New Products
111. Steps in Incorporating a Business
161. Proving Fidelity Losses
162. Keeping Machines and Operators Productive
169. Designing Small Plants for Economy and Flexibility
170. The ABC's of Borrowing
174. Is Your Cash Supply Adequate?
176. Financial Audits: A Tool for Better Management
177. Planning and Controlling Production for Efficiency
178. Effective Industrial Advertising for Small Plants
179. Breaking the Barriers to Small Business Planning
180. Guidelines for Building a New Plant
181. Numerical Control for the Smaller Manufacturer
182. Expanding Sales Through Franchising
185. Matching the Applicant to the Job
186. Checklist for Developing a Training Program
187. Using Census Data in Small Plant Marketing
188. Developing a List of Prospects
189. Should You Make or Buy Components?

190. Measuring the Performance of Salesmen
191. Delegating Work and Responsibility
192. Profile Your Customers to Expand Industrial Sales
193. What Is the Best Selling Price?
194. Marketing Planning Guidelines
195. Setting Pay for Your Management Jobs
196. Tips on Selecting Salesmen
197. Pointers on Preparing an Employee Handbook
198. How to Find a Likely Successor
199. Expand Overseas Sales with Commerce Department Help
200. Is the Independent Sales Agent for You?
201. Locating or Relocating Your Business
203. Are Your Products and Channels Producing Sales?
204. Pointers on Negotiating DOD Contracts
205. Pointers on Using Temporary-Help Services
206. Keep Pointed Toward Profit
207. Pointers on Scheduling Production
208. Problems in Managing a Family-Owned Business
209. Preventing Employee Pilferage
211. Termination of DOD Contracts for the Government's Convenience
212. The Equipment Replacement Decision
214. The Metric System and Small Business
215. How to Prepare for a Pre-Award Survey
216. Finding a New Product for Your Company
217. Reducing Air Pollution in Industry
218. Business Plan for Small Manufacturers
219. Solid Waste Management in Industry
220. Basic Budgets for Profit Planning
221. Business Plan for Small Construction Firms
222. Business Life Insurance

## *SBA Small Business Management Series*

The booklets in this series provide discussions of special management problems in small companies. The fees for these booklets are listed below.

| | *Catalogue No.* | *Pages* | *Price* |
|---|---|---|---|
| AN EMPLOYEE SUGGESTION SYSTEM FOR SMALL COMPANIES<br>Explains the basic principles for starting and operating a suggestion system. It also warns of various pitfalls and gives examples of suggestions submitted by employees. | SBA 1.12:1 | 18 | $ .40 |
| HUMAN RELATIONS IN SMALL BUSINESS<br>Discusses human relations in relation to finding and selecting employees, developing them, and motivating them. | SBA 1.12:3 | 68 | $ .60 |

IMPROVING MATERIAL HANDLING IN SMALL BUSINESS

| | | | |
|---|---|---|---|
| A discussion of the basics of the material handling function, the method of laying out workplaces, and other factors essential to setting up an efficient system. | SBA 1.12:4 | 42 | $ .60 |

BETTER COMMUNICATIONS IN SMALL BUSINESS

| | | | |
|---|---|---|---|
| Designed to help smaller manufacturers help themselves in winning cooperation by means of more skillful communications. Also seeks to explain how communications within the firm can improve operating efficiency and competitive strength. | SBA 1.12:7 | 37 | $ .65 |

COST ACCOUNTING FOR SMALL MANUFACTURERS

| | | | |
|---|---|---|---|
| Stresses the importance of determining and recording costs accurately. Designed for small manufacturers and their accountants. Diagrams, flow charts, and illustrations are included to make the material easier to use. | SBA 1.12:9 | 163 | $1.60 |

THE SMALL MANUFACTURER AND HIS SPECIALIZED STAFF

| | | | |
|---|---|---|---|
| Stresses the necessity of building a competent staff through the use of staff specialists and outside professional advisers, so that the small business owner can be relieved of routine work. | SBA 1.12:13 | 36 | $ .65 |

HANDBOOK OF SMALL BUSINESS FINANCE

| | | | |
|---|---|---|---|
| Written for the small business owner who wants to improve his financial-management skill. Indicates the major areas of financial management and describes a few of the many techniques that can help the small business owner. | SBA 1.12:15 | 80 | $ .95 |

NEW PRODUCT INTRODUCTION FOR SMALL BUSINESS OWNERS

| | | | |
|---|---|---|---|
| Provides basic information that will help the owners of small businesses to understand better what is involved in placing a new or improved product on the market. | SBA 1.12:17 | 69 | $1.10 |

RATIO ANALYSIS FOR SMALL BUSINESS

Ratio analysis is the process of determining the relationships between certain financial or operating data of a business to provide a basis for managerial control. The purpose of the booklet is to help

| | Catalogue No. | Pages | Price |
|---|---|---|---|
| the owner/manager in detecting favorable or unfavorable trends in his business. | SBA 1.12:20 | 65 | $ .90 |
| PROFITABLE SMALL PLANT LAYOUT<br>Help for the small business owner who is in the predicament of rising costs on finished goods, decreasing net profits, and lowered production because of the lack of economical and orderly movement of production materials from one process to another throughout the shop. | SBA 1.12:21 | 48 | $ .80 |
| PRACTICAL BUSINESS USE OF GOVERNMENT STATISTICS<br>Illustrates some practical uses of federal government statistics, discusses what can be done with them, and describes major reference sources. | SBA 1.12:22 | | |
| GUIDES FOR PROFIT PLANNING<br>Guides for computing and using the break-even point, the level of gross profit, and the rate of return on investment. Designed for readers who have no specialized training in accounting and economics. | SBA 1.12:25 | 52 | $ .85 |
| PERSONNEL MANAGEMENT GUIDES FOR SMALL BUSINESS<br>An introduction to the various aspects of personnel management as they apply to small firms. | SBA 1.12:26 | 79 | $1.10 |
| PROFITABLE COMMUNITY RELATIONS FOR SMALL BUSINESS<br>Practical information on how to build and maintain sound community relations by participation in community affairs. | SBA 1.12:27 | 36 | $ .70 |
| SMALL BUSINESS AND GOVERNMENT RESEARCH AND DEVELOPMENT<br>An introduction for owners of small research and development firms that seek government R and D contracts. Includes a discussion of the procedures necessary to locate and interest government markets. | SBA 1.12:28 | 41 | $ .75 |

| | | | |
|---|---|---|---|
| MANAGEMENT AUDIT FOR SMALL MANUFACTURERS<br>A series of questions that will indicate whether the owner/manager of a small manufacturing plant is planning, organizing, directing, and coordinating his business activities efficiently. | SBA 1.12:29 | 58 | $ .75 |
| INSURANCE AND RISK MANAGEMENT FOR SMALL BUSINESS<br>A discussion of what insurance is, the necessity of obtaining professional advice on buying insurance, and the main types of insurance a small business may need. | SBA 1.12:30 | 72 | $ .95 |
| MANAGEMENT AUDIT FOR SMALL RETAILERS<br>Designed to meet the needs of the owner/manager of a small retail enterprise. 149 questions guide the owner/manager in an examination of himself and his business operation. | SBA 1.12:31 | 50 | $ .80 |
| FINANCIAL RECORDKEEPING FOR SMALL STORES<br>Written primarily for the small store owner or prospective owner whose business doesn't justify hiring a full-time bookkeeper. | SBA 1.12:32 | 131 | $1.30 |
| SMALL STORE PLANNING FOR GROWTH<br>A discussion of the nature of growth, the management skills needed, and some techniques for use in promoting growth. Includes a consideration of merchandising, advertising, and display, and checklists for increases in transactions and gross margins. | SBA 1.12:33 | 99 | $1.35 |
| SELECTING ADVERTISING MEDIA—A GUIDE FOR SMALL BUSINESS<br>Intended to aid the small business owner in deciding which medium to select for making his product, service, or store known to potential customers and how to best use his advertising money. | SBA 1.12:34 | 120 | $1.40 |
| FRANCHISE INDEX/PROFILE<br>Presents an evaluation process that may be used to investigate franchise opportunities. The Index tells what to look for in a franchise. The Profile is a worksheet for listing the data. | SBA 1.12:35 | 56 | $ .65 |

| | Catalogue No. | Pages | Price |
|---|---|---|---|
| CASH PLANNING IN SMALL MANUFACTURING COMPANIES<br>Reports on research that was done on cash planning for the small manufacturer. Designed for owners of small firms and the specialists who study and aid them. | SBA 1.20:1 | 276 | $2.70 |
| THE FIRST TWO YEARS: PROBLEMS OF SMALL FIRM GROWTH AND SURVIVAL<br>This discussion is based on the detailed observation of 81 small retail and service firms over a 2-year period. The operations of each enterprise were systematically followed from the time of launching through the end of the second year. | SBA 1.20:2 | 233 | $2.40 |
| EXPORT MARKETING FOR SMALLER FIRMS<br>A manual for owner/managers of smaller firms who seek sales in foreign markets. | SBA 1.19: EX7/971 | 134 | $1.30 |
| U.S. GOVERNMENT PURCHASING AND SALES DIRECTORY<br>A directory for businesses that are interested in selling to the U.S. government. Lists the purchasing needs of various agencies. | SBA 1.13/ 3:972 | 169 | $2.35 |
| MANAGING FOR PROFITS<br>Ten chapters on various aspects of small business management—for example, marketing, production, and credit. | SBA 1.2: M31/11 | 170 | $1.95 |
| BUYING AND SELLING A SMALL BUSINESS<br>Deals with the problems that confront buyers and sellers of small businesses. Discusses the buy/sell transaction, sources of information for buyer/seller decision, the buy/sell process, using financial statements in the buy/sell transaction, and analyzing the market position of the company. | SBA 1.2:898 | 122 | $1.60 |
| STRENGTHENING SMALL BUSINESS MANAGEMENT<br>Twenty-one chapters on small business management. This collection reflects the experience that the author gained in a lifetime of work with the small business community. | SBA 1.2: M31/14 | 158 | $2.25 |

*SBA Starting and Managing Series*

This series is designed to help the small entrepreneur in his effort "to look before he leaps" into a business. The first volume in the series—*Starting and Managing a Small Business of Your Own*—deals with the subject in general terms. Each of the other volumes deals with one type of business in detail. Available titles and prices are listed below.

| | *Catalogue No.* | *Pages* | *Price* |
|---|---|---|---|
| Starting and Managing a Small Business of Your Own | SBA 1.15:1 | 97 | $1.35 |
| Starting and Managing a Service Station | SBA 1.15:3 | 80 | $ .70 |
| Starting and Managing a Small Bookkeeping Service | SBA 1.15:4 | 64 | $ .90 |
| Starting and Managing a Small Building Business | SBA 1.15:5 | 102 | $1.40 |
| Starting and Managing a Small Restaurant | SBA 1.15:9 | 116 | $1.20 |
| Starting and Managing a Small Retail Hardware Store | SBA 1.15:10 | 73 | $1.10 |
| Starting and Managing a Small Retail Drugstore | SBA 1.15:11 | 103 | $1.25 |
| Starting and Managing a Small Dry Cleaning Business | SBA 1.15:12 | 80 | $ .95 |
| Starting and Managing a Small Automatic Vending Business | SBA 1.15:13 | 70 | $ .75 |
| Starting and Managing a Carwash | SBA 1.15:14 | 76 | $1.10 |
| Starting and Managing a Swap Shop or Consignment Sale Shop | SBA 1.15:15 | 78 | $ .95 |
| Starting and Managing a Small Shoe Service Shop | SBA 1.15:16 | 86 | $1.00 |
| Starting and Managing a Small Retail Camera Shop | SBA 1.15:17 | 86 | $ .95 |

| | Catalogue No. | Pages | Price |
|---|---|---|---|
| Starting and Managing a Retail Flower Shop | SBA 1.15:18 | 121 | $1.20 |
| Starting and Managing a Pet Shop | SBA 1.15:19 | 40 | $ .60 |
| Starting and Managing a Small Retail Music Store | SBA 1.15:20 | 81 | $1.30 |
| Starting and Managing a Small Retail Jewelry Store | SBA 1.15:21 | 78 | $ .90 |
| Starting and Managing an Employment Agency | SBA 1.15:22 | 118 | $1.30 |
| Starting and Managing a Small Drive-in Restaurant | SBA 1.15:23 | 65 | $ .75 |
| Starting and Managing a Small Shoestore | SBA 1.15:24 | 104 | $1.35 |

## *SBA Field-Office Addresses*

*New England*

| | |
|---|---|
| Boston | 150 Causeway Street, Boston, Massachusetts 02114 |
| Holyoke | 326 Appleton Street, Holyoke, Massachusetts 01040 |
| Augusta | Federal Building, U.S. Post Office, 40 Western Avenue, Augusta, Maine 04330 |
| Concord | 55 Pleasant Street, Concord, New Hampshire 03301 |
| Hartford | Federal Office Building, 450 Maine Street, Hartford, Connecticut 06103 |
| Montpelier | Federal Building, 2nd Floor, 87 State Street, Montpelier, Vermont 05602 |
| Providence | 702 Smith Building, 57 Eddy Street, Providence, Rhode Island 02903 |

*New York, New Jersey, and Puerto Rico*

| | |
|---|---|
| New York | 26 Federal Plaza, Room 3100, New York, New York 10007 |
| Hato Rey | 255 Ponce de Leon Avenue, Hato Rey, Puerto Rico 00919 |
| Newark | 970 Broad Street, Room 1635, Newark , New Jersey 07102 |
| Syracuse | Hunter Plaza, Fayette and Salina Streets, Syracuse, New York 13202 |
| Buffalo | 111 West Huron Street, Buffalo, New York 14202 |
| Albany | 99 Washington Avenue, Albany, New York 12207 |
| Rochester | 55 St. Paul Street, Rochester, New York 14604 |

*Mid-Atlantic*

| | |
|---|---|
| Philadelphia | One Bala Cynwyd Plaza, Bala Cynwyd, Pennsylvania 19004 |
| Harrisburg | 1500 North Second Street, Harrisburg, Pennsylvania 17108 |
| Wilkes-Barre | 34 South Main Street, Wilkes-Barre, Pennsylvania 18703 |
| Baltimore | 7800 York Road, Towson, Maryland 21204 |
| Wilmington | 844 King Street, Wilmington, Delaware 19801 |
| Clarksburg | Lowndes Bank Building, 109 North 3rd Street, Clarksburg, West Virginia 26301 |
| Charleston | Charleston National Plaza, Suite 628, Charleston, West Virginia 25301 |
| Pittsburgh | Federal Building, 1000 Liberty Avenue, Pittsburgh, Pennsylvania 15222 |
| Richmond | Federal Building, 400 North 8th Street, Richmond, Virginia 23240 |
| Washington | 1030 15th Street, N.W., Room 250, Washington, D.C. 20417 |

*Southeast*

| | |
|---|---|
| Atlanta | 1401 Peachtree Street, N.E., Atlanta, Georgia 30309 |
| Biloxi | 111 Fred Haise Building, Biloxi, Mississippi 39530 |
| Birmingham | 908 South 20th Street, Birmingham, Alabama 35205 |
| Charlotte | Addison Building, 222 South Church Street, Charlotte, North Carolina 28202 |
| Columbia | 1801 Assembly Street, Columbia, South Carolina 29201 |
| Coral Gables | 2222 Ponce de Leon Boulevard, Coral Gables, Florida 33134 |
| Jackson | Petroleum Building, Pascagoula and Amite Streets, Jackson, Mississippi 39205 |
| Jacksonville | Federal Office Building, 400 West Bay Street, Jacksonville, Florida 32202 |
| Louisville | Federal Office Building, 600 Federal Place, Louisville, Kentucky 40202 |
| Tampa | Federal Building, 500 Zack Place, Tampa, Florida 33607 |
| Nashville | 404 James Robertson Parkway, Nashville, Tennessee 37219 |
| Knoxville, | 502 South Gay Street, Knoxville, Tennessee 37902 |
| Memphis | Federal Building, 167 North Main Street, Memphis, Tennessee 38103 |

*Midwest*

| | |
|---|---|
| Chicago | Federal Office Building, 219 South Dearborn Street, Chicago, Illinois 60604 |
| Springfield | 502 East Monroe Street, Springfield, Illinois 62701 |
| Cleveland | 1240 East 9th Street, Cleveland, Ohio 44199 |
| Columbus | 34 North High Street, Columbus, Ohio 43215 |
| Cincinnati | Federal Building, 550 Main Street, Cincinnati, Ohio 45202 |
| Detroit | 1249 Washington Boulevard, Detroit, Michigan 48226 |
| Marquette | 201 McClellan Street, Marquette, Michigan 49855 |
| Indianapolis | 575 North Pennsylvania Street, Indianapolis, Indiana 46204 |
| Madison | 122 West Washington Avenue, Madison, Wisconsin 53703 |
| Milwaukee | 735 West Wisconsin Avenue, Milwaukee, Wisconsin 53203 |
| Eau Claire | 500 South Barstow Street, Eau Claire, Wisconsin 54701 |
| Minneapolis | 12 South Sixth Street, Minneapolis, Minnesota 55402 |

*South Central*

| | |
|---|---|
| Dallas | 1100 Commerce Street, Dallas, Texas 75202 |
| Albuquerque | 5000 Marble Avenue, N.E., Albuquerque, New Mexico 87110 |
| Houston | 808 Travis Street, Houston, Texas 77002 |
| Little Rock | 611 Gaines Street, Little Rock, Arkansas 72201 |
| Lubbock | 1205 Texas Avenue, Lubbock, Texas 79408 |
| El Paso | 109 North Oregon Avenue, El Paso, Texas 79901 |
| Lower Rio Grande Valley | 219 East Jackson Street, Harlingen, Texas 78550 |
| Corpus Christi | 3105 Leopard Street, Corpus Christi, Texas 78408 |
| Marshall | 505 East Travis Street, Marshall, Texas 75670 |
| New Orleans | 1001 Howard Avenue, New Orleans, Louisiana 70113 |
| Oklahoma City | 50 Penn Place, Oklahoma City, Oklahoma 73118 |
| San Antonio | 301 Broadway, San Antonio, Texas 78205 |

*Plains*

| | |
|---|---|
| Kansas City | 911 Walnut Street, Kansas City, Missouri 64106 |
| Des Moines | New Federal Building, 210 Walnut Street, Des Moines, Iowa 50309 |
| Omaha | Federal Building, 215 North 17th Street, Omaha, Nebraska 68102 |
| St. Louis | Federal Building, 210 North 12th Street, St. Louis, Missouri 63101 |
| Wichita | 120 South Market Street, Wichita, Kansas 67202 |

*Mountain*

| | |
|---|---|
| Denver | 721 19th Street, Room 426, Denver, Colorado 80202 |
| Casper | 100 East B Street, Casper, Wyoming 82601 |
| Fargo | 653 2nd Avenue, North, Fargo, North Dakota 58102 |
| Helena | 613 Helena Avenue, Helena, Montana 59601 |
| Salt Lake City | Federal Building, 125 South State Street, Salt Lake City, Utah 84138 |
| Sioux Falls | National Bank Building, 8th and Main Avenues, Sioux Falls, South Dakota 57102 |

*West*

| | |
|---|---|
| San Francisco | Federal Building, 450 Golden Gate Avenue, San Francisco, California 94102 |
| Fresno | Federal Building, 1130 O Street, Fresno, California 93721 |
| Honolulu | 1149 Bethel Street, Honolulu, Hawaii 96813 |
| Agana | Ada Plaza Center Building, Agana, Guam 96910 |
| Los Angeles | 849 South Broadway, Los Angeles, California 90014 |
| Las Vegas | 301 East Stewart, Las Vegas, Nevada 89121 |
| Phoenix | 112 North Central Avenue, Phoenix, Arizona 85004 |
| San Diego | 110 West C Street, San Diego, California 92101 |

*Northwest*

| | |
|---|---|
| Seattle | 710 Second Avenue, Seattle, Washington 98104 |
| Anchorage | 1016 West Sixth Avenue, Anchorage, Alaska 99501 |

| | |
|---|---|
| Fairbanks | 501½ Second Avenue, Fairbanks, Alaska 99701 |
| Boise | 216 North 8th Street, Boise, Idaho 83701 |
| Portland | 921 Southwest Washington Street, Portland, Oregon 97205 |
| Spokane | Courthouse Building, Room 651, Spokane, Washington 99210 |

## *Bank of America—Small Business Reporter*

The Bank of America Small Business Reporter series may be ordered for $1.00 each from Bank of America, Department 3120, P.O. Box 37000, San Francisco, California 94137.

### *Business Operations Series*

Advertising
Vol. 9, No. 1
Avoiding Management Pitfalls
Vol. 11, No. 5
Business Management: Advice from Consultants
Vol. 11, No. 3
Crime Prevention for Small Business
Vol. 13, No. 1
Exporting
Vol. 12, No. 6
Financing Small Business
Vol. 8, No. 5
Franchising
Vol. 9, No. 9
How to Buy or Sell a Business
Vol. 8, No. 11
Management Succession
Vol. 10, No. 12
Marketing New Product Ideas
Vol. 10, No. 5
Opening Your Own Business: A Personal Appraisal
Vol. 7, No. 7
Personnel for the Small Business
Vol. 9, No. 8
Retail Financial Records
Vol. 10, No. 4
Steps to Starting a Business
Vol. 10, No. 10
Understanding Financial Statements
Vol. 7, No. 11

### *Business Profiles*

Apparel Manufacturing
Vol. 10, No. 3
Apparel Stores
Vol. 12, No. 2
(Includes men's, women's, & children's wear)
Auto Parts and Accessory Stores
Vol. 8, No. 12
Bars & Cocktail Lounges
Vol. 11, No. 9
Bicycle Stores
Vol. 12, No. 1
Bookstores
Vol. 11, No. 6
Building Maintenance Services
Vol. 12, No. 3
Coin-Operated Drycleaning
Vol. 8, No. 7
Convenience Food Stores
Vol. 9, No. 6
Equipment Rental Business
Vol. 12, No. 6
Hairgrooming/Beauty Salons
Vol. 12, No. 9
The Handcraft Business
Vol. 10, No. 8
Health Food Stores
Vol. 11, No. 2
Home Furnishings Stores
Vol. 11, No. 1
Independent Camera Shops
Vol. 12, No. 7
Independent Drug Stores
Vol. 9, No. 12
Independent Liquor Stores
Vol. 11, No. 4

Independent Pet Shops
Vol. 10, No. 2
Independent Sporting Goods Stores
Vol. 10, No. 11
Mail Order Enterprises
Vol. 11, No. 7
Mobile Home and Recreational Vehicle Dealers
Vol. 9, No. 11
Plant Shops
Vol. 12, No. 4
Proprietary Day Care
Vol. 11, No. 8
Repair Services
Vol. 10, No. 9
Restaurants and Food Services
Vol. 12, No. 8
Service Stations
Vol. 10, No. 7
Sewing & Needlecraft Centers
Vol. 11, No. 10
Shoe Stores
Vol. 12, No. 5
Small Job Printing
Vol. 9, No. 5
Toy and Hobby/Craft Stores
Vol. 12, No. 10